"

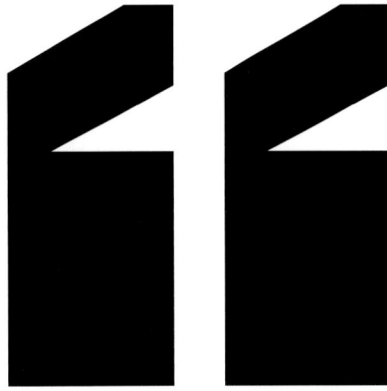

A WOHA building is recognizable not so much for its colour or shape or material usage, but for the graphic expression of its programme for sustainability. With no little panache, WOHA have turned that expression into their own art form.

WOHA

New Forms of Sustainable Architecture

Patrick Bingham–Hall

Essays by Nirmal Kishnani and Timothy Beatley

With over 370 illustrations

T&H

Projects

Prototypology
The Architecture of WOHA
Introduction

PATRICK BINGHAM-HALL

'**It** *may well be that WOHA have set a template for architecture in the 21st century which will be globally embraced. They have not shirked the issues that face our world ... An individual architectural practice can only do so much to remediate the difficulties faced by a city, or by society itself, but relentless imagining and iconoclastic problem-solving may be architecture's great contribution to human life.'*

I wrote those words in 2012, and it is now more than pertinent to remind everybody what WOHA were up to back then, and to note what they have subsequently achieved. Global warming and urban dysfunction are upon us – these circumstances are widely acknowledged – and one no longer needs to bang the drum of doom in books such as this. The issues that WOHA refused to shirk are now central to any discourse in relation to architectural relevance: the climate has changed, and architectural thinking really has been forced to change too.

The realization has dawned that we are now trapped in a world of our own making (almost apologetically categorized as the Anthropocene epoch) and as a consequence, possibly for the first time in its history, the fundamental meaning of architecture is not aesthetic but programmatic, and any assessment of its validity is now predicated by that notion. The climate and the demography of our planet have changed decisively, and as a consequence, so have the ways in which we think about and look at the built environment. We have passed a tipping point, and architecture now has an overriding ethical mandate.

WOHA work in Asia, home to twelve of the sixteen metropolitan areas or conurbations in the world that are currently adjudged to have a population of over twenty million.[1] As only three Asian cities would have featured in the top sixteen in 1990 – the year that free trade (capitalism) effectively commandeered the global economy – the relative growth rate has been staggering, and in terms of environmental and social sustainability, the potential consequences are quite frightening.

WOHA understand this new reality only too well. They accept that it may be impossible to achieve a geopolitical resolution to uncontrolled urbanization, and they are working to resuscitate and remediate the damage created by unenlightened planning policies and construction methods. They have proposed fully sustainable and highly sociable mini-cities within mega-cities, and they have already designed and completed several buildings-as-towns that engage with and contribute to the surrounding city. All these projects utilize passive ventilation and

> **A WOHA building is recognizable, not so much for its colour or shape or material usage, but for the graphic expression of its programmatic strategies. With an ongoing series of notable public buildings, WOHA have turned that expression into their own art form.**

sun-shading, and provide sizeable community spaces, often high above ground in the form of sky gardens, sky villages and sky parks. And it must be stressed that WOHA's schemes are inherently healthy and antiviral: fresh rather than recycled, open rather than enclosed, natural rather than artificial.

So many architects have for so many years simply transplanted their designs from one global locale to another with little modification: an ongoing and remorseless process that has, astonishingly, singled out the cities of tropical Asia and the sweltering Middle East as repositories for cold-climate buildings. At the forefront of a localized resistance movement, WOHA have instead responded directly to the culture, climate, micro-environment and urban networks that define the location of each of their projects, and those external considerations are taken to be part of the architectural package. The phrase 'inside/outside' has become something of a cliché in the reportage of tropical architecture, but WOHA have taken the notion several steps further by inviting biodiversity and vegetation into the structure and by extruding the building's elements back out to the landscape and the city.

WOHA's architecture has an identity bequeathed by the consistency and validity of their principles. As to whether WOHA have a style, it is revealing to look back on their oeuvre and note that the aesthetic of their architecture is appreciably more discernible now than it was at the time of a project's completion. One can view WOHA's built works as a succession of prototypes – a prototypology – whose ideas built upon each other, and as this evolution became increasingly apparent, so did their visual signature and their contribution to the urban environment. A WOHA building is recognizable not so much for its colour or shape or material usage, but for the graphic expression of its programmatic strategies. With an ongoing series of notable public buildings, WOHA have turned that expression into their own art form.

Aesthetics and the City: the Folly of Follies

'The quest for sustainability now makes it urgent that architectural education be designed to also develop the student psychologically and culturally. Architecture might then lift itself out of the egocentric shaping of icons, the competitive elaboration of obfuscatory theory and all other such trivia. Instead it can focus on the larger and now urgent concerns that are best understood and solved by designers who have evolved both psychologically and intellectually to reach a world- or biosphere-centric level of cultural and personal development.'
—**Peter Buchanan**[2]

Over the last few decades, the role and symbolic value of a monumental building has been supplanted by the straightforward desire for an icon, for an edifice whose *raison d'être* is to say, 'look at me'. The only symbolic value is symbolism as an end in itself, and like a Ferrari stuck in a traffic jam, an iconic building wedged into a congested cityscape looks like nothing more than an exercise in pointless vanity.

So many cities all over the world have been trying to look different, to establish a distinctive presence, but in doing so, they have ended up looking much the same as each other. Twisted slabs, pointed shards and contorted trapezoids – cheek-by-jowl and clad in

1   The statistical assessment of a conurbation's population can vary, according to whether or not it is determined by administrative boundaries. However, in terms of patterns of settlement, the most relevant population count would be that of an autonomous urban entity, which might include several cities. Using this metric, the Shanghai-Nanjing-Hangzhou metropolitan area is considered to have at least ninety million inhabitants. The other Asian mega-cities with a population of more than twenty million are (in descending order) Guangzhou-Shenzhen-Hong Kong, Tokyo-Yokohama, Jakarta, Delhi, Seoul, Mumbai, Karachi, Manila, Beijing, Osaka-Kobe, Dhaka.

2   Peter Buchanan, 'The Big Rethink', in *The Architectural Review*, 28 May 2012.

'We wanted landscape and architecture to come together... we were reconceptualizing cities and architecture as entities that could be interwoven with nature, so they had to be civic buildings as well as organic buildings.'

—WOHA

↑
Parkroyal
on Pickering.
Singapore,
2007–13.

These WOHA towers are overtly eco-friendly, climatically attuned and highly conspicuous: they are eye-catchingly sustainable and must be seen as the aesthetic expression of environmental resilience.

tinted glass – have become the skylines of emerging cities everywhere, while discordantly intruding into the urban fabric of old-world cities trying to keep pace. Dubai, Shanghai, New York, London, Sydney, Singapore ... the architectural circus comes to town.

Of course, iconic architecture has always existed; it just wasn't thought of in such terms, because the purpose and representation of monumental buildings built over the ages was never ambiguous. Any structure whose function or meaning was indecipherable was referred to as a folly, and as all architecture is inevitably and reductively evaluated as part of a historic continuum, it will surely be acknowledged that most contemporary monumental buildings are follies. They do not even attempt to express their function or their meaning, unless you contend that geometric abstraction is an honest expression of modern capitalist endeavour or spiritual inclination.

The majority of 21st-century iconic buildings do not engage with or objectify the realities of our time and, as such, their architects are swimming against the tide of architectural history. Architects have all availed themselves of the latest digital technology, and they are imposing the global-branding desires of their clients but, no matter how showy their creations, they have categorically failed to move beyond the modernist template for building development. The architecture is outdated, and very few recent designated icons could be regarded as worthy successors to the Sydney Opera House or the Seagram Building, never mind San Pietro or Hagia Sophia.

It might seem paradoxical, but structural innovation and expressive delight have actually been stymied by the recent waves of technological advances,

and the digitally inspired aesthetic representations of our new age are literally only skin-deep, confined to the building's surface. In the field of high-rise design – where most of the icons can be found – few architects have veered from the constructional super-highway of a stack of floor plates cantilevered from a central core and completely sealed by glass curtain walls.

These monumental edifices are wearing the emperor's new clothes at a time when urban construction and building operations account for more than half the planet's use of fossil-fuel energy. Although they might appear as 'how did they build that?' symbols of a gee-whiz hi-tech universe of infinite warp-and-weave possibilities ... just strip away the tinted glass and the buildings remain the same. The starchitects and their imitators have marginalized their environmental obligations in favour of what might be described as parametric bling, which will be remembered in due course as a rather curious aesthetic representation of our efforts to mitigate global warming.

For over two decades, cities have been transformed by a proliferation of regressive reactionary architecture, which in spite of its apparent flash, actually constitutes a counter-reformation intent upon asserting the conservative outlook of its corporate and political patronage. All that glitters is not gold ... if we do need to indulge the ego or sate our desire for beauty while saving the planet, it could be suggested that a new set of prototypes for iconic architecture is required. Buildings as monuments would then be both eye-catching and sustainable and, to revert to the form-follows-function appraisal of architectural integrity, iconic buildings would thus be eye-catchingly sustainable.

WOHA's iconic city buildings have charted a new course. The designs respond to the desire for a distinctive architectural presence, but they derive their monumental expression from the strategies used to engage in environmental responsibility (for the city at large, not just the building). These WOHA towers are overtly eco-friendly, climatically attuned and highly conspicuous: they are eye-catchingly sustainable and must be seen as the aesthetic expression of environmental resilience.

The site of the Parkroyal on Pickering hotel (2007–13) occupies an entire city block in downtown Singapore, and the northern elevation of the hotel rises above the lawns of a public park as an explicit representation of a new green city. Three levels of gigantic curvaceous shelves stretch between the protruding blocks of the E-planned building, festooned with all manner of tropical foliage – trees, vines, creepers and flowering plants – to present a layered vertical landscape as a new vista for the surrounding city, while providing the guests of a high-rise hotel with rooms in a garden. The architectural expression is consummately organic: a variety of cornices in the hotel's public spaces are comprised of contoured, sinuous mouldings, while the external floor slabs and walls were carved and etched to form meandering soffits and provide crevices with gardens and waterfalls. The five-storey podium had been sculpted to form an elaborate piece of topographic architecture, an eroded, striated rockface providing a home for all manner of flora and fauna.

When completed, the consummately 'greened' building represented a great leap forward in urban design: it was a tangible realization at a grand scale of WOHA's idealistic visions of an environmentally sustainable and aesthetically pleasing urban environment for 21st-century Asia.

> # " We are dreaming of cities as rainforest.

The nearby tower of the Oasia Downtown hotel (2011–16) is coloured crimson and scarlet. As every other tower in the Singapore skyline is toned in muted shades of grey and/or blue, Oasia Downtown can thus be immediately distinguished from any distance and it stands proud as a monumental piece of urban pop art. The aluminium mesh that wraps around the façades was painted red, but it is turning green. Vines creep and crawl over every surface, spreading out from planter boxes placed on each level, so that the tower performs as a living artwork, as a herbaceous installation in a minimalist urban gallery of concrete and glass. The colours and textures of the façades change with the winds and rainfall, and with the natural cycles of plant life: sometimes the tower is green and bushy, sometimes it's red and bony.

The tower is a prototype; one where the need for climatically responsive architecture has converged with the desire for an iconic presence. The building's efficacy as a hotel is secondary to its significance as a piece of urban design, and (although they don't need to be painted crimson) it might be hoped that within the foreseeable future every skyscraper will be this green. The tower contains three large atria, which are open to the elements – they do not need to be enclosed in Singapore's equatorial climate – and their layers of parkland and cloaks of vines dramatically increase the biodiversity levels of a downtown environment. The cumulative amount of greenery contained within the structure and wrapped around its surface is calculated to be eleven times that of the site in its natural state, which provides the tower with a possibly unprecedented Green Plot Ratio of 1100%.

The unashamedly tropical attributes of Oasia Downtown currently appear anti-contextual in a generic CBD environment, and while its 'shock of the new' appearance signifies the mark of a genuine prototype, it might be more pertinent to think of it as the 'shock of the old'. In essence, WOHA have reapplied the fundamental principles of tropical vernacular architecture – cross-ventilation, site orientation, perforated structure, sun-shading, rain protection and environmental integration – to a 21st-century tower.

Sustainability and the City: New Forms of Beauty

In response to the 21st-century scenario wherein the procedures of urban development are becoming increasingly entangled in a mess of their own making, WOHA are sailing into uncharted waters. They are going where few architects have gone before, propelled

> **The tower is a prototype, conflating the need for climatically responsive architecture with a desire for an iconic presence. The building's efficacy as a hotel is secondary to its significance as a piece of urban design, and it might be hoped that within the foreseeable future every skyscraper will be this green.**

by a methodology that conflates urban planning with architecture. Throughout the developing world, new cities, new suburbs and new precincts are being built at a rate never before seen, but even if the plans are commendably sustainable, they will inevitably serve as grids or matrixes for unsustainable components, plugged in by architects subservient to the confines of a specific site and their client's brief. And the reverse procedure – fully sustainable buildings plugged into an unsustainable masterplan – is equally problematic. WOHA see this state of affairs as an abrogation of civic responsibility, and they advocate that planners should think like architects and architects should think like planners.

It can be observed that this notion has always lain behind the work of their practice, no matter what the size or typology. WOHA are now working at the largest possible scale, but their practice began with a series of private houses, and they insistently point out that their fundamental principles were always in place: *'Our approach, our strategies, were scaled up and up. We haven't changed, we have been very consistent. Now we are working at such a large scale, we describe it as "form follows systems", but actually that's how we have always approached design.'*

The floating roofs, the voluminous breeze-ways, the communal spaces, the integration of nature, the synthesis of programme with aesthetics ... they were always there, they simply became more and more evident as the scale increased. To take a case in point, the Kampung Admiralty project (2013–17) is primarily

residential, it is naturally ventilated in all dimensions, its facilities care for the elderly and for infants, it has a food court and supermarkets, it contains community gathering and circulation spaces, and it has a beautiful set of gardens. Scale it right down, and what do you have? You have an early WOHA house, say the House at Maple Avenue (1999–2002), wherein the food court is the dining room, the community spaces are the family spaces, and so on. The early houses were in fact the micro-prototypes for WOHA's later macro-prototypes, which were to plug into the city at large, and which would then attempt to prescribe what a city might comprise and how it might operate.

Twenty years ago, WOHA set out to propose a new typology for mega-city living, which would constitute an interconnected set of densely populated yet highly amenable high-rise towers: the structures would be sustainable as well as sociable. They unveiled their initial proposal with the Duxton Plain competition entry in 2001, and went on to design The Met in 2003 and SkyVille @ Dawson in 2007, which were then completed in 2009 and 2015 respectively as variants of their megastructural prototype. The Met, located in central Bangkok, has an unambiguous, uncompromising and unprecedented structural expression. The design of the sixty-six-storey set of towers pays no heed to established aesthetic codes as it was instead explicitly directed by strategies for passive environmental control: by wind directions, thermal displacement, one-room-thick apartments and sunlight protection. In fact, The Met had done nothing less than introduce a new aesthetic to architecture, as acknowledged by the Royal Institute of British Architects, who awarded the 2011 Lubetkin Prize to the project. One of the jurors, Deborah Saunt, observed that: *'This is where sustainability steps in, because it is here that new forms of beauty emerge. The true beauty of a sustainable building is that it is forever.'*

A contemporaneous building in Singapore was to be equally uncompromising in terms of its structural parti and appearance. The School of the Arts (2005–10) is a ten-storey building with an intransigent bulk, whose internal configurations comprise what was a calculated experiment in monumental space-framing, with voids and atria overlooked by galleries of naturally ventilated classrooms and linked by open circulation routes. The structure is not enclosed, no passageways are sealed in, and the breezes are constant and occasionally very strong. With its resolute complexity of scaling and connections, the entire volume is a self-contained communal organism, and as such it was a prototype for a tropical 'city within a city'.

←
Oasia
Downtown.
Singapore,
2011–16.

The scale, appearance and strategies for sustainability of Kampung Admiralty (2013–17) are not markedly different from those of the School of the Arts, but the scope of the programme had expanded, and the building was effectively a prototype for a new typology, that of environmentally responsible design twinned with public sociability. The School of the Arts had been conceived as a multi-layered private village for its students, but Kampung Admiralty was built as a very public multi-storeyed town for the residents of northern Singapore. The stratified eleven-storey complex contains an underground car park, a basement shopping centre, a double-height community space on the ground floor overlooked by a food court on a mezzanine level, two levels of medical facilities and two apartment towers for the elderly. The crowning glory – the building's signature – is the rooftop parkland, a set of luxuriantly landscaped terraced gardens open to the public at large. An oasis surrounded by a concrete desert of suburban apartment blocks, the sky park offers a seemingly remarkable and wondrous experience, but it is only natural, and that is the WOHA position.

All Things Work Better When They Are Working Together

In light of the biggest picture, that of mitigating and/or adapting to climate change, true sustainability must be achieved as quickly as possible, and in order to do that, some form of pact is required at the communal, national and global levels. If nothing else, the Covid-19 pandemic has shown us that many governments and their constituents could not be trusted to save themselves (the leaders were incompetent and the citizens misguided), and when seen in that harsh light it is clear that political responsibility and societal reciprocity must be urgently re-established. Sustainability begins in the city, where most of us live and where the greatest environmental damage is being done, and it cannot be realized without a large number of citizens agreeing to work towards the greater good.

The Punggol Digital District (2017–), a massive project instigated and financed by the Singapore government for the 'cross-fertilization of knowledge and collaboration opportunities among student, faculty and industry professionals' is currently under construction, and it was conceived as a template for large-scale urban development built with strategies employed to counteract climate change. Comprising a continuous array of internal and external spaces, layered and interconnected in fabulous complexity –

> **WOHA's thinking has gone back to the past, to the days when seeking shelter from the rain and the sun didn't chew up energy and raise the temperature, when human beings could intermingle without hindrance, when nature was our environment, and when being alive was to be happy and healthy.**

> 'You are undone if you once forget that the fruits of the earth belong to us all, and the earth itself to nobody.'
> —Jean-Jacques Rousseau

organic, tropical, sociable and megastructural – this is potentially WOHA's most momentous project to date. Here they could innovate with regard to the benefit of the community at large, at a level that transcends the idealism previously displayed in isolated prototypes funded by private developers. Intrinsic to this new paradigm for urbanization is the notion that true sustainability can only be achieved by resolving human issues, by providing an environment that might be termed highly optimistic and highly sociable. With such a project, the meaning and value of architecture have thus changed. In such troubled and uncertain times, architecture at this scale has a transformative role, socially and politically, which is ultimately responsible for us doing our best to beat climate change. For WOHA, the way forward is clear: effective remediation – both environmental and social – can only be

↑
Kampung
Admiralty.
Singapore,
2013–17.

implemented by working with and improving all the systems that make up a city. Genuine innovation will not come through architecture itself, which can only provide the framework.

It may sound a little too elemental for an age of rampant technology, but the fact is that we need to go back to the past to plan for the future. As shown by our ongoing succession of cataclysmic events and doomsday episodes, human beings are no less susceptible to the vicissitudes of existence and planetary conditions than they ever were. WOHA's thinking has gone back to the past, to the days when seeking shelter from the rain and the sun didn't chew up energy and raise the temperature, when human beings could intermingle without hindrance, when nature was our environment, and when being alive was to be happy and healthy.

Such imaginings might sound hopelessly romantic yet desperately desirable, but WOHA have now reached the point where they can prove that their strategies and principles have been effective; that they work. Humanist ideals have been underpinned by structural pragmatism. WOHA's prototypes have been built and they have been successful, not just as pieces of architecture but as programmes for societal remediation and advancement. WOHA have been able to demonstrate what a building can do, rather than what it might do, and they are intent upon extending their vision to the macro scale of Asia's urban conglomerations: 'We are dreaming of cities as rainforest.'

Essays

Virtuous Architecture

As this book documents the trajectory of a practice set up in 1994 by two architects who were students during the 1980s, the subsequent shift in the critical understanding of architecture's meaning and value inevitably underscores the impact of WOHA's approach. When Wong Mun Summ and Richard Hassell were at university, architecture was still considered by its practitioners and its critics to be an intellectualized aesthetic, and to allow one's eye and mind to wander from the poetic to the prosaic – to dwell upon the usability and performance of a building – was to devalue the noble art and the credibility of the observer. The rationale for such a purview had been set in stone, as it were, by Nikolaus Pevsner forty years earlier when he famously wrote: 'A bicycle shed is a building, Lincoln Cathedral is a piece of architecture. Nearly everything that encloses space on a scale sufficient for a human being to move in is a building; the term architecture applies only to buildings designed with a view to aesthetic appeal.'[1]

As the high-modernism and structural expressionism of the mid-20th century transmuted (or reverted) into what might be charitably termed mannerism, it is now clear that the principled equation of 'form follows function' – which did take pains to accord with the Pevsner observation – was becoming passé. This entropic process was at its most perplexed during the 1980s, when the 'less is a bore' carnival of postmodernism took centre stage with protagonists whose essential concerns appeared to be colourful shape-making, tectonic linguistics (!) and historical references. Architects (and polemicists)[2] were navel-gazing, and it was a curious time to be a student.

In a formal sense, the standard of architecture over the last few decades has been notably high (the word 'starchitecture' was coined for good reason), but the 1980s preoccupation with appearance and/or expression without consideration for function – and a building's programme in particular – has lingered. We are now twenty years into the 21st century, times have changed, and this represents quite a problem. Aesthetics without ethics (form without function?) really should be dismissed as artifice at an intellectual level and as counterproductive at the level of implementation, which must prioritize environmental sustainability and, ipso facto, communal wellbeing. In that respect, WOHA were ahead of their time: they have never had any doubts as to the relative values of aesthetics and meaning (beauty and truth).

This is the sixth book published on WOHA, but the previous books must all be regarded as partial, if not total, proclamations of intent, which focused on a particular phase of their evolution. Indeed, when

> **It has become clear that one type of 'good' architecture cannot be achieved without the other. Like sustainability and sociability, the two need to go hand in hand, and WOHA are adamant that 21st-century architecture needs to be 'good' ... both ethically and aesthetically.**

the most recent of those books, *Garden City Mega City*, was launched in 2016 at the Aedes Gallery in Berlin, the esteemed architect Matthias Sauerbruch pronounced that the publication was 'nothing less than a manifesto for our times'. This volume, however, is not a manifesto per se; it is intended as a comprehensive and reflective mid-career assessment of WOHA's oeuvre, but it will also serve as a documentation of their (ongoing) proclamations of intent, which are inextricably intertwined with the project chronology. Although the word 'manifesto' does have a nicely retro revolutionary connotation, it must be borne in mind that neither Wong nor Hassell is a confrontational or provocative protagonist: on the contrary, their 'polemic' is always well-considered, well-researched and, above all, practical and worldly.

The worldliness of Wong and Hassell is a manifestation of a duality specific to their hometown. Singapore has never been a cultural epicentre and its architects (among others) are thus detached from the established and residually parochial mainstreams of global discourse. But every successful Singaporean is plugged into a global network, as the city-state is surrounded by much larger nations with which it has an almost fraternal relationship, and it is one of the world's leading financial and trading centres. Singaporeans are effectively obliged to take the initiative, to plan well ahead, to punch above their weight and to take the lead.

When seen in this light, it can be understood that the polemic of Wong and Hassell is quite simply their rationale, pragmatic rather than provocative, but the changes they are intent upon instigating are formidable, self-evidently unprecedented and genuinely radical.

Wong and Hassell are grateful for the opportunities that Singapore presented, acknowledging that they were always encouraged to think ahead, to understand that urban restructuring might well take the form of a quantum leap: 'We were able to push the boundaries and we were very very persistent.' As Anna Johnson observed, Singapore's processes of planning and construction had emerged as a template for developing cities, and it was thus a very good place for architects to push the boundaries in the face of climate change and urban alienation, if they were so inclined. WOHA were so inclined, and their persistence in pushing those boundaries for the greater good of Asian society has been the constant theme of their career to date.

The notion of the 'greater good' conspicuously fell out of favour in the Western world after a short-lived spirit of emancipation and brotherhood of man flowered in the 1960s: the 1970s were labelled the 'Me Decade' and the 1980s are probably best remembered for the phrase 'greed is good'. In what used to be

1   Nikolaus Pevsner, *An Outline of European Architecture*, Pelican Books, 1943.

2   Charles Jencks, a prolific and voluble high priest of the postmodernist discourse, wrote these words in 1982 at the conclusion of his book *Current Architecture*: 'Exotic new environments constructed over the sea are not discussed, nor are the pressing issues of building economics, land control, and patronage. I have discussed such issues only insofar as they have led to buildings or projects which I consider relevant architecturally.' He was acknowledging that buildings do have a purpose, but he was implying that to focus on that purpose, on the civic or environmental role of architecture, was to miss the point.

'The emergence of Singapore as a template for developing cities has been mirrored in WOHA's evolution. This background has provided them with the prerequisites for the extension and implementation of their own strategies as the 21st century progresses, in a world of realignment and reassessment, overlooked by the spectre of global warming.'[3]

referred to as the Third World, an implicit acceptance of the greater good had essentially underpinned most communities until 'emergence' recast the nature of aspiration and expectation, and the newfound material wealth of a previously unseen upper middle class stealthily recalibrated the gap between the haves and the have-nots. Now, as the world lurches into what might be described as a set of challenging problems, the logic of advocating a policy of all-encompassing communal benefit is, you would have to say, difficult to dispute: everybody would be better off. It doesn't matter how much money you have, you don't want to live in a dysfunctional city on a dying planet.

When interviewed in 2011, Hassell quite candidly explained WOHA's philosophy of mutual benefit: 'We wanted to put our gifts to the maximum use and for maximum personal satisfaction, but as architects, altruism must be part of that mix. We conflated "good" in terms of good quality with "good" in its ethical meaning.'[4] WOHA's attitude was ostensibly unremarkable, but to revert to the way in which architecture was perceived, even as recently as 2011, it put them out of step with their peer group and, oddly enough, with the next generation of architects. Form-making (often cloaked in the garb of what was confusingly referred to as theory) had been taught, it had been prescribed, it had taken hold, and it was apparent that WOHA's thinking had more in common with scientists and sociologists than with architects and urban planners.

WOHA's motivation to enhance the greater good at a greater scale requires little explanation, but it must be said that the thoughts, processes and strategies that facilitate such an outcome are unusually complex to elucidate in terms of architectural analysis. Architecture has traditionally been assessed as an art form or as a set of efficient and/or expressive buildings co-opted for a particular programme, but Wong and Hassell talk of systems rather than tectonics, and an intrinsic feature of systems is their overlapping and intertwining in a multiplicity of dimensions and complex interactions. The DNA of WOHA is thus singularly difficult to portray in a series of two-dimensional images, and any written analysis – as opposed to polemic – tiptoes cautiously across the thin ice of convolution.

The content of this book (the architecture) is determined by its context, by the times and the places to which WOHA have responded, and no analysis of their projects should be undertaken without painting a picture of that context. As well as providing a compendium and chronology of WOHA's projects, this book attempts to identify, if not isolate, WOHA's philosophical and architectonic DNA. As one is constantly reminded by the architects themselves, the fundamental principles – the strands of their DNA – have been evolving ever since the inception of the practice in 1994.

The determination to continually conceive and nurture prototypes has placed WOHA in a curiously invidious position. By its very nature, an architectural prototype will look different, maybe even awkward, maybe even ugly, when first erected in its public setting. No matter how efficacious and beneficial the building's programme, it will instinctively be judged for its aesthetics, using criteria that possibly no longer apply. Such is the nature of architectural innovation, as noted by Deyan Sudjic of Norman Foster, Richard Rogers and James Stirling back in 1986: 'It is an unfortunate vanguard role that [they] have all found themselves forced to play.'[5] WOHA have frequently been frustrated, if not exasperated, when their competition entries were rejected because they veered too far from the tried-and-tested, and they often struggled to persuade potential clients and fellow architects that problem-solving was fast becoming the primary objective. It now appears that they are closer to winning that battle, as a younger generation (two steps removed) of architects had been absorbing their ideas before going into practice and, as Wong and Hassell cheerfully acknowledge: 'We are now seeing WOHA-type buildings all around the world.'

Many years ago, I observed that Wong and Hassell 'operated in an almost rarefied atmosphere of virtuous creativity', and it was plain to see that there was something special going on; there was something that would set them apart. 'Virtuous' was the crucial word, and in order to serve the greater good, virtue has been a constant factor, but WOHA were also good architects. As Hassell points out, 'good' architecture has two meanings for WOHA, and as the role and the value of an architect have been transformed so comprehensively over the last twenty-five years, it has become clear that one type of 'good' architecture cannot be achieved without the other. Like sustainability and sociability, the two need to go hand in hand, and WOHA are adamant that 21st-century architecture needs to be 'good' ... both ethically and aesthetically.

3   Anna Johnson, 'Context and Connection: Local Identities and Global Desires', WOHA, edited by Patrick Bingham-Hall, Pesaro Publishing, 2009, p. 44.

4   As quoted in Patrick Bingham-Hall, WOHA: Selected Projects Vol. 1, Pesaro Publishing, 2011, p. 29.

5   Deyan Sudjic, Norman Foster, Richard Rogers, James Stirling, Thames & Hudson, 1986, pp. 190–91.

Wong Mun Summ and Richard Hassell

Wong Mun Summ and Richard Hassell met in late 1989 at the Singapore offices of Kerry Hill Architects, where both were working on the practice's stock-in-trade, the design of hotels and resorts across Southeast Asia. Both had graduated that year, Wong (born 1962) from the National University of Singapore and Hassell (born 1966) from the University of Western Australia in Perth. In terms of their ability to work at a large scale and to regard masterplanning as part of an architectural package, the four years spent with Kerry Hill were invaluable, and as Wong and Hassell had worked on over thirty projects in their four years with the practice, they were not exactly what you would call naïve when they set up their own business, nor were they intimidated by the workload. Another legacy, which would prove to be crucial, was their appreciation of localized vernacular architecture: *'When we were designing resorts, we were required to tell a cultural story ... we had to give the resorts a meaningful form. The existing cultural expression was at a vernacular scale, where the forms are determined by the climate, so we realized that cultural meaning could be expressed through climate-responsive architecture.'*

Wong departed Kerry Hill Architects in 1994, after playing a key role in the design of the highly acclaimed Datai Langkawi resort. Hassell linked up with him six months later to form WOHA[1] as a partnership, and although the pair may have harboured grand ambitions, their immediate desire was to engage in the day-to-day processes of architecture and construction; an activity denied to them while designing resorts in foreign lands. Both wanted to be hands-on operators; they wanted to be involved with every little detail, and in that they were displaying a latent inclination for supervisory control and a knowledge that true craft could only be realized through rigorous application. This shared attitude revealed their respective upbringings, which despite geographical and cultural dissimilarities, had crucial aspects in common. Wong's father owned a metal engineering business in Singapore, and as a teenager, he spent much of his extracurricular time working on the factory's production line. He was essentially fascinated by the intersection of design and production, as was Hassell, whose father ran a steel distribution company in Perth and devoted much of his downtime to issues of sustainability: *'My dad was a prototypical greenie ... he developed a completely solar-powered air-conditioning system for his business in the 1970s.'* As teenagers, Wong and Hassell were actively encouraged to indulge their artistic inclinations and appreciation of the finer things, and as a corollary, both took it as written that mathematical rigour should be applied to any intellectual and/or creative pursuits. Wong was directed by

→
Wong Mun Summ and Richard Hassell. Photo taken in WOHA's Singapore office in 2009.

1 Singaporeans are fond of using acronyms, whether for expressways, government departments, cultural events or people's names. Architecture is not exempt, and most Singapore practices have an acronym for a name. WOHA is quite simply comprised of WO for Wong and HA for Hassell.

government policy into the technical rather than the artistic educational stream, but forsook his enrolment in computer science at university because he realized that *'it was ridiculous, I should be doing architecture'.* Meanwhile, Hassell studied fine art at university for a year before switching to architecture: *'I loved drawing buildings, but because I'd always been focused on art, I hadn't thought about architecture until that point.'*

The personalities, predilections and talents of the two young architects overlapped in a fashion that was remarkable, their synergy and empathy were readily apparent, and their left-hand right-hand understanding has now endured for twenty-five years. Both Wong and Hassell have an engaging and optimistic disposition, the tiresome Randian arrogance of the successful architect has been misplaced (or conscientiously avoided), and a pervading sense

WOHA: NEW FORMS OF SUSTAINABLE ARCHITECTURE

16

> # "
> **The personalities, predilections and talents of the two young architects overlapped in a fashion that was remarkable, their synergy and empathy were readily apparent, and their left-hand right-hand understanding has now endured for twenty-five years.**

of open-mindedness dovetails with their range of interests beyond the formalities of architecture. At a purely creative level, Wong has always designed furniture, while Hassell continues to paint (now as a digital artist), and both pursuits are constantly intertwined with their architecture, from bookcases, tables and crafted joinery to the façade patterning of many notable buildings. Hassell is now obsessed by the infinite potential of geometric tessellation and has had solo exhibitions of his work, which comprises a singular and often very amusing continuation of the explorations made by Roger Penrose and MC Escher. WOHA furniture has been marketed under the moniker 'wohabeing' since 2017, and the range combines the craft of Wong with the geometrically abstracted fabrics of Hassell.

Hassell has always been voluble and impassioned when explaining his inspirations, and in a 2020

↑
Sanya InterContinental Resort. Hainan, 2006–10. The precast concrete screen on the façade was composed as a geometric tessellation by Richard Hassell.

←
Furniture by wohabeing on display at Maison et Objet 2017, Paris.

panel discussion he claimed: *'If I had not become an architect, I'm sure I would have been a natural scientist.'* He also declared his fascination with *'the philosophical implications of mathematics and physics'*, and his increasing interest in systems theory, stating that *'complex systems give rise to emergence, where the properties of the system cannot be predicted by the properties of its components'*; an observation that underpins both his geometric artwork and WOHA's thinking with regard to the city. Wong is not inclined to speak so confessionally, and one might say that his principal means of expression is quite simply the resolution of his architecture. Wong is essentially an intuitive thinker and the parti of any building represents the distillation of all that he has observed and devised: *'Parti is just an abstraction to clarity; it's when everything has been boiled down into one very clear idea.'*

WOHA's Residential Architecture
Rigour and Certitude

HOUSE AT MERRYN ROAD
SINGAPORE, 1994—98

The House at Merryn Road was the closest WOHA ever came to unambiguously expressing the vernacular forms of tropical architecture. With three timber–clad pitched–roof pavilions surrounding and protruding into a luxurious swimming pool, the house had a resort–style ambience, augmented by WOHA's built–in furnishings and cabinet work. More significantly, the planning was that of a compound, with indoor and outdoor 'rooms' merging to form a sequence of family (community) spaces. Although the photos attracted some publicity for the 'tropical modern' genre, when seen in retrospect the architecture was uncharacteristic, most notable for the planar compositional rigour that would become a WOHA signature.

F ollowing the formation of the practice in 1994, WOHA completed a rigorously resolved batch of residential projects over a period of eight years, and it was a collection with a most distinctive emanation of certitude, which firmly established the first iteration of the practice's reputation and identity. The Houses at Watten Estate Road (1995–98), the partnership's first commission, was a decidedly large project for a couple of novices, stepping down a low hillside in a leafy suburb as a set of twelve semi-detached three-storey townhouses with an assured presence, one that clearly evidenced the degree of self-confidence possessed by the young architects. Seen as a whole, the grouping has a robust abstracted expression, derived from the orthogonal arrangement of the walls, screens and elements required for heat protection and comprehensive cross-ventilation in the tropics.

→
House at Merryn Road. Three cross–ventilated pavilions open out to the pool in the manner of a traditional Southeast Asian courtyard house.

↘
Ground–floor plan.

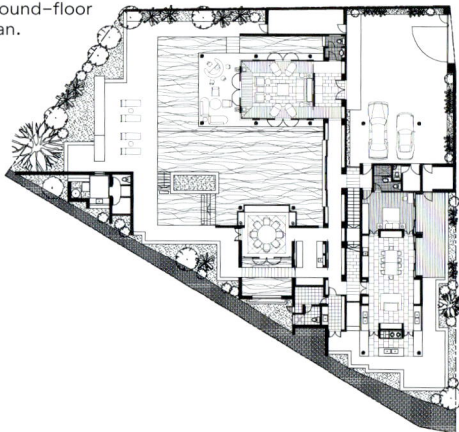

Ⓝ 5 10 20 m

SHOPHOUSE AT EMERALD HILL
SINGAPORE, 1995—98

The Shophouse at Emerald Hill was a commission that constitutes a rite of passage for Singapore architects: the conversion of a rundown shophouse into an elegant modern residence. When stripped of its commercial function (the shop), the Singaporean shophouse is the typological equivalent of the row house, the terrace house, the Georgian townhouse and the New York brownstone, with the added joy of an internal lightwell or courtyard, which disperses daylight and fresh air into the stuffy recesses of the volume. WOHA's initiation into shophouse conversion was to prove highly influential, and Wong Mun Summ candidly explains the impetus for its design: 'We were walking back from lunch when I spotted an old burned-down shophouse which revealed the beautiful party walls on either side of an empty space, and I thought it was a wonderful setting for a freestanding box.' WOHA were to do just that on Emerald Hill Road, a sloping street leading up from Orchard Road, by inserting an entirely new, crisply detailed structure within the long and narrow three-storey volume. The 'box' sat clear of the party walls, the levels were connected by lightweight stairs, and one of the courtyard walls was tilted to bounce daylight into the newly open-planned interior spaces.

↑
Three Houses at Victoria Park Road. The living areas of each house extend into a private courtyard and swimming pool.

↖
View from the courtyard back to the smooth sandstone box placed in the street-front volume.

←
Shophouse at Emerald Hill. Looking towards the courtyard from the new internal structure, which sits clear of the party walls.

THREE HOUSES AT VICTORIA PARK ROAD
SINGAPORE, 1998—2001

The Three Houses at Victoria Park Road had a striking planar composition, but the true significance of the project was to be found in the three-dimensional planning of the spaces. The houses were conjoined on a tight suburban site with a triangular plan, and the architects had the dichotomous challenge of providing outdoor living areas that could be privately enjoyed. Richard Hassell says that the design was '... planned as a matrix of spaces — internal, external and in-between — that have a variety of characteristics and take their cue from the structure of Paul Klee's rhythmic tonal paintings'. This project was the most complex undertaken to date, and it does indeed confirm Wong and Hassell's insistence that their approach and strategies have remained consistent: '... they were scaled up and up'. The parti of the composition at Victoria Park Road was effectively that of a building complex on a larger scale, where many factors are taken into account and then resolved by utilizing spatial configurations that maximize ventilation and natural lighting while enhancing occupant amenity.

↑
The bedrooms are screened for privacy, while the living areas are open to the garden.

↓
The house has a bipartite appearance, with two volumes separated by the entry hall and circulation space.

HOUSE AT MAPLE AVENUE
SINGAPORE, 1999—2001

The House at Maple Avenue and the House at Hua Guan Avenue are best considered as a twinset: as well as being sited close to one another, they display similar preoccupations and share a material language, even though the formal expressions are quite different. The two houses were notable for the quality of their workmanship, an issue that had been bothering

Wong and Hassell, as they had come to realize that local contractors were unwilling to risk their profitability and timetable when subjected to the architects' rigorous demands. WOHA approached a firm called Daiya Engineering, which specialized in rebuilding service stations within a month: 'We rationalized that if they could manage the reconstruction of a petrol station so well over a short period of time, they must have very good subcontractors and efficient working schedules.' Their hunch proved correct: 'Daiya embraced our ideas and loved our obsession with details, and they went all out to build them ... they then went on to become one of Singapore's top residential contractors.' The two houses in the Bukit Timah area were visible from the street, and the programme of each house was legible in the external composition, which clearly delineated the public spaces and private volumes. The expression may have been formally diagrammatic, but the houses had a quirky individual presence: the composition of Maple Avenue was deliberately naïve and homely, while Hua Guan Avenue was classically proportioned and elegantly austere. In both cases, WOHA had treated an enclosed family home as they would a public compound, with well-defined communal spaces, private spaces and service areas. The expression of the articulation is in fact the architectural parti, whereby all of the spaces, even the transition zones, of two private houses were imbued with a distinct tectonic identity and defined purpose.

→
The formally
composed entry
and circulation
gallery.

↓
The exterior was
designed as a
giant verandah,
with all rooms
overlooking the
swimming pool.

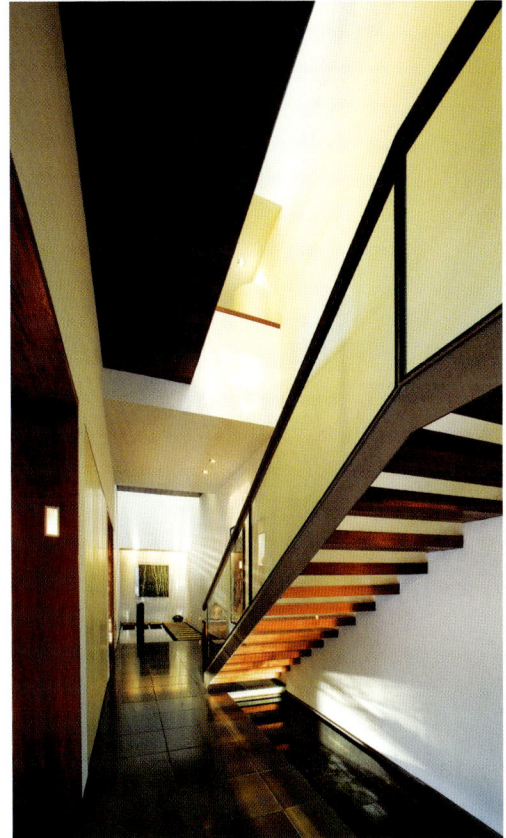

HOUSE AT HUA GUAN AVENUE
SINGAPORE, 1999—2001

"

In both cases, WOHA had treated an enclosed family home as they would a public compound, with clearly articulated communal spaces, private spaces and service areas. The expression of the articulation is in fact the architectural parti, whereby all of the spaces, even the transition zones, of two private houses were imbued with a distinct tectonic identity and clearly defined purpose.

THREE HOUSES AT BERRIMA ROAD

SINGAPORE, 2000—02

The Three Houses at Berrima Road faced a similar challenge to the Victoria Park Road project, but the site permitted a more detached plan, and the three identical lengthy volumes maintained a degree of separation. Although privacy was enhanced by staggering the plans of the houses, the overwhelming sensation when inside them is of the transparent connection with the forested landscape and glimpses of the other houses. A rich array of materials was selected, with warm oak panelling and floor-boards, glass curtain walls supported by slender steel columns, and rough grey stone steps and common floors. A great expressive gesture is made by the extremely thin cantilevered aluminium roofs, which extend five metres beyond the street elevation to form a modern rendition of the umbrella roofs seen in tropical vernacular architecture.

↑
View from the street showing the breadth of the slender cantilevered roofs.

→
The stairway is treated as a landscaped gallery, which leads down from the bedroom level to the living areas.

HOUSE AT ROCHALIE DRIVE

SINGAPORE, 2000—03

The orthogonal volumetric composition of the House at Rochalie Drive was also dramatically enlivened by a wafer-thin cantilevered roof form, which sailed above an outdoor family area extending from the notionally internal living room. As with the House at Maple Avenue, this house has two conspicuously contrasting elevational expressions: open and inclusive when viewed from the gardens, but blank and closed off when viewed from the street. The corridors and rooms are bright and airy, striated and dappled by the patterns of sunlight shining through a variety of louvres and screens, and the house has an expansive and adaptable spatial arrangement; it is very much a gathering place for extended family — a house as a community centre — where even the private bedrooms look over the public areas and the large lawn.

→ Viewed across a lawn used for large gatherings, the house is naturally ventilated and shielded by a huge floating roof.

→ The street façade was designed to maintain privacy, with solid walls perforated by screens that encourage airflow and provide daylight.

↓ The architecture is light, airy and transparent, framing internal/external communal areas.

The Gilstead Brooks project didn't just indicate the direction in which WOHA were heading; it also effectively marked the end of their low-rise residential work in Singapore's suburbs. They were to design only a handful of private houses over the next two decades, and their condominiums and apartment blocks would all be high-rise. The House at Cluny Park (2003–06) constituted the final instalment of WOHA's period as domestic architects, but as by now they were busy designing high-density mega-city schemes, their new preoccupations could not help but show through. Like Gilstead Brooks, the completed house was a beautifully detailed and deliberately over-scaled assemblage of formations, proportions, juxtapositions and paths of circulation, but the programme was public, or at least semi-public, rather than private, which was somewhat incongruous in such a setting. WOHA were advocating social inclusivity and environmental sustainability across the breadth of the city, but a luxurious villa self-evidently signifies exclusivity and a retreat from communal reciprocity. WOHA were now urban architects, and their thinking lay well beyond the confines and comforts of the private house.

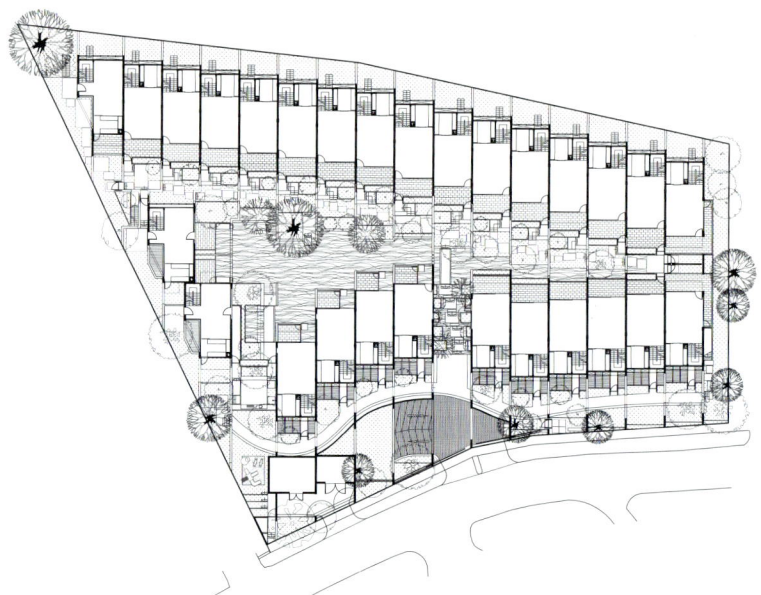

> **WOHA were now designing for a community, rather than a family, and as the two rows of four-storey houses were ranged either side of a large swimming pool and a set of gardens, they were introducing a principle of high-density high-amenity for the first time.**

↖
Each of the houses opens out to a shared landscape of watercourses and plantings of Brazilian fern trees.

←
Site plan.

↗
Paved walkways wend across the site between rows of houses that display a variety of screens, masonry and glazing.

GILSTEAD BROOKS
SINGAPORE, 2000—04

Gilstead Brooks, a cluster housing development tucked away on a quiet street in the middle-class Novena district, was of a style with a mannerist intention. WOHA were taking their planar wall expression as far as it could go, creating almost illusory vistas and viewpoints by over-scaling and over-delineating in repetitive sequences that appeared infinite within the grounds of the compound. At a purely visual level, this composition was quite delightful and slightly eccentric — a game played with fixed-point perspective that exaggerated the identikit repetitions of suburban job-lot housing and then subverted the 'genre' with perfect detailing and luscious landscaping. At a programmatic level, however, WOHA were using architecture as a social device. It was the first commission where they were required to address issues of density, as

twenty-eight houses were compacted on to a site previously occupied by two, and the over-scaling of the walls was in fact a strategy utilized to enable privacy, reduce noise and provide a coherent backdrop for the shared landscaping. WOHA were now designing for a community, rather than a family, and as the two rows of four-storey houses were arranged either side of a large swimming pool and a set of gardens, they were introducing a principle of high-density high-amenity for the first time. The pool and gardens were in themselves mannerist compositions, taking their cue from the over-scaled orthogonal geometries of the architecture, and the compound as a whole had an aesthetic assurance and ambience that would come to define many of WOHA's upcoming projects.

WOHA at the Turn of the Millennium

It could be said that the WOHA story really began back in 1975, when a little-publicized but hard-headed act of Singaporean policymaking set up a sequence of events that would determine the long-term direction of architectural practice in Southeast Asia. Following the years of post-Second World War turbulence, most nations had attained independence by the 1960s, and a swelling of local and regional pride was to surface in the form of architectural expression. The heroic geometries of the prevailing International Style were inflected by regional forms and motifs, and a series of public buildings built in concrete displayed an assertive interpretation of vernacular architecture. Unsurprisingly, the economies of the fledgling nations were to languish during their early years, several countries were devastated by conflict, and the erection of such concrete assertions of localized pride was more or less discontinued. But under the stewardship of the redoubtable Lee Kuan Yew, the small island-state of Singapore quickly decided to languish no longer, and embarked upon a programme of geopolitical acceleration which would, as Lee would later phrase it, take the nation 'From Third World to First.'[1]

Architecture and building construction were critical to this process, and the first phase consisted of a comprehensive slum clearance programme, which saw residents rehoused in the public housing blocks of a series of new towns radiating across the island from the city centre. The next phase had the rather more

1   After 140 years of British rule, Singapore gained self-governance in 1959 and joined the Federation of Malaysia in 1963, before seceding two years later to assert complete independence in 1965. In that year, its per capita GDP was US$517, by 1975 it was $2,490, by 1985 it was $7,000 and by 1995 it was $24,914.

2   In 1967, the Singapore government enacted the Land Sales Policy, whereby development proposals for the central city had to be submitted to the Urban Renewal Department of the HDB. The proposal for the OCBC Centre was submitted to the URD in 1968 after the Second Sale of Sites. With the appointment of IM Pei as lead designer, it was formally approved in 1975 by the URA (which had replaced the URD in 1974), and from then on, the

winning bids for all significant sites had a well-known international architect as lead designer. Tay Kheng Soon, an eminent local architect, observed in 1987: 'Foreign expertise has not broken any new ground. No new design issues or themes intrinsic to Singapore have emerged.'

cosmetic intention of transforming the image of the city itself, specifically its downtown skyline. Singapore had set its sights on becoming the region's leading financial centre, positioning itself as what we would now describe as a world city, and in order to attract world-class corporations, the government decided to commission world-class architects. Under the aegis of the Urban Redevelopment Authority (URA), the door was opened to international architects in 1975,[2] and IM Pei designed the first of the requisite towers – the OCBC Centre – which was completed the following year. In due course, as it became clear that Lee's objective had been consummately achieved, Singapore's neighbours followed suit and the modern skyline of every emerging Asian city has, more or less, been shaped by American, European and Japanese architects. In Singapore itself, as a result of the foreign-architects-preferred policy, the door had now been closed to locals when it came to designing large-scale projects: their role at a civic level was now to provide logistical support for the likes of Kenzo Tange, and so it remained.

The years leading up to the URA change in direction had actually seen something of a flowering of local architecture in Singapore, with semi-monumental and programmatically ambitious structures designed by the likes of Alfred Wong, Design Partnership and Archurban, but those blooms quickly withered. A generation of architects then busied themselves by attempting to define what a local architecture might

ST MARY OF THE ANGELS
BUKIT BATOK, SINGAPORE, 1999—2003

The buildings and gardens of St Mary of the Angels remain in pristine condition, laid out across a small plateau overlooking the public housing blocks of Bukit Batok, 14 kilometres to the northwest of Singapore's city centre. The lengthy rectangular compound does have something of the nature of a resort about it, in formal terms if not social, with the landscaping and the architecture combining to create another world, a retreat from the city. In terms of WOHA's subsequent oeuvre, the complex is significant in many ways, and Wong and Hassell now prefer to assess the project with regard to its spatial and community qualities rather than those of the immediately apparent devotion to crafting and detailing. The interaction between the internal and external spaces on two ground levels was a revelation, and with their first large-scale public project WOHA had achieved a programmatic resolution that would serve as a template for future works, most notably the community schemes devised over a decade later. For example, their Kampung Admiralty project (2013—17) can be seen as a scaled-up version of St Mary's, especially when the layering is revealed in cross-section. The terraced gardens at Admiralty are ramped above public areas lit by a giant skylight, and they look across to the residential blocks, just as the gardens of St Mary's gaze towards the church and down to the columbarium.

↗
Looking to the church from the outdoor congregational area, which also serves as a public plaza.

←
The interior of the church. All the furniture and light fittings throughout the complex were designed by WOHA.

comprise, but their commissioned projects were small and out of the way, their styles were derivative rather than interpretive, and a malaise spread across the profession – and it was one that extended throughout Southeast Asia. The only large-scale work to be had was designing the luxury resorts that were proliferating across the region, and significantly, these commissions inspired a renewal of interest in contextually appropriate architecture and the inherently sustainable forms of vernacular construction. As a direct consequence, the design of similarly luxurious private houses and condominiums reflected this predilection, and a desire for a tropical resort lifestyle took hold in the urban enclaves of wealth. A plethora of publications[3] ensured that Southeast Asian architecture was now perceived as 'exotic' (with a sustainability twist), the resorts and the houses for the affluent were categorized by such phrases as 'tropical modern', and Singapore architects, in particular, now had a reputation, but they continued to miss out when landmark projects were commissioned for their hometown.

WOHA emerged from the 1990s with a tropical modern reputation and quite some degree of eminence. The practice, which had only been formed three years earlier, had not been adversely affected by the 1997 financial crisis in Southeast Asia, and it could be observed that as a result of developers turning to architects of burgeoning repute in order to attract newly discriminating investors, WOHA tangibly benefited from the ensuing marketplace adjustments. They were already perceived as part of a select coterie that might offer more of a cutting edge than the established firms, the corporate architects who had been designing most of Singapore's apartments, condominiums and other medium-scale projects, although it was taken for granted that the policy direction taken by the URA in 1975 still denied local architects the opportunity to work as lead designers on the public stage. However, in a bolt from the blue at the turn of the millennium, WOHA were able to bridge that great divide, and the practice was then to receive a steady flow of commissions for urban projects in Singapore: some would be bona-fide city landmarks, and all would be exercises in sustainability, sociability and contextual awareness. At the turn of the millennium, WOHA were very ambitious, committed in their desire to move on up from private houses to the public realm, and the precursors to their first civic projects were two mould-breaking designs: one for a large religious complex and one for a residential tower.

" At the turn of the millennium, WOHA were very ambitious, committed in their desire to move on up from private houses to the public realm, and the precursors to their first civic projects were two mould-breaking designs: one for a large religious complex and one for a residential tower.

3   During the 1990s, Tan Hock Beng and Robert Powell were prolific authors of books on contemporary architecture, with such titles as *Tropical Resorts* and *Contemporary Vernacular: Evoking Traditions in Asian Architecture* (Tan), and *The New Asian House* and *The Tropical Asian House* (Powell).

→ With only two apartments on each floor, cross–ventilation is unimpeded, and shade is provided by projecting ledges and perforated metal cladding.

1 MOULMEIN RISE
NOVENA, SINGAPORE, 1999—2003

St Mary of the Angels can now be seen as WOHA's initial prototype for programmatically integrated medium–rise community buildings, and a project commissioned in the same year must be acknowledged as the equivalent of another urban typology WOHA knew to be in need of a rethink. Now surrounded by a discordant assemblage of high–rise buildings, 1 Moulmein Rise stands as a sleekly elegant silver–toned tower whose impact and enduring legacy stemmed from WOHA's back–to–basics approach to tropical architecture. The slender structure had only two apartments on each floor, which were screened and shaded on their lengthy elevations to the north and south, and cooled by unimpeded cross–ventilation. The strategy worked as effortlessly as it should, and it was remarkable to discover how pleasant high–rise living could be without air–conditioning, taking advantage of the smoother and cooler airflows above street level. The tower was also notable for its discreetly abstracted external expression, whereby a complex pattern was created by the seemingly random juxta–position of standard elements — such as window framing and overhangs — within a vertically bipartite composition.

'We wanted to change high-rise buildings in Singapore, as we realized that the existing buildings had not really been designed for the tropics. We looked at the curtain wall and the enclosure of the building, and decided to do something new. We thought in terms of vernacular form, where the façades and the roof are the most critical elements for sustainable construction and comfortable living, and we decided to apply this approach to a high-rise tower.'

—WOHA

In the context of Singapore's processes of architectural procurement, a pair of commissions awarded in 2000 were to serve as a game-changer, for WOHA at least, if not for their peer group. As noted, it had been pretty much set in stone that landmark architecture – public and/or civic – could only be designed by foreign architects with an acknowledged pedigree, and since 1975, no locals had slipped through the net. Some imaginative and innovative buildings had been designed by Singaporeans – the Kandang Kerbau Hospital (1988–97) by Tay Kheng Soon of Akitek Tenggara springs to mind – but none had what you would call 'world city' branding potential. A previously unseen window of hope opened when the Land Transport Authority (in conjunction with the Singapore Institute of Architects) held an open competition in 2000 for each of two MRT stations on the new Circle Line that, due to their location, would play a leading civic role: they would indeed be landmark buildings. Up against a line-up of well-known and not-so-well-known foreigners and locals, WOHA won both competitions. The window then closed again, very quickly, but WOHA had got their big break, even though they have since expressed their disappointment that the circumstance was a one-off: 'That was a shame. The process was seen as too risky.' The two stations did not open for another eight years, but WOHA's winning designs were widely published, their reputation was in the ascendant and they were now positioned to obtain additional projects that might also be categorized as landmarks.

So, why did WOHA win these two competitions? What was so special, so persuasive about their proposals? The locations and contexts were markedly different, and so too were the materials, but the design intentions and resultant expressions of the two stations were essentially the same. Both schemes formed a synthesis of contextual awareness and respect; rational and efficient planning; urban generosity and reciprocity; bold and assured architectonics; and maybe most importantly, a wonderfully un-conditioned conviction that lateral thinking can be the mainspring of inspiration. To visit the stations twenty years later, one is struck by the recognition that the architecture does not have a date-stamp: there is little, if any, evidence of when the stations were designed and built. It might be observed that, as the programme was so utilitarian, WOHA's innate adherence to rigour precluded any inclination to affectation, and quite possibly (and perhaps at a subliminal level) that is why the two competition entries were so persuasive.

→
Stadium MRT Station. Looking up from the platforms to the ribbed aluminium walls and a skylight that curves over the length of the station.

←
Bras Basah MRT Station. View from the concourse. Sunlight passes through a pool above the glass roof and over the escalators and a sloping limestone wall.

BRAS BASAH MRT STATION
SINGAPORE, 2000—08

The site for the Bras Basah MRT Station was smack in the middle of one of Singapore's best-preserved historic precincts, and as a few encroaching modern developments had somewhat lowered the tone over the past few decades, WOHA decided that they simply could not impose another piece of contemporary architecture. Apart from a few discreet entry volumes, their station cannot be seen; it resides beneath a massive glass ceiling that supports a gently rippling set of reflection pools. A remarkably grand urban experience is to be had from within the station, where a series of escalators convey commuters to the platforms 35 metres below through a giant void flooded with daylight, dappled by its passage through a glass-bottomed pond.

STADIUM MRT STATION
KALLANG, SINGAPORE, 2000—08

WOHA's proposal for the Stadium MRT Station actually used 'canyon' as the key word, and as Wong and Hassell fondly recall: *'This was our topographic architecture. We specifically discussed using natural forms to create a journey into the underworld.'* The site was located on the reclaimed flatlands that form the eastern shore of Kallang Basin, home to the National Stadium and the Singapore Indoor Stadium, and the station's operation would be determined by waves of sports fans and concertgoers, rather than commuters and tourists. The internal journey is the dramatic equal of that at Bras Basah, but this is truly an underworld — or underwater — experience, which takes place in a great, glowing crescent-shaped void. Visiting either station is an event in itself, and it must be said that in the supremely functional context of modern Singapore, such phenomena are most unexpected, and all the more stimulating for that.

WOHA AT THE TURN OF THE MILLENNIUM

WOHA's early 21st-century incursions into the city were not confined to the MRT stations, as they were now seeking out and securing commissions for what might be described as urban infill or revitalization. Such work would help to sustain the practice from now on, and two initial projects were to be found in near adjacency, in the Bras Basah precinct of central Singapore, which was ostensibly being regenerated as an arts and entertainment district. Over a period of eight years, WOHA would design eight buildings to be completed in this area, and although they had sharply differing programmes, they shared a morphological intention, one of civic reintegration and connectivity. Wong and Hassell had perceived that the post-independence modernization of Singapore had sucked much of the life out of the city: the street-life and communal interaction in public and semi-public spaces had been shut down and closed off by hermetically sealed private developments. Many of WOHA's inner-city projects were thus characterized by the insertion of semi-public spaces and pedestrian linkages, which aimed to encourage the re-creation of extended networks throughout their neighbourhoods.

→
A glazed furniture showroom and a spectacular lightbox were built either side of a new entry plaza for the existing Odeon Towers.

↓
The new entry plaza forms a crisply detailed modernist landscape, bringing a fresh design rigour to an undistinguished neighbourhood.

ODEON TOWERS EXTENSION

BRAS BASAH, SINGAPORE, 2002—03

The Odeon Towers Extension was an exuberant piece of public architecture, with a huge fluorescent Ginza-style lightbox bringing colour and life to an unremarkable streetscape. The giant billboard was set apart from an elegant new furniture showroom by a public pathway, which ran through the site with a series of right-angled turns and deviations to connect North Bridge Road with Victoria Street. En route, this landscaped passageway — featuring roughly hewn stone walls, reflective pools, granite paving and timber decking — linked up with the entrance to a food court and the very public spaces of the Bras Basah shopping complex. The elegance of WOHA's tectonic approach suggested how the reinstallation of urban connections could be enhanced by using a contemporary architectural language.

→
At the entry to Odeon Towers, the pathway turns at right angles and passes as a timber boardwalk through a set of reflection pools.

> **Many of WOHA's inner-city projects were characterized by the insertion of semi-public spaces and pedestrian linkages, which aimed to encourage the re-creation of extended networks throughout their neighbourhoods.**

↗
Clad with a sleek aluminium skin, the new apartment block rises above the tiled roofs of the conserved shophouses.

→
Appearing as a shimmering curtain wall in the rear laneway, the aluminium skin can be adjusted by occupants to control ventilation and shading.

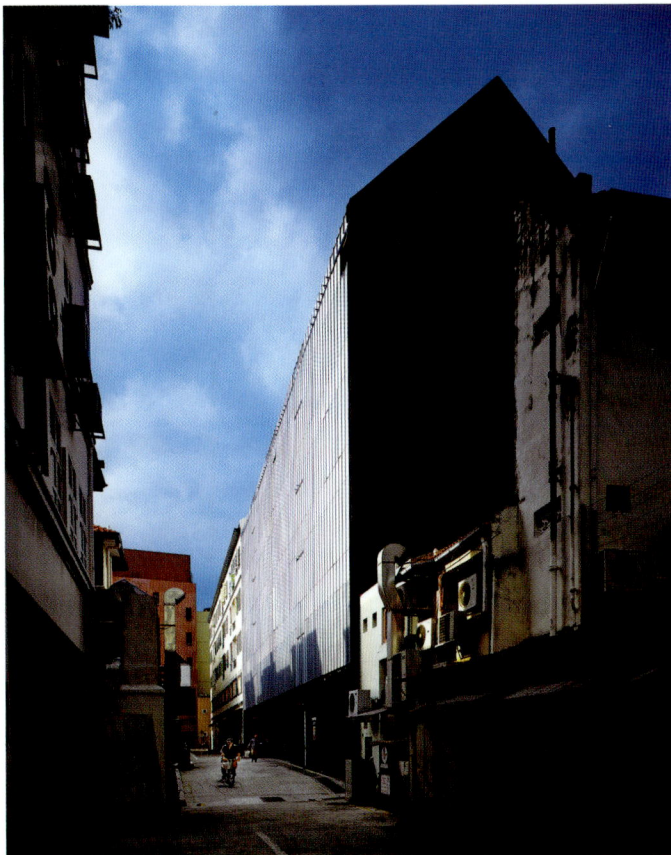

TAN QUEE LAN SUITES
BRAS BASAH, SINGAPORE, 2002—05

Five hundred metres away from the Odeon Towers Extension, this adaptive reuse of a row of shophouses was not concerned with urban connectivity so much as density, amenity and appearance. A six-storey 'box' clad with a perforated aluminium skin pops up behind a row of restored shophouses, and the aesthetic juxtaposition of sleek and silver modernism with terracotta roof tiles and dark timber shutters is more than acceptable; it is in fact quirky and refreshing. The modernist addition, which doubled the density of the residential development, backed on to a service lane for the restaurants on Liang Seah Street, and WOHA's sheer wall of permeable aluminium provides an austere, yet somehow quite appropriate, backdrop to the grimier side of the city's urbanity.

Sky Cities and Towers of Green

By the end of 2000, WOHA had designed a large church complex, a high-rise residential tower and two downtown MRT stations, all of which were under construction: the practice had now made the leap from private house design to public architecture and had procured work in three very different typologies. They were, however, established typologies. The opportunities for innovation when designing religious buildings, apartment blocks and railway stations are to be found in the rethinking of existing models, not in proposing a completely new typology, but at the beginning of the 21st century in Asia the notion of devising a brave new architecture was not entirely fanciful.

Many Asian countries had now 'emerged' geopolitically and economically, and the remainder were doing their best to catch up. The most dramatic demographic consequence was the extraordinary growth of the cities and many, such as Mumbai, Jakarta and Manila, would triple their populations between 1990 and 2020 to become bona fide megacities, while even Singapore, that paragon of orderly expansion, would double its population over the same time span, from three to six million. Confronted by this surge of urbanization, planners had stuck to the established template of housing residents in rows or clusters of high-rise apartment blocks. The citizens of Singapore had fared quite comfortably, as the New Town decentralization strategy had been rolled out in a satisfyingly beneficial manner by the Housing and Development Board in the 1960s, but by the turn of the century, most Asian mega-cities were densely settled with poorly designed high-rise blocks that had little in the way of amenity. Infrastructure and transport networks and social services were lagging way behind the population growth curves, and although the likes of the United Nations, the World Health Organization and the World Bank were ringing humanitarian alarm bells, it appeared that the nexus between architecture, urban planning, climate change and mega-city dysfunction had not yet been acknowledged, never mind acted upon.

If the increasing problems of the cities of Asia could be remediated by architecture, it was clear to WOHA that the typologies – particularly with regard to housing – needed to change completely, not just rethought but designed anew, as if on a blank slate, a *tabula rasa*. The two fundamental words were 'sustainable' and 'sociable', and the initial iteration of WOHA's proposed strategies for reinventing the city-living typology on a grand scale was revealed in a 2001 competition for a public housing scheme in Singapore. Most appropriately, however, the first WOHA project to demonstrate that such a new typology might actually work began construction in the mega-city of Bangkok two years later.

> " Infrastructure and transport networks and social services were lagging way behind the population growth curves, and although the likes of the United Nations, the World Health Organization and the World Bank were ringing humanitarian alarm bells, it appeared that the nexus between architecture, urban planning, climate change and mega-city dysfunction had not yet been acknowledged, never mind acted upon.

DUXTON PLAIN
TANJONG PAGAR, SINGAPORE, 2001 (SCHEME)

The Duxton Plain competition entry of 2001 for a public housing (HDB) project in Tanjong Pagar, on the southern edge of Singapore's CBD, proposed a socially activated and environmentally sustainable city in the sky. The renderings and the rhetoric would have probably resurfaced from time to time, in the way that all such provocatively prototypical but never-built schemes are, to be cited by academics bemoaning the absence of innovative thought processes, but this particular vision of the future now occupies an honourable position in Asia's architectural canon of works. Every idea proposed for Duxton Plain has been subsequently realized, time and again, in WOHA's completed projects and in countless buildings by other architects, all through the region and, eventually, all around the world. The project was a prototype for a new typology, which could be called a 'sky city', and it was flagrantly too great a risk for the Housing and Development Board to consider as a viable proposition, although the competition entry did receive a merit award. The HDB did eventually come around, six years later, and commissioned WOHA for a similar (and in many ways, even more radical) development, which would be called SkyVille @ Dawson.

To use 20th-century architectural terminology, the Duxton Plain proposal was a megastructure, whose antecedents had only been built in fragments, mainly by a Japanese group known as the Metabolists who were active in the 1960s. The most audacious schemes had a truly mega scale, and it was assumed that they would never be built, but the notion of a set of interconnected structures forming a massive and potentially self-sufficient building was only a few decades ahead of its time. WOHA had

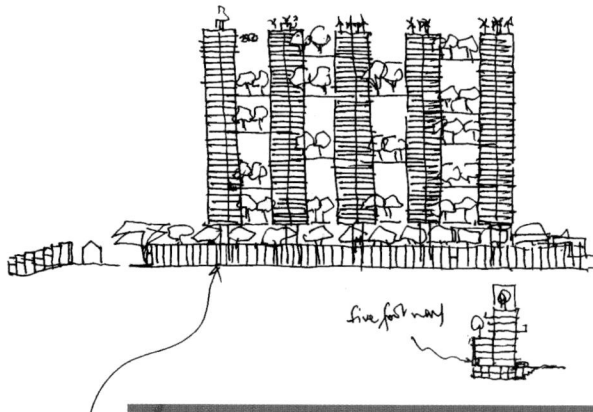

five foot way

↗
Eastern eleva-
tion. Sky streets
are layered on
every fifth floor
and the blocks
are raised ten
floors above
ground level.

perceived that the essential parti of a megastructure would be ideal for the tropical climate,
where the 'Lego' style arrangement of horizontal
and vertical components would stimulate airflow,
provide shade and shelter, and could support
communal biodiverse environments. If the
Duxton Plain competition entry had a specific
precedent, it was Akira Shibuya's vision of an
Urban Megastructure (1966), which referred to
spaces between aerial horizontal housing blocks
as 'vicinity plazas', although it was not clear how
the plazas could be accessed, and his drawings
showed helicopters buzzing around.

　　　The Duxton Plain scheme comprised
nine fifty-storey towers, which were placed on a
staggered plan and linked to each other at every
fifth level by 'sky streets', whose platforms
would also serve as 'sky parks' and 'sky villages'.
WOHA's renderings show forests of trees and
large open communal courtyards, forty floors
above the street, yet the architecture and the
ambience look disarmingly normal and there's
no hint of futurist dreaming, and this approach
was critical. WOHA had treated each aerial
ground plane as if it were at street level — a
village, a kampung, an urban neighbourhood —
and the architectural form and appearance did
not respond to the increasing verticality; it
remained domesticated and familiar. In essence,
the creation of a multiplicity of interconnected
neighbourhoods was the new typology, because

←
An early concept
sketch, which
shows the over-
riding intention
of constructing
a large–scale
vertical
landscape.

it had been done within a vertical high-density
building envelope: this was not an apartment
tower whose residents only had a view to enjoy.
Arranged in clusters of four and separated from
one another by small breezeways, the apartments were completely cross-ventilated, and
oriented in accordance with the needs for daylight and sun-shading. By raising the base level
of the apartment blocks ten floors above the
street, the complex minimized its impact on
the existing cityscape of Tanjong Pagar and
provided a public plaza as an extension of
Duxton Plain Park.

　　　Apart from its superstructural
composition, the Duxton Plain proposal was
most notable for its greenery. WOHA had
emphatically, and rather disarmingly, depicted
the massive edifice as a set of vegetated towers,
covered vertically by walls of vines and horizontally by groves of trees and extensive gardens.
It might seem surprising twenty years later,
but this was not exactly the standard procedure at the time, and WOHA were to encounter
a degree of scorn for what was regarded as
the architectural version of greenwashing, for
sticking a few trees on a building and insisting
that amounted to sustainability. With their next
built residential tower, WOHA would assert the
credentials of 'greening' a building by providing
statistical proof of its virtues, both for residents
and the city at large.

DUXTON PLAIN

TANJONG PAGAR, SINGAPORE, 2001 (SCHEME)

→
The sky streets were planned as sky parks with groves of trees and landscaped communal areas.

←
Site plan.
The towers are connected on every fifth level by a network of sky streets and gardens.

↑
The residents look out to a typical street scene, even though the apartments are many levels above ground.

←
Multiple ground levels serve as platforms for sky villages arrayed between the apartment towers.

←
The southeast façade features cantilevered sky gardens and a 100-metre-high wall of flowering vines.

→
Five floors above the street, communal gardens spread across the roof of the car park podium.

NEWTON SUITES
NOVENA, SINGAPORE, 2003—07

The thirty-six-storey Newton Suites apartment block was a singular piece of architecture. Located only 600 metres from 1 Moulmein Rise (designed three years earlier), it eschews that tower's shimmering elegance for an altogether more complex and intricate composition, while maintaining similar strategies for sustainable construction. The external appearance is defined by a bristling armature of horizontal black steel sunscreens, cantilevered U-shaped balconies and a full-height (100-metre) wall of continuous greenery. Arrayed three per floor, the framed-mesh sunscreens are precisely detailed, and when viewed from below the assemblages present a dynamic perspective of elemental climate control at work. As seen in the Duxton Plain proposal, four apartments on each floor are separated by breezeways, and they are shaded by protruding balconies, while a series of broader balconies at every fourth level on the southeast façade serve as communal sky gardens, or mini sky villages. The great wall of greenery is also located on the southeast façade, with a continuous vertical carpet of thunbergia vines rising alongside the external fire stairs and passing by frangipani on the communal balconies. The notion of segregating the apartments from the public spaces below, also seen in the Duxton

Plain scheme, was realized by partially support-ing the mass of the building on lofty circular columns in the porte-cochère. This gesture was a knowing appropriation of Paul Rudolph's entry sequence to the nearby Colonnade Apartments (1985), a tribute to the American architect's expressive essays in climate-responsive design, in both Singapore and Indonesia.[1]

Although a private development that catered to an affluent marketplace, Newton Suites saw the initial implementation of many of WOHA's sky city ideas, but its most tangi-ble achievement was in ensuring that 'green' was taken seriously. The northwestern entry forecourt was densely landscaped, but the main innovation was to be found at the southeast of the site, where large communal gardens were emplaced on the roof of a car park podium completely wrapped in vines. The public area on the roof comprised reflection pools, swim-ming pools and timber decking, all sheltered by palm trees and frangipani, and this vegetation formed a horizontal extension of the great green wall and its adjoining series of sky gardens. The 100-metre vertical garden was the largest in the world when completed, and the landscaped surface was 130% larger than the original area of the site, which, so far as anyone knew, was the first time that the amount of vegetation on a Singapore development had exceeded that of its natural environment if left undisturbed. WOHA

were to codify this equation as the Green Plot Ratio and it was eventually enshrined as part of the Urban Redevelopment Authority's assess-ment of proposed developments.

The lavish display of greenery at Newton Suites was not primarily intended as an aesthetic expression nor as a piece of envi-ronmental art, but as an ecological tool. The screens of vines worked as filters to absorb airborne pollution, the foliage greatly reduced heat levels, the overall 'parkland' served to re-introduce biodiversity to the city, and as a welcome corollary, residents and passers-by were reconnected to nature itself. For the first time in WOHA's career, the publicity that ensued when the building was completed in 2007 extended well beyond Singapore and the region. Architecture's worldwide web was intrigued and somewhat perplexed by such an exuberant expression of sustainable strategies, as indi-cated by Peter Schmal (juror for an international high-rise award), who observed that '... *this Singapore building was something else. It was untamed and, in concept, ran completely counter to Eurocentric norms*'.

1   Although Paul Rudolph (1918-97) is best remembered for his Brutalist-style buildings in the USA, designed between the mid-1950s and the mid-1970s, he had a late-career flourish in Singapore and Indonesia with four buildings that could be acknowledged as his best work: The Colonnade (1980-87) and The Concourse (1987-94) in Singapore, and the Wisma Dharmala Towers (1982-88) in Jakarta and (1994-97) in Surabaya.

"
The 100-metre vertical garden was the largest in the world when completed, and the landscaped surface was 130% larger than the original area of the site, which, so far as anyone knew, was the first time that the amount of vegetation on a Singapore development had exceeded that of its natural environment if left undisturbed. WOHA were to codify this equation as the Green Plot Ratio and it was eventually enshrined as part of the Urban Redevel-opment Authority's assessment of proposed developments.

← Looking up to the southeast façade from the street, with the vine-covered wall of the car park at left.

→ Looking down to the gardens on the car park roof. The 100-metre-high wall of thunbergia vines can be seen at right.

↓ The apartment block is raised above the porte-cochère and the public gardens of the northwest entry.

NEWTON SUITES
NOVENA, SINGAPORE, 2003—07

THE MET

BANGKOK, 2003—09

The Met was designed at the same time as Newton Suites, but although it was also a private residential development, it had a more rugged and raw disposition, and it was much larger. The Met was incontrovertibly a megastructure and, when seen from a distance, its powerful, self-assertive presence in the disappointingly bland high-rise skyline of Bangkok remains rather disconcerting, as if it belongs to an alternative visualization of the city. Although it has the appearance of a single sixty-six-storey slab, it is actually comprised of six slender towers rising from a staggered plan, and linked on every fifth floor by small sky gardens and on the 9th, 28th and 47th levels by communal sky streets, which extend across the length and breadth of the structure. All the apartments and external spaces are ventilated by the winds that pass between the towers, a process that is further enabled by the upward airflow generated by thermal displacement, and the structure essentially operates as a giant cooling machine: no bad thing in a city whose temperature tends to hover around the 35°C mark. And The Met is a green building: the towers are festooned with frangipani on the balconies and in the sky gardens, the nine-storey car park podium is wrapped in vines, and it scored 180% on the Green Plot Ratio.

The sustainable benefits for the city at large and the sociable benefits for the residents have now become evident, and Wong Mun Summ and Richard Hassell regard The Met as their breakthrough — the project where their ideas for a new typology were applied at a scale where their impact was indisputable: 'When we were invited to enter the competition for The Met, we went there to have a look and we were disappointed to see the developments designed by foreign architects ... they were American-model high-rise with bathrooms at the core, surrounded by the other rooms, all mechanically ventilated. We knew instantly that we could make a difference in Bangkok. We wanted to pull the core apart to ventilate and open up the spaces, and to use our one-room-thick approach in the apartments ... we had always done that in our houses and resorts, and we wanted to do it in a high-rise.'

The Met. View from the south-east showing the sky gardens and sky streets that link the six towers.

SkyVille @ Dawson. The forty-seven-storey towers enclose three full-height diamond-shaped voids. The car park podium is roofed by a public park.

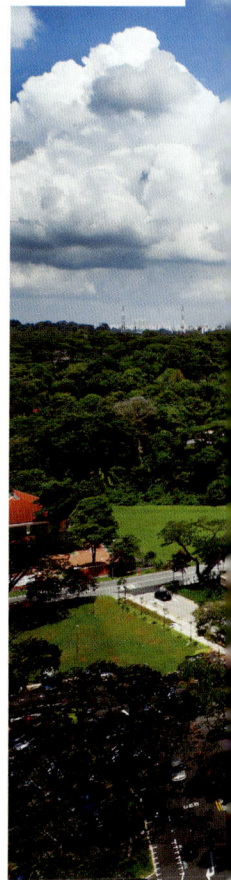

SKYVILLE @ DAWSON

QUEENSTOWN, SINGAPORE, 2007—15

Wong and Hassell were delighted that so many of the ideas first aired in their Duxton Plain proposal came to fruition with The Met, and this 2007 commission for an HDB public housing project in Singapore saw a further flourishing. Sky streets, sky gardens and sky terraces were all inserted within a forty-seven-storey megastructure capped by a sky park on the roof. However, the most striking innovation was the structural parti: twelve slender apartment towers formed an external carapace

that enclosed three diamond-shaped voids rising the full height of the structure, and these spaces were segmented by site-wide 'aerial' ground planes at every eleventh level. This hollowed-out structural arrangement had a manifestly sustainable agenda: winds and breezes blow continually through the large slots between the towers, and comprehensive shading is provided by the carapace, the sky streets and the sky park. Above all, the structural parti had been determined by an

> **Above all, the structural parti had been determined by an overriding social programme, whereby community interaction could take place in three-dimensional sky villages. The project was essentially envisaged as a collection of eleven-storey precincts, which could be overlooked (and overseen) by each of the residents' apartments, in the manner of any neighbourhood or small village.**

overriding social programme, whereby community interaction could take place in three-dimensional sky villages. The project was essentially envisaged as a collection of eleven-storey precincts, which could be overlooked (and overseen) by each of the residents' apartments, in the manner of any neighbourhood or small village.

The external architectural expression was not overly decorative, which is deemed appropriate for all HDB developments: motivated by an egalitarian agenda, the Singapore government has shied away from encouraging aesthetic competitiveness in public housing design. The relative sobriety of the external expression serves to heighten the visual impact of the internal spaces, which is breathtaking. One is taken aback by WOHA's audacity, by the realization that they actually did devise and build something so new on this scale. Initially, one could sense that the residents were also taken aback, unsure of how and when to use high-rise spaces for which there were no precedents. However, as borne out by independent research studies that compared the residents' satisfaction levels with those in other recently completed HDB projects, that 'shock of the new' uncertainty has been vanquished. The quantification of happiness and liveability is a sign of the times, one welcomed and actively encouraged by WOHA as they work to likewise quantify their ambitions, and post-occupancy evaluations show that the residents of Skyville's 960 apartments have endorsed the typological template.

→
The 264-storey-
high sky city
for five million
residents
contains layers
of mass transit
systems, park-
lands and farms.

PERMEABLE LATTICE CITY

SINGAPORE, 2011 (SCHEME)

Conceptualized in 2011, the Permeable Lattice City formed WOHA's wildest and most beguiling proposal for high-rise tropical living. It was a sky city in extremis, and two wonderful renderings show a cluster of great green towers rising from islands south of Singapore at a scale that was, to all intents and purposes, infinite. The vision of the Permeable Lattice City was beyond utopian; it was the stuff of sci-fi fairy tales, with layers of luxuriant sun-drenched parklands and farm-lands coiling around the green-walled towers like rainforests and rice paddies high in the sky. The apartment towers were reiterations of The Met in Bangkok; they were used as components to build a city, much as tropical houses had been used as components to build the towers of The Met. The scale had jumped up a notch: houses had been stacked to form towers, and now towers were stacked to form vertical cities. And as the towers were stacked four Mets high, the mega-mega-complex reached a height of **264 floors and could accommodate five mil-lion residents,** with railway networks operating on each of the four site-wide platforms in the sky. As with the most fabulous schemes of the Japanese Metabolists, it was clearly understood that the Permeable Lattice City would never be built, but the fantasy had more than a hint of reality, and WOHA's imagining would resurface several years later (from 2019) in a potentially realizable form with a series of competition entries in China.

WOHA: NEW FORMS OF SUSTAINABLE ARCHITECTURE

A New Way of Building in the Tropics

The First Decade of Public Architecture

By the standards of any architectural practice, the first decade of the 21st century was very productive and very successful for WOHA. It was a comfortable decade for architects all around the world, propped up by the money-falls-off-trees dissemination of easy credit, and this came as a great relief to Southeast Asian practices, most of which had been hit hard by the regional financial crisis of 1997. A plethora of commissions were to keep WOHA busy, and they were in an ideal position to accelerate their creative momentum. A variety of programmes, and increasingly, a variety of locations, presented new challenges and opportunities, which were welcomed and actively encouraged by Wong Mun Summ and Richard Hassell.

The completion of the Church of St Mary of the Angels and the 1 Moulmein apartment tower in 2003 provided WOHA with a surge in publicity. As this came soon after the MRT station competition victories of 2000 and the unapologetically ambitious Duxton Plain proposal a year later, it meant WOHA were gaining a credibility above and beyond the prevailing 'tropical modern' categorization of the region's architects. Two smaller-scale urban projects designed in 2001, the Odeon Towers Extension and Tan Quee Lan Suites, were completed in 2003 and 2005 respectively, and WOHA were to quickly expand their Singapore public building portfolio with a range of projects designed more or less simultaneously. Several of these buildings were highly conspicuous, occasionally verging upon the flamboyant, but they were all primarily concerned with urban morphology and liveability. Along with the Bras Basah and Stadium MRT stations, each of these projects was completed between 2008 and 2010, and WOHA had tangibly transformed much of Singapore's urban and civic identity.

> **Everything was a learning curve for us ... we really enjoyed trying something new and something different.**

WILKIE EDGE
BRAS BASAH, SINGAPORE, 2005—09

Wilkie Edge, a mixed-use development in a mixed-use inner city precinct at the edge of the Bras Basah district, set out to redress the neighbourhood's underlying lack of coherence and cohesion, and WOHA's approach was fundamentally an exercise in applying a degree of order to the processes of urban morphology. Although quite large, commanding a corner site on a busy intersection, the building doesn't have an assertive presence; it is not a standalone object but an assemblage of uncompleted forms and geometries, which respond amorphously to the multifarious typologies and architectural styles that surround it. In architectonic terms, Wilkie Edge is a curious building: it's there but somehow it's not there, partly clad in an ethereal shimmering silver skin that opens up to reveal pocket parks, terraces and layers of glazing with brown-toned sunscreens. WOHA were building a three-dimensional diagram of urban reciprocity and connectivity without imposing the architecture as a form or an aesthetic, and from that the building derives its own value. Wilkie Edge knits the neighbourhood together without subverting its existing patterns, and the crispness of the building's external detailing refreshes a succession of streetscapes that had been looking increasingly torn and frayed.

The School of the Arts was a prototype for a comprehensive form of passive environmental control.

↑
The existing building was opened out and converted into an apartment block clad with perforated aluminium panels. The car park podium now contains commercial space.

←
Wilkie Edge is located at the intersection of several precincts and establishes a degree of morphological coherence in a loosely defined sector of the inner city.

↑
Separated by massive breezeways, the vine–clad classroom blocks were placed above the school's public areas, which appear to be hewn from stone.

NOMU

ORCHARD ROAD DISTRICT, SINGAPORE, 2003—09

The adaptive reuse of a nearby building at the city end of Orchard Road had a similar agenda to Wilkie Edge. Although the locale of NOMU was not exactly rundown, it was ripe for revitalization, and WOHA provided a gleaming and finely detailed, though noticeably reticent, expression of sleek modernity. The concrete framework of the existing building, which contained six levels of apartments above a seven–floor car park podium, was retained and opened out to support a range of apartments with cantilevered sky gardens and communal terraces. As with Wilkie Edge, the geometries were abstracted and deliberately misaligned, with protruding and receding forms that allowed sunlight and breezes to splay throughout the structure. Neither of the buildings were architectural statements *per se*: they were considered, they were polite, they were environmentally sustainable, and they were quietly yet effectively reinvigorating the morphological direction of their urban contexts.

SCHOOL OF THE ARTS

SINGAPORE, 2005—10

The School of the Arts rears up abruptly from a major traffic intersection and effectively marks the transition point between Singapore's historic precinct and the Orchard Road retail district. The building's programme is clearly legible from the street, with a cavern–ous five–level public podium supporting a six–storey classroom block wrapped in a cloak of green vines. The manner in which the building 'operates' is also clearly legible, as the upper six levels are segmented by two great atria that serve as gigantic breezeways, thoroughly venti–lating every space and room in the school. It does appear over–scaled, but that was indeed the point: the building was a prototype for a comprehensive form of passive environmental control, and it was conceived as a machine for zero–energy ventilation and as a shell for self–shading. By constructing a new typology, WOHA were pre–empting an urban morphology.

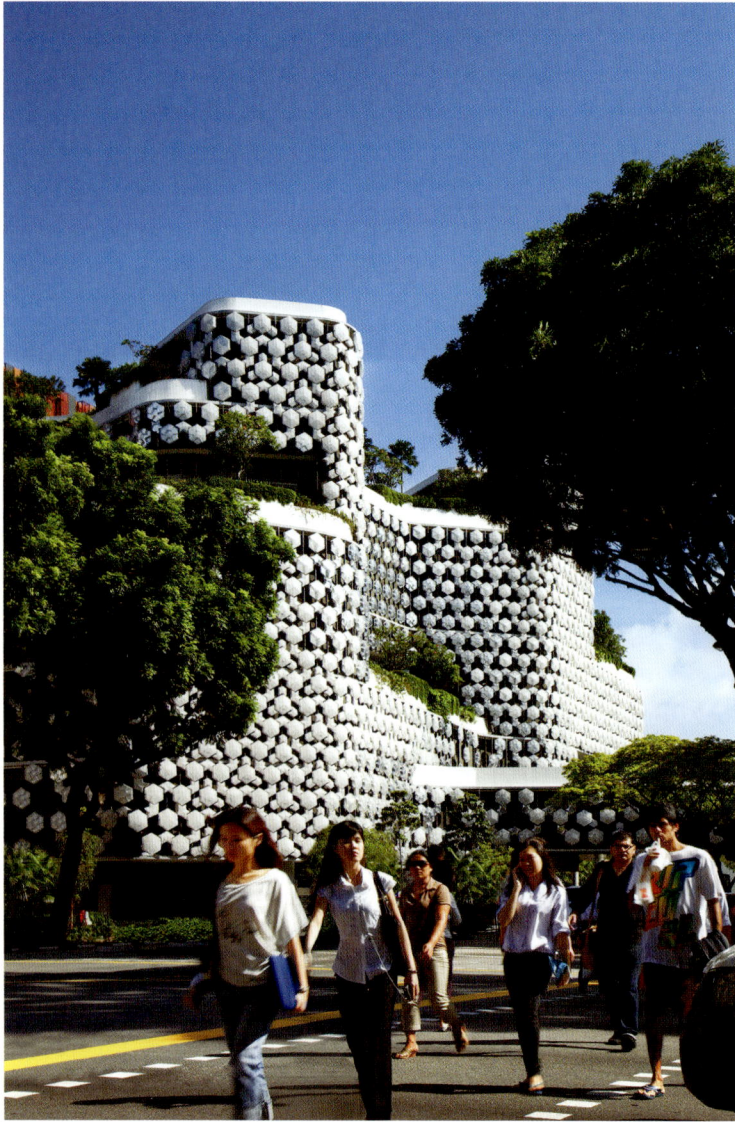

ILUMA

BUGIS, SINGAPORE, 2005—09

The Iluma complex, which is split neatly between an open-plan shopping mall and a closed box containing a car park and cinemas, has a striking appearance in the heart of the colourful and heterogeneous Bugis precinct. It is resplendent in a 'crystal mesh'[1] diaphanous gown that wraps tightly around the curvaceous shopping mall elevation, while the other (rear) façade presents itself to the street as a sheer orthogonal multi-hued, multi-panelled wall. Although it is ostensibly the entry point to the mall and the cinemas, the ground floor serves as an extension of the many laneways that cross through the neighbourhood, so it is beneficial to pedestrians and to the commercial interests of the shop owners. A six-storey central void between the shopping arcades was horizontally segmented by platforms with giant elliptical perforations and framed by escalators and curving galleries, so that the entire space has an alluring but rather disorienting quality, much in the manner of the Stadium MRT Station.

↑
The ten-storey shopping mall elevation is comprised of faceted hexagons mounted on a steel frame.

↗
At night, the undulating exterior of the shopping mall glows and flickers as an urban-scale public artwork.

→
Within the atrium of the shopping mall, the floor plates twist and overlap each other with looping amoebic patterns and shapes.

1   The crystal mesh façade was designed in conjunction with the Berlin-based architects realities:united gmbh.

↑
The organic forms of the shopping mall spiral out from the rigidly orthogonal volume of the cinema complex.

→
Overlaid CAD plans, with the cinema complex above the curving forms of the shopping mall levels.

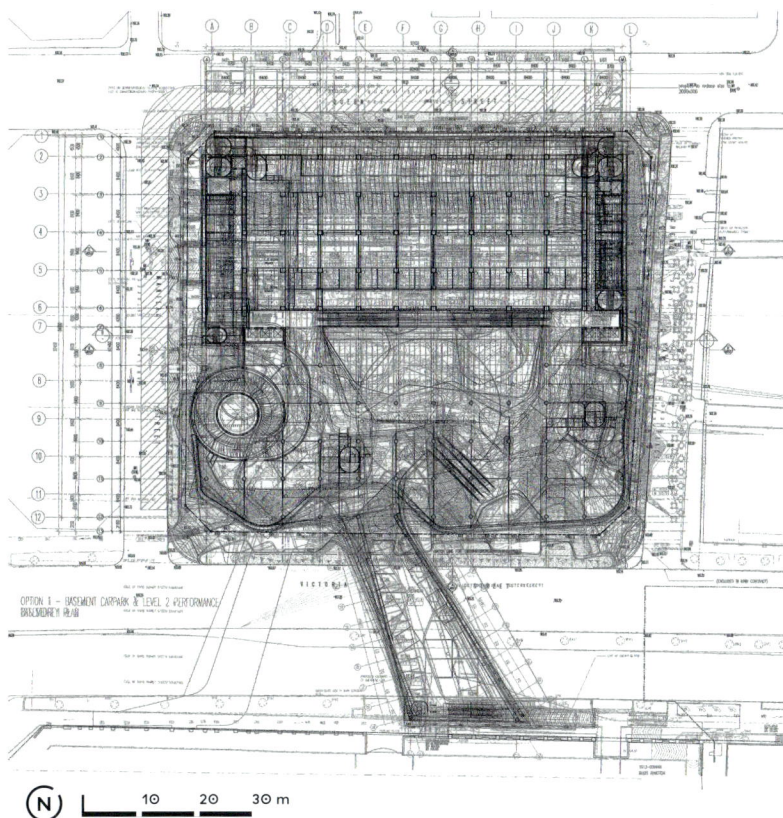

N ⊢— 10 20 30 m

CROWNE PLAZA HOTEL

CHANGI AIRPORT, SINGAPORE, 2006—08

Both internally and externally, the Crowne Plaza Hotel remains one of WOHA's most artfully composed pieces of architecture; one that takes advantage of its airport setting to provide a welcoming and very public manifestation of a newly urbane tropicality. A charcoal drawing by Richard Hassell of a female nude was the literal starting point for the voluptuous planning and interior design of the lobby areas, while the orthogonal exterior is encased within an exuberant yet highly functional sunscreen of white floral motifs that dance across the breadth of the façades and above the public gardens. Directed by strategies for sustainability and environmental integration, the guest rooms are placed either side of a continuous corridor with a rigid S-shaped plan, which enabled the creation of two gardens on the roof of the lobby podium. The larger northeastern courtyard forms a wonderful tropical land-scape, replete with palm trees, frangipani, and a series of ponds and pools, all bathed in the sun shining through a huge eyeball-shaped cutout in the external screen. The corridors and public spaces above the podium are all naturally ventilated, and screened by multi-coloured metallic mesh and abundant planting.

←
The lobby areas are wrapped in bands of timber veneer, glazed Thai tiles, batik fabric and Chinese metallic mesh.

→
Looking down from the open-air guest room corridors into the gardens on the roof of the lobby.

← The orthogonal volume of the hotel is veiled by a sunscreen placed on a steel framework and decorated with a continuous floral pattern.

→ The north–eastern courtyard on top of the lobby podium is encircled by black steel frames that contain twisting ribbons of white polymer–gypsum.

→ Typical guest room floor plan. Ground–floor plan.

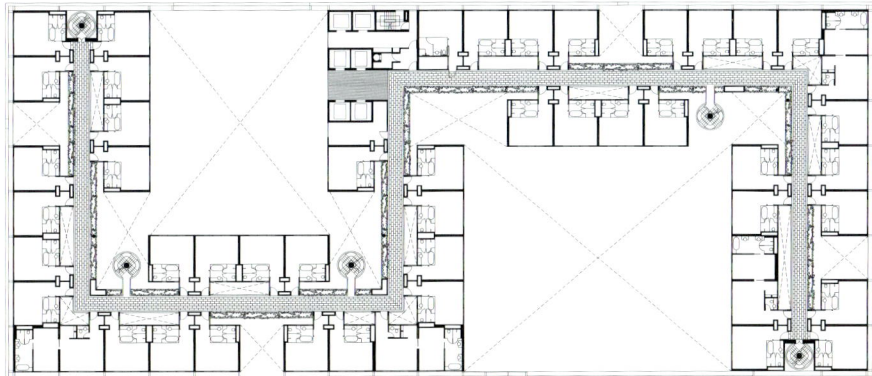

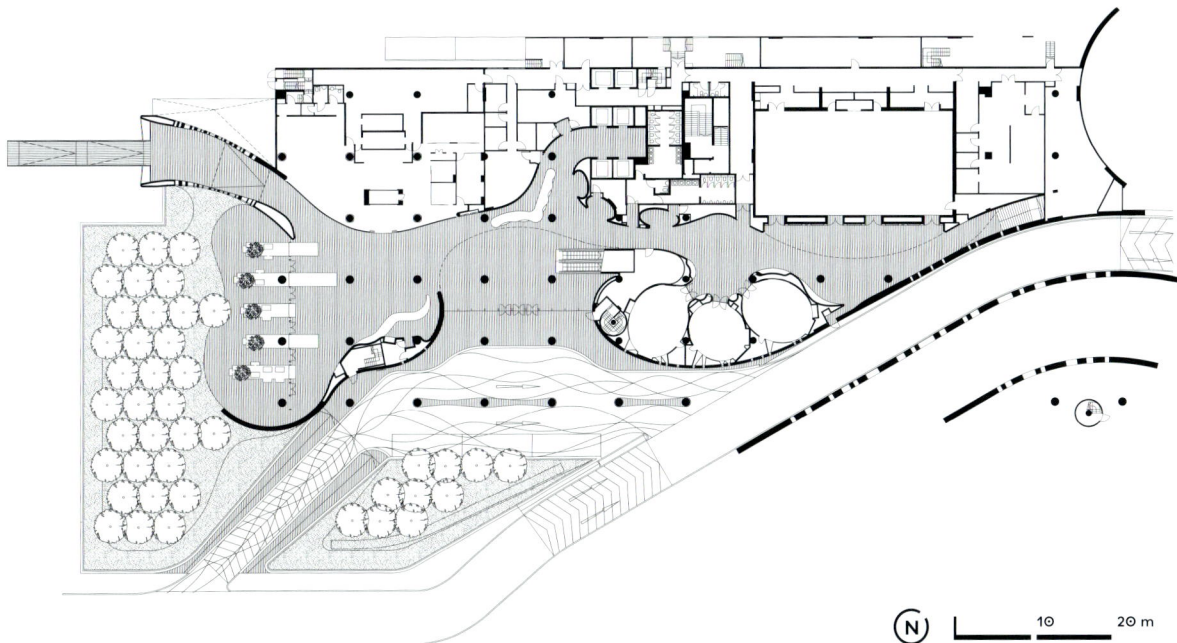

↑
Wooden beads
crafted in an
Indonesian
village wrap
around the walls
of the theatre
to promote
acoustic
harmony.

→
The walls and
ceilings of the
theatre lobby
are comprised
of an array
of undulating
timber fins.

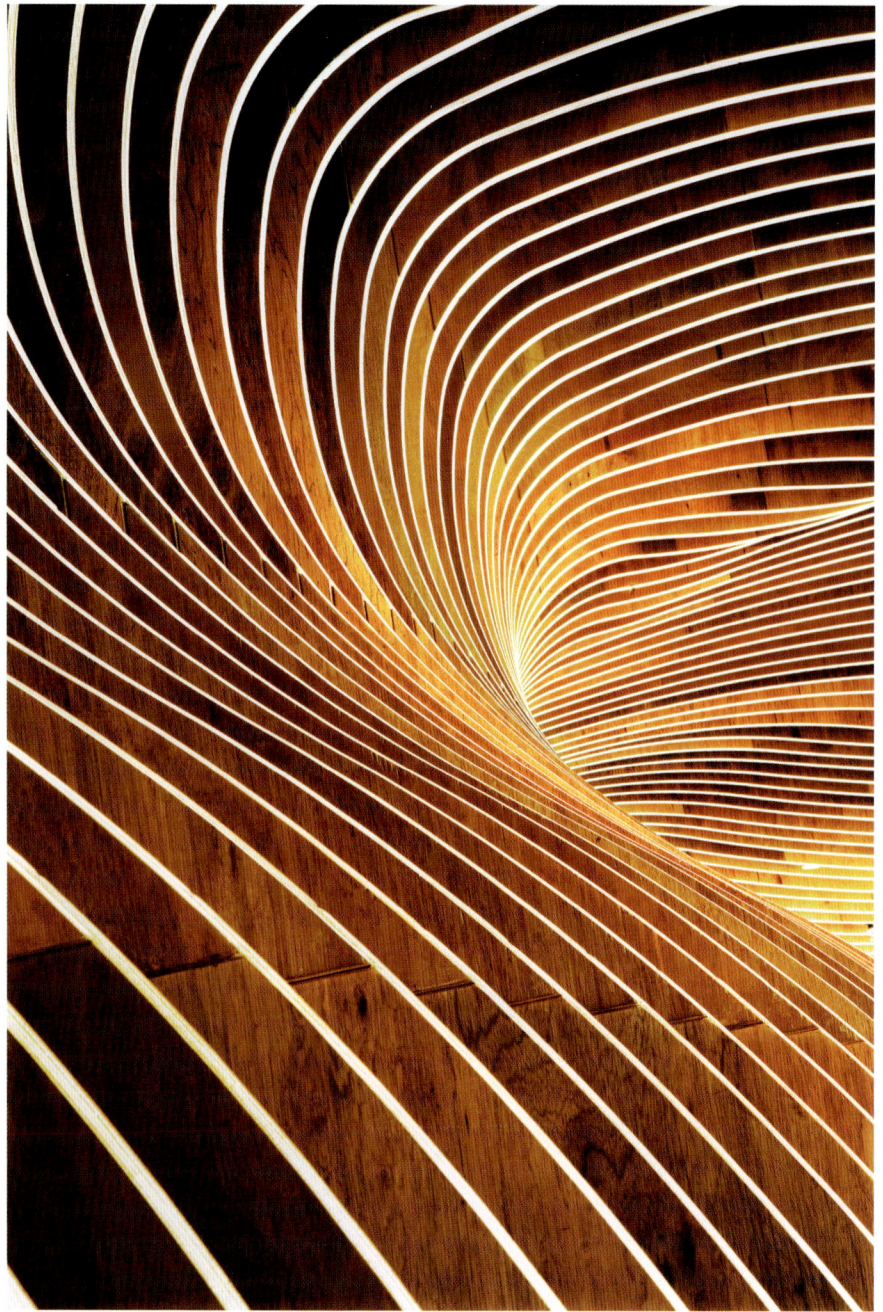

GENEXIS THEATRE

ONE NORTH, SINGAPORE, 2005—08

As a project solely concerned with craft and artistic composition, the Genexis Theatre forms something of an anomaly in WOHA's architectural production line, but it quite splendidly reveals the range of Wong and Hassell's interests and inclinations. They have long been avid collectors of Asian artefacts. They are fascinated by traditional joinery and craftsmanship, and whenever possible they have revelled in designing the furniture for their built projects. The theatre and its lobby are defined by timber, and WOHA shaped and sculpted it to produce two 'stage sets' that form dramatic compositions in their entirety and in their minutiae. The theatre, set in an egg-shaped capsule designed by Kurokawa Architects as part of an office complex, was lined with 400,000 timber beads that clung to the walls and served to resolve the less-than-satisfactory acoustics to be found within the shell of a large egg. The lobby has a cave-like topographic ambience, roofed and walled by a remarkable assemblage of rippling timber fins that enclose a collection of benches and settees shaped like boulders, and its swirls and curves were highly photogenic, to say the least.

29 HONGKONG STREET

SINGAPORE, 2007

Wong and Hassell's eclectic tastes were also quite splendidly displayed in the conversion of a 1940s shophouse near Boat Quay, which was conceived of as an exposition of their fascinations, and it remains to this day as WOHA's office, studio and occasional testing ground. The lobby areas, meeting rooms and anterooms have been treated as galleries for collected artefacts and Hassell's oil paintings, while the joinery and furniture that are spread over each of the five floors were all devised by WOHA. At the heart of the building, a glass-framed four-storey lightwell has hanging gardens that glow in the midday sun.

↑
The central lightwell serves as an ongoing site for experimentation in the development of green wall systems.

←
The lobby contains objets d'art collected throughout Asia. An oil painting by Richard Hassell of an abstracted mega-cityscape can be seen in the background.

→
The renovated shophouse is located in Singapore's old mercantile district. The rooftop was transformed as an entertainment area and vegetable garden.

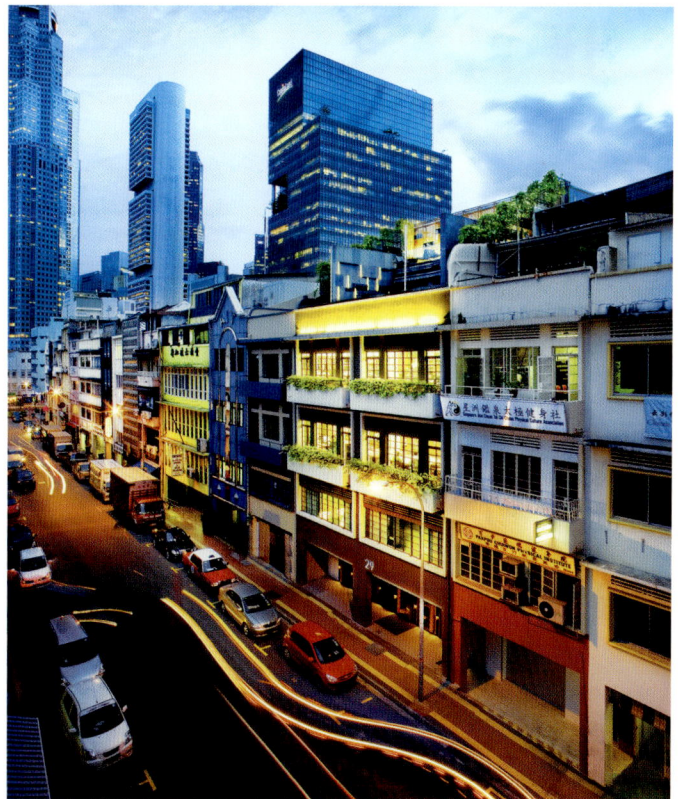

WOHA's range of work during this period was not just confined to Singapore, as several projects across the region were also completed between 2008 and 2011, a process kickstarted in 2003 by the commissions for The Met apartments in Bangkok and the Alila Villas Uluwatu resort in Bali. Two further apartment towers were commissioned in Bangkok and one in Sydney, along with a large beachfront resort in Sanya, China. This regional diversification was to be followed by a rapid expansion over the first few years of the next decade, as WOHA moved on to a variety of schemes and projects in China and two huge apartment complexes in India. Wong and Hassell are the first to admit that overall, the results have been mixed: 'All our projects are based on clear ideas, but there are such challenges with building in developing countries, which we fully embraced. If we had twenty ideas, but only three were seen through as we intended ... well, that's still a very successful outcome for us. We realized that we needed to have a large number of initial proposals in order to figure out which ones will ultimately rise to the challenges of a project.'

Of the initial batch of overseas projects, The Met and Alila Villas Uluwatu could be regarded as unqualified successes; the other two Bangkok towers were let down by the construction quality; the Sydney apartment block was distinguished though formally reticent; and the Sanya resort was a truly wonderful sight to behold, even though WOHA were precluded from input when many features were modified on site prior to completion.

> **The reason that Alila Villas Uluwatu worked – the reason that wealthy patrons could accept a sustainable environment and lifestyle – was that in terms of its ambience, its landscaping and its architecture, the resort was singularly beautiful.**

ALILA VILLAS ULUWATU

BALI, 2003—09

The Alila Villas Uluwatu resort was a one-off, an extraordinary project that provided WOHA with an opportunity to indulge their aesthetic predilections and implement strategies for sustainability on a very blank slate. The site was seriously unlike the mythical Bali of popular imagination, but it had a charm and magic all its own. Instead of swaying palm trees, golden sands and lush vegetation, Uluwatu (meaning land's end) is formed of a scrubby and rocky, almost arid plateau at the south of the island overlooking the ocean from an extended sheer cliff-face, and it had been left well alone by tourists. A resort in this region could not conform to the Balinese resort template — it was not possible in such a landscape — so WOHA had the scope to invent something new, and they had the chance to create a prototype out of necessity.

'We wanted to implement passive sustainability in a holistic fashion, and we wanted to "reposition" luxury. Before Alila Villas, we had rejected resort commissions because our clients would not embrace sustainability. We decided that luxury must equate with sustainability, and it worked... Alila Villas completely changed the hospitality landscape, and now all the big operators and hotel chains embrace sustainability. We proved that wealthy patrons could accept less in the way of material consumption if their surroundings were something special.'

The reason that Alila Villas Uluwatu worked — the reason that wealthy patrons could accept a sustainable environment and lifestyle — was that in terms of its ambience, its landscaping and its architecture, the resort was singularly beautiful. WOHA had made a virtue out of the site's vegetation and topography by using planning geometries that echoed the hilly landforms and by using an all-encompassing design language that took many cues from the rudimentary appearance of the small farms scattered across Uluwatu. The vistas at the resort are not of traditional Balinese pitched-roof pavilions and beachfront swimming pools, but of roughly hewn stonework, flat-roofed timber cabanas, rigidly orthogonal watercourses and a notably idiosyncratic architectonic disposition. The architecture of the public buildings was both historicist and modern, defined by a sequence of quasi-classical colonnades built in creamy white stone.

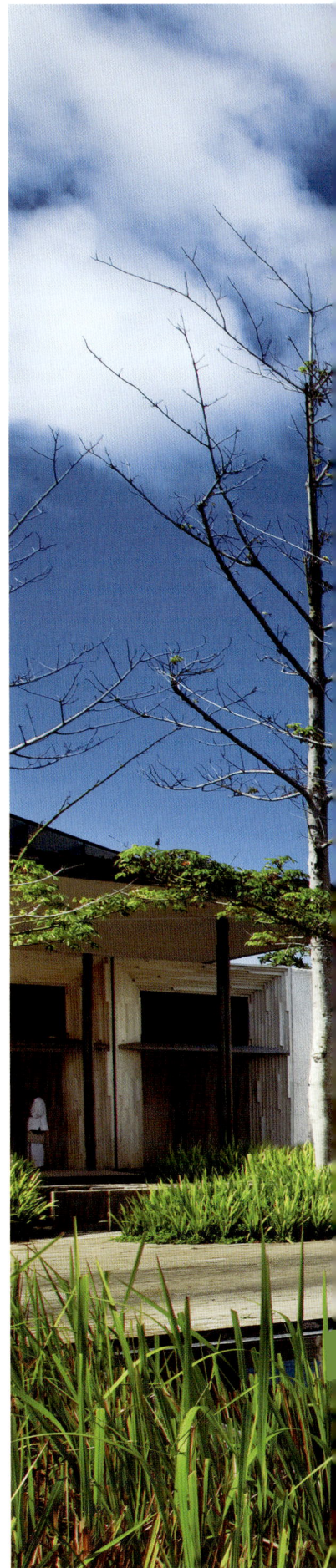

WOHA: NEW FORMS OF SUSTAINABLE ARCHITECTURE

'We imagined that Mies van der Rohe and Carlo Scarpa paid a visit to a Majapahit[1] emperor ... we were drawing romantic visual and compositional connections, and we made this a conversation between Balinese architecture, Javanese architecture and the canon of modern architecture.'

—WOHA

1   The Majapahit empire lasted from c.1300 to c.1530. From its base near present–day Surabaya in East Java, the Hindu empire ruled much of Southeast Asia. Bali remains a Hindu 'outpost' in the mainly Islamic modern–day Indonesia, and the stepped brick profiles of its temples are a legacy of the Majapahit period.

←
As seen in the entry courtyard, the formal colonnades were inspired by the proportions of Majapahit–era Balinese architecture.

SANYA INTERCONTINENTAL RESORT

HAINAN, 2006—10

The Sanya InterContinental Resort occupies most of the beachfront of a sizeable bay in Sanya, on the southern tip of the tropical Chinese island of Hainan. The previously unremarkable port city of Sanya has been drastically remodelled as a tourist destination, and the InterContinental was one of the first large resorts to be built, although the architects' determination to minimize its scale emerged as one of the project's defining aspects: 'The site provided us with an opportunity to do something where a large hotel would feel like a small hotel. We created multiple ground planes, and it is not really a building with a scale. Each courtyard is a hectare in size and the building is only two storeys high.' A vast continuous structure appears to comprise two separate buildings, one of which rises ten storeys as a slab with a hooked linear plan, while the other sprawls from the lobby areas across the remaining breadth of the site as a three-pronged collection of low-rise guest rooms. As the site was perfectly flat, the potential for the landscape to serve as a giant artwork — a mosaic, a tapestry, a tableau — was seized upon, and aerial views of the abstracted water-forms and roof gardens have become the ubiquitous images of the resort. This geometric abstraction is in fact a literal depiction of the resort's rigorous plan: the diamond-shaped roof gardens on each of the three prongs reveal that every guest room is oriented at 45 degrees to the ocean views,

and that the connecting corridors are formed of a sequence of similarly diamond-shaped atria.

Two magnificent water gardens recline like bays between the three low-rise 'headlands', with planter beds and lotus ponds contained by an extruded slipping and sliding rectangular framework, and the guest rooms look over or directly into this artfully romanticized landscape. As the low-rise block only had two floors, the rooms could be accessed from a single mid-level corridor — half the guests go up, half the guests go down — and the perfect symmetry of this planning led to an imposing geometric expression: 'We were looking back to the buildings of Louis Kahn and IM Pei.' As opposed to the fecund coloura-tion of the gardens, the semi-monu-mental corridors and public entrances are grey-toned and austere, evoking a more traditional Chinese sense of Imperial propriety. As with Alila Villas Uluwatu, WOHA were respon-sible for the interior design, the furnishings and the joinery, embel-lished by an array of ornamental screens and ceilings that refer to both Eastern and Western mani-festations of opulence. The entire western land-side façade of the ten-storey guest block is sheathed by a screen made from precast con-crete, with a geometric composition derived from an Ammann tiling pat-tern that had long intrigued Richard Hassell. The resort comprised many things, but the landscape-as-an-artwork is the memory that lingers,

and one might suggest that it was in fact the project's fundamental parti: 'We thought of it as a pleasure garden, and one that would perform well ecologically. We were influenced by both the rice paddies and the tribal geometric weaving of Hainan ... and we imagined the roofs and the gardens as an inhabited textile, as an environment to be explored.'

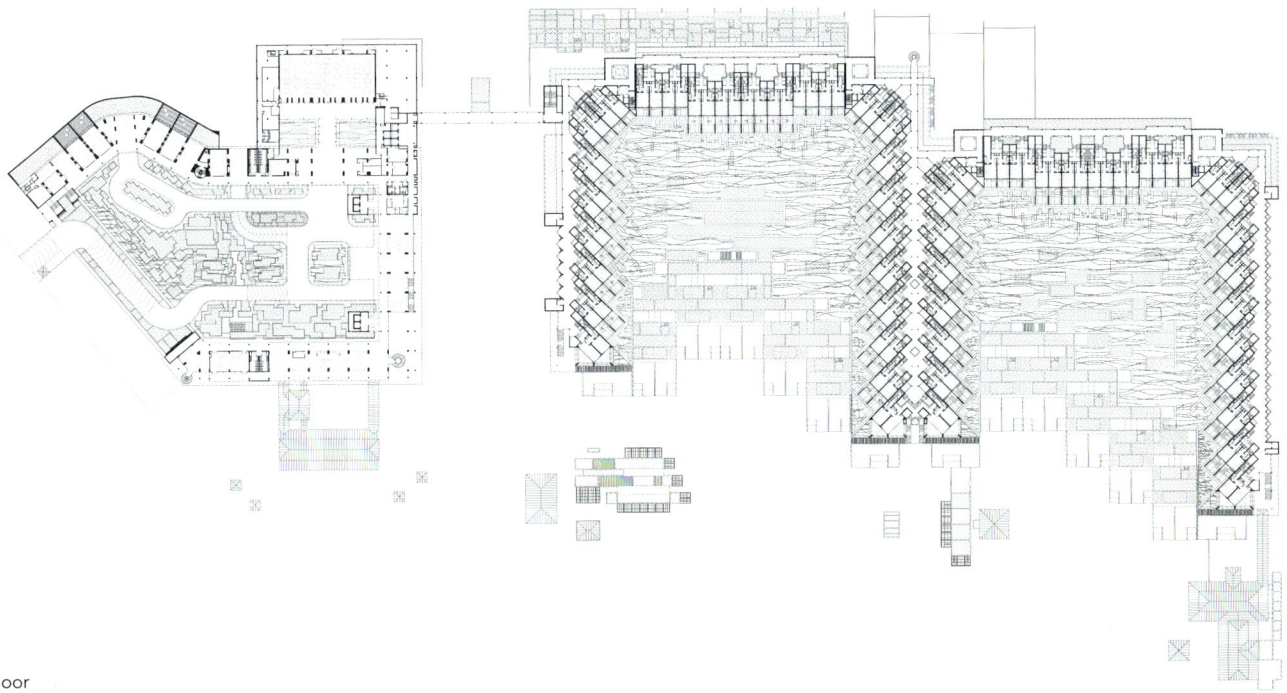

↗
Second-floor
site plan.

(N) 20   50   100 m

'We thought of it as a pleasure garden, and one that would perform well ecologically. We were influenced by both the rice paddies and the tribal geometric weaving of Hainan … we imagined the roofs and the gardens as an inhabited textile, as an environment to be explored.'

—WOHA

↖
The guest rooms look directly into the large water gardens that lie between the three prongs of the low-rise block. This rooftop landscape can also be viewed by residents of the tower blocks recently erected on the Sanya beachfront, as seen in the background.

← The Pano. The apartment tower rises above a car park podium sculpted as a geological landform to be overgrown with foliage.

THE PANO

BANGKOK, 2006—10

The Pano apartment tower was commissioned shortly after WOHA commenced work on The Met in central Bangkok, and it was located some six kilometres south on the banks of the Chao Phraya River. The original scheme comprised three towers, each with a 'propeller' plan, but eventually only one was built. The construction was rudimentary, not to say crude, but WOHA's design strategy was innovative and they regard the seminal idea as a '*breakaway ... a point of departure.*' In order to reduce exposure to flooding, all tower blocks in Bangkok are required to sit above a car park podium, and WOHA decided to 'sculpt' that prosaic block into what they describe as '*... a geological form, as a rock which could be carved to provide crevices and waterfalls*'. This topographic moulding and modelling of a building's base fitted neatly with WOHA's evolving notions of a garden city, and the 'geological form' was to reappear in a more refined fashion in subsequent projects, most notably at the Parkroyal on Pickering (2007—13) and the 443 Queen Street tower in Brisbane (2015—).

↑ Hansar. The apartments are screened by panels of aluminium mesh, and sky gardens for all residents extend from the common areas.

← Hansar is entered beneath the large wall of greenery that cloaks the car park podium.

↑
The Hyde. The apartments are completely open to the northern sun and the tower can be seen as a set of high-rise verandahs.

HANSAR

BANGKOK, 2005—11

In an exclusive neighbourhood near Lumphini Park, the Hansar hotel and apartment tower formed an elegant and glistening addition to the Bangkok skyline, sheathed in a golden veil of expanded aluminium mesh. As with The Met, the apartments were raised above a car park podium draped in greenery, which did much to mitigate the grit and pollution of the busy streets, while the apartments, public spaces and corridors were opened out to receive constant ventilation from breezes. WOHA, however, rued the project as a missed opportunity, as the construction progress proceeded with modifications they were unable to control, and the building stands as a transitional work: most of its features were more clearly resolved on other projects.

THE HYDE

SYDNEY, AUSTRALIA, 2005—10

The Hyde apartment tower stands as possibly WOHA's most visually restrained building, which was in many ways quite a shame, given that it was their first non-Asian project and it occupied a prominent site overlooking Sydney's only downtown park. As the building faces north, the design was primarily concerned with admitting as much sunlight as possible during the winter months and ensuring unimpeded views of Sydney Harbour. Neatly segmented by strips of projecting sunscreens and deep-set balconies, the clean, sharp-edged formality of the façade distinguishes the tower from its bulky neighbours and serves as a delicately filigreed backdrop to the lawns, trees and axial pathways of Hyde Park.

Aesthetics and Sustainability

A conundrum that faced 21st-century architects when the implications of climate change began to dictate their design strategies was, historically speaking, pretty much unprecedented. Aesthetics – style, form, appearance, representation – had always been the fundamental criteria for architectural innovation and critical assessment. Architects over the ages had immediately taken advantage of any structural breakthroughs, and more recently, advances in technology; they had reflexively responded to the twists and turns of patronage and to the needs of society at large, but they had never been obliged to acknowledge that one universal programme must override any other consideration. The phrase 'form follows function', coined by Louis Sullivan in 1896, had become a modernist mantra, but the philosophy was only applied to individual buildings: a factory or warehouse should not resemble the Palazzo Pitti, an office tower should not pretend to be the Lighthouse of Alexandria, and so on. The trouble with the 21st-century paradigm – architecture must follow sustainability – was that environmental awareness and zero-energy construction do not provide or require a certain form, or indeed appearance. Sustainability is a programme, not a function, and aesthetics are intrinsically extraneous.

WOHA had spent their first five years conscientiously implementing a programme of sustainable strategies in their private house commissions, but these were luxury developments, and as Wong Mun Summ and Richard Hassell candidly admit: 'We smuggled in the sustainability without anybody noticing.' To look back at those houses, and to their first public commissions – the Church of St Mary of the Angels and the 1 Moulmein Rise apartment tower – the strategies for passive environmental control are plain to see; in fact that's probably the way in which they are now assessed. At the time, however, those projects were essentially appraised in terms of their architecture, and the awareness of sustainability was acknowledged as a virtue but not the primary attribute. Smuggling in sustainability was the most feasible tactic: even though environmental accountability (LEED ratings and the like) was beginning to form part of the building codes, it was basically factored in as a commendable step forward, but one to be implemented by engineers and specialist consultants. With WOHA's next round of buildings, designing for sustainability was more than evident, and the practice was to find itself in a dichotomous position. Although acclaimed for their aesthetic appeal and architectonic strength, the buildings were overtly green in appearance and (for those in the know) the exposed structure was informed specifically by the need for passive environmental control. WOHA were not smuggling any more; they were expressing (and advocating) sustainability, and for many, this was as perplexing as it was unprecedented. WOHA were regarded as very good architects, but they were perceptibly straying from the prevailing discourse, and this led to some degree of discomfort among those who regarded architecture as an end in itself.

The conundrum – and WOHA's dichotomy – was new territory, as sustainable design had never really been considered in an aesthetic sense at a holistic level, at the scale of the building itself rather than its components. Before the advent of air-conditioning, most tropical buildings embodied strategies for passive environmental control, but aside from humble vernacular structures, their appearance was not defined by the methods utilized for sun-shading, rain protection and cross-ventilation. Whether colonial or modernist, the bungalows, shophouses and public buildings were all modifications of internationally accepted architectural styles, and although the 'tropicalized' proportions were often exaggerated as a design gesture, the overall composition was never intended to be a consummate expression of what we now call sustainability. The first WOHA building to display such an expression was the Newton Suites apartment tower (2003–07) and it did so with greenery, lots of it, as great walls of vines and as cantilevered sky gardens with frangipani trees. However, the tower had many other architectonic attributes (all of which were, in fact, directed by sustainability), and one could have assumed at the time that the greenery was just one element of the architectural expression, but from now on, every WOHA building incorporated trees, walls of vines and swathes of multifarious plantings and gardens. For a time, putting plants on buildings became something of a signature for WOHA, but going green in such a literal fashion was only part of the story.

The structure of The Met (2003–09) in Bangkok was directed only by its functionality, by its passive energy performance, and although it was tempting to classify the concrete massing as Brutalist, it was in its megastructural monumentality far more brutal than that. The intentionally stark, unadorned structure of the Brutalist buildings of the 1950s and 1960s was tempered by the attention paid to sculptural geometry in particular, and that cannot be said of The Met, whose geometry was purely performance-related. However, if you looked past the structural heft, The Met was carefully scaled and delicately composed: the expression in diminution was actually quite intimate, it was anything but brutal, and WOHA were to describe this aesthetic duality as 'domesticating the megastructure'.

WOHA's prioritization of megastructural liveability (domesticity) was especially pronounced in their design for SkyVille @ Dawson (2007–15), a public housing development in Singapore, and it was

> **"** If you looked past the structural heft, The Met was carefully scaled and delicately composed: the expression in diminution was actually quite intimate, it was anything but brutal, and WOHA were to describe this aesthetic duality as 'domesticating the megastructure'.

WOHA: NEW FORMS OF SUSTAINABLE ARCHITECTURE

rather hard to see what they were getting at when the building was under construction. The heroic structure appeared to be anything but liveable in the absence of gardens, trees and people; with sheer concrete walls soaring high above giant scale-less voids, it looked more like a rocket-launching facility than a homely collection of apartments. When the completed building was finally seen by the public, its presence was imposing but there was something indisputably noble about the architecture: 'SkyVille was self-consciously a megastructure ... it didn't pretend to be a small building, it was confident in its largeness and it expressed its size; it was not trying to minimize itself.' By 2015, the external expression seemed markedly less 'shocking' than that of The Met, as it was now understood that far from being an uncompromising and brutal statement, the structure had been devised to ventilate and shade. SkyVille @ Dawson did not look like a solid block – it was quite evidently a perforated exoskeleton that shielded the living spaces within – and it did not look large, because the size of the perforations relieved the scale of the mass. The internal spaces were the point of the exercise, however, and once the concrete platforms had been transformed into tropical gardens, it could be adjudged that WOHA had again introduced a new aesthetic. The internal architecture provided a vista of repetitive geometries, all of which had a human scale with plants and trees, chairs and tables, joggers and students, and it was apparent that a heroic structure had been domesticated: 'We were dealing with a mega density and scale. We knew we had to come up with something that dealt with all the complexities and issues of a megastructure, and we could only do that by getting the spatial qualities right, by making people feel at home.'

'We became well known because our buildings were well resolved as objects, but we noticed that when we started to talk about programme and sustainability, people thought we'd lost interest in formal innovation and we no longer regarded aesthetics as important. But our strategies don't come at the expense of aesthetics ... we love to search for an architectural language that shows off those strategies in its expression.'

—WOHA

> **We got a mixed reaction ... many thought it was an ugly building, but we were OK with that ... it looked ugly because it was a completely new type of building. It was just ahead of its time, that's all. People will adjust to the architecture, and they will appreciate new forms of beauty ... ones that are natural expressions of these new functions.**

Far removed from the high densities and social challenges of the cities, the design of the Alila Villas Uluwatu resort (2003–09) in Bali was inspired by WOHA's determination to implement sustainable strategies for a typology where designers had not shown much inclination to reconsider the methods for providing creature comfort. Hotel and resort operators put the customer first, and the provision of air-conditioning and the distancing of nature were taken to be prerequisites. In a manner reminiscent of their private house commissions, WOHA's only possible method would be to deliver (smuggle) sustainability into an architecture that supplied the required creature comforts. Apart from sustainability, the architects were obliged to ensure that the resort would be regarded as a 'must stay' destination. Unlike The Met and SkyVille @ Dawson, the resultant aesthetic expression was not determined by the strategies for sustainability, but by how WOHA used them to create an unfolding sequence of wonderful vistas and architectural 'artefacts'. As all the landscape elements were localized, the huge compound – sprawling down a hillside to a small plateau at the edge of a cliff – felt entirely of its place, and furthermore, it quite deliberately celebrated the 'different' Balinese environment of Uluwatu with an architectural language that paid scant attention to the established styles of Balinese resort design. Wong and Hassell conjured up a multiplicity of geometries, historical references and material juxtapositions that were something to behold, and the intended outcome, that of combining sustainability with desirability, looked like it had been almost effortlessly realized. Before the completion of the resort in 2009, the consensus held that you either designed something sustainable or something beautiful, and it was assumed that something environmentally sustainable would only attract backpackers and underfunded eco-tourists, which was not economically sustainable for a large hotel operator. But Alila Villas Uluwatu demonstrated that something beautiful could be environmentally sustainable, the resort did become a 'must stay' destination, and this WOHA prototype had an immediate impact.

The aesthetics of sustainability are not yet universally recognizable, and no style in particular has obtained what might be termed a critical mass of identification, in the manner that curtain-walled towers signal 'commercial offices', or cantilevered roofs with slender steel elements indicate 'sporting stadia'. But then, sustainability is not a typology *per se*, and the lines remain blurred. By 2020, possibly the only widespread form of sustainability identification has been 'putting plants on buildings', a now more than acceptable gesture that brings a wry smile to the faces of Wong and Hassell.

It would be naïve to think that architects will shun millennia of evolution and abandon form and aesthetics for structures that are purely modular, driven by programmatic considerations and nothing else: the joys of architecture will not be suppressed and nor should they. In the face of this 21st-century conundrum, it is intriguing to note the reaction accorded to WOHA's built prototypes, not all of which has been positive or supportive. There were few, if any, precedents for the megastructural form of The Met, so Wong and Hassell were not overly concerned by peer group appraisal, pointing out that '*architects, particularly in the developed world, in the West, are much more comfortable with a smaller scale ... we were dealing with urgent issues that just didn't exist there ... so our strategies didn't have an immediate impact*'. Alila Villas Uluwatu, the Church of St Mary of the Angels, 1 Moulmein Rise and Newton Suites were all highly regarded and duly awarded for their aesthetics, and eventually for their sustainability programmes, but an equally significant contemporaneous project was greeted with a more equivocal response. Upon completion, the School of the Arts (2005–10) was regarded with some unease and received a dose of outright criticism. For many observers, the building appeared as an affront to architectural taste and to the established processes of urban morphology, and Wong and Hassell were to devote much time to explaining the overriding intentions of the structure, which were to provide passive environmental control in a comprehensive fashion and to think of a building in self-referential urban terms, as if it were a town within a city. '*We got a mixed reaction ... many thought it was an ugly building, but we were OK with that ... it looked ugly because it was a completely new type of building. It was just ahead of its time, that's all. People will adjust to the architecture and they will appreciate new forms of beauty ... ones that are natural expressions of these new functions.*'

Macro-
Architecture
Micro-
Urbanism

At a micro scale, in their initial, mainly domestic projects, WOHA's fundamental principles for sustainability and sociability in architecture and planning were clearly apparent. Now, over twenty years later, when Wong Mun Summ and Richard Hassell explain their mega-city projects, they still use the same phrases they used back then: natural ventilation, community spaces, cultural patterns, vernacular forms, macro/micro, one room thick, environmental connections, and so on. When used in the early explanations of the rationale that lay behind their work, some of that phraseology did seem to be slightly presumptuous (and unexpectedly intellectualized) for what comprised little more than a collection of residential developments and a handful of medium-scale public buildings. Architecture takes time to reveal itself, however, and when Wong and Hassell were speaking broadly of community lifestyle and cultural patterns, they were using those small projects as exemplars of the strategies they were now extending to the larger-scale projects on their drawing boards.

At a macro scale, the implementation of WOHA's underlying structural matrix for social and environmental sustainability was formally inaugurated with their design for the School of the Arts (2005–10), a building they now pinpoint as a breakthrough: '*It was our first significant inner-city building. It was very urban, and it appeared to have a great bulk, because it had huge spaces for fresh air to circulate ... it was naturally ventilated, and it was very sociable for the students. Right from the start of this project, we wanted to come up with a new way to design for a tropical city ... we built on that from one project to the next.*'

From then on, WOHA would formulate a set of proposals, of which several were built, that posited the notion of developments as mini-cities within a

'In our search for solutions we are driven by the desire to innovate, but we encounter roadblocks that lie outside the project. When we are trying to figure out the solutions to our own projects, we uncover a whole lot of city-related problems on the way.

'Our technique is really a process of reverse engineering ... we need to envisage the city of the future in order to design our own buildings. Unless you can define your ambition and the likely outcome, you will find it impossible to overcome the ingrained mechanisms of urban development.'

—WOHA

↑
Self–Sufficient
City. Jakarta,
2014 (scheme).

mega-city. As the schemes were reconfigured and incrementally elaborated, the ideas that lay behind the designs for these mini-cities extended to the mega-city itself. WOHA were adamant that urban planning and architecture must be hand-in-glove, they must be symbiotic, and that systemic sustainability and reme-diation could not be achieved by isolated exercises in responsible architecture: *'There is no point in producing one building that tries to solve its own problems when it is embedded in a city which is doing all the wrong things.'* The strategies, structures, networks and systems of their mini-cities (as first glimpsed at the School of the Arts) were then conceptualized, inevitably, as components of a 'city of the future', and WOHA would codify the evolution of their prototypes as a process of 'Macro-Architecture Micro-Urbanism'.

'We submitted competition entries for univer-sity campuses and community town hubs in Singapore, and we did several proposals in China and Malaysia and Indonesia. It was a process of experimentation and testing ideas. We were addressing very different locations, soci-eties and levels of development ... but the same thinking and the same principles lay behind them all. As we worked on ideas of social spaces and community spaces, we were constantly using urban analogies within a building and inevitably we enlarged our buildings to the point where they genuinely had the scale of a city.'

Most of the proposals, which inched ever closer to all-inclusive city planning, were of a medium scale – especially in Singapore – and, like the School of the Arts, many had a voluminous orthogonal dimen-sion. Irrespective of their height, the schemes were conceived of as a stack of horizontal planes, which could be staggered and layered if the structure should extend or expand in any direction. Above all, WOHA were striving for a form of humanist, personalized architecture, working to alleviate what they described as 'the harshness of an abstracted cityscape', and they referred to many of their proposals as 'domesticated megastructures'.

SCHOOL OF SCIENCE AND TECHNOLOGY
SINGAPORE, 2008 (SCHEME)

A diagrammatic formalization of WOHA's nascent strategies for tropical community architecture appeared in a 2008 competition entry for the School of Science and Technology in western Singapore. A broad and rigidly orthogonal structure accommodated all the (private) academic facilities on the top floor, and as with the fifth floor at the School of the Arts, this horizontal plane served as a rooftop for the public areas below. The floor slabs, walls and roof were perforated by a variety of voids and openings, which stimulated continuous cross−ventilation and provided ambient daylight.

| 10 | 20 | 30 m |

> **"** This scheme was the first in which layering and permeability, on a very large site, set up a parti that was simultaneously organic and modular, natural and human-made, and it would be comprehensively revisited when WOHA received the commission for the Punggol Digital District in 2017.

SUTD STUDENT HOUSING

SINGAPORE UNIVERSITY
OF TECHNOLOGY AND DESIGN,
2010 (SCHEME)

Another competition entry, for the Student Housing at the Singapore University of Technology and Design, was a more elaborate and ambitious exercise, comprised of a set of long snaking blocks raised on cylindrical columns above an undulating landscape of parks and community spaces. The project was conspicuously 'greened', with each structure wrapped by vines and capped by lawns, while the rolling parklands drifted into, out of and through the structural matrix. This scheme was the first in which layering and permeability, on a very large site, set up a parti that was simultaneously organic and modular, natural and human-made, and it would be comprehensively revisited when WOHA received the commission for the Punggol Digital District in 2017.

↑
Three long housing blocks form the spine of an interconnected cluster of buildings veiled by hanging gardens.

←
The buildings serve as massive umbrellas above the sculpted landscape, which itself performs as a collection of giant breezeways.

→
A fusion of landscape and architecture was conceived to stimulate sociability and enhance environmental sustainability.

TAMPINES COMMUNITY TOWN HUB

SINGAPORE, 2011 (SCHEME)

A pair of competition entries for community hubs in northeast Singapore displayed a distinctly similar appearance, form and structural rationale, and it could be observed that WOHA's proposals for such civic projects were now looking eminently buildable. It would be difficult to deny their social and sustainable validity on the grounds of impracticality, overly idealistic imagining or, indeed, expenditure for much longer. (It should be noted that an equivalent circumstance had occurred with their public housing proposals before SkyVille @ Dawson was commissioned by the Housing and Development Board in 2007.) The Tampines Community Town Hub scheme of 2011 integrated all of its commercial, civic, recreational and retail facilities within (or on top of) one massive seven-storey orthogonal volume. The other competition entries, including the winning scheme, had proposed a collection of buildings, but WOHA surprised everyone by placing the sporting stadium and swimming pools on the roof of their building, thus allocating extensive parks and plazas to the now-vacant residual space on the site. The vine-clad structure was carved apart along its length by five huge breezeways, which were bridged at different heights by walkways and socializing areas, with airflow stimulated in every direction by open-ended arcades and four-storey atria.

↓
A stadium was placed on the roof of the Tampines Community Town Hub, above a comprehensively ventilated open-ended volume.

↓↓
Tampines Community Town Hub. Second-floor plan.

" The most remarkable feature was a layered aerial parkland, which rose up through the structure as a set of terraces and courtyards, segmented by a light-filled void (or canyon) that slashed through the length of the building.

PUNGGOL COMMUNITY PARK STATION

SINGAPORE, 2013 (SCHEME)

Likewise, the Punggol Community Park Station proposal of 2013 was very much a 'city within a city', with components layered as strata inside an elongated eleven-storey rectangular block wrapped in greenery. A load-transfer space frame on the fifth level supported six floors of offices and roofed a community club, a library, a medical centre, a police station and a public housing office, each of which appeared to be an individual building at ground level, adjacent to a bus interchange. The most remarkable feature was a layered aerial parkland, which rose up through the structure as a set of terraces and courtyards, segmented by a light-filled void (or canyon) that slashed through the length of the building.

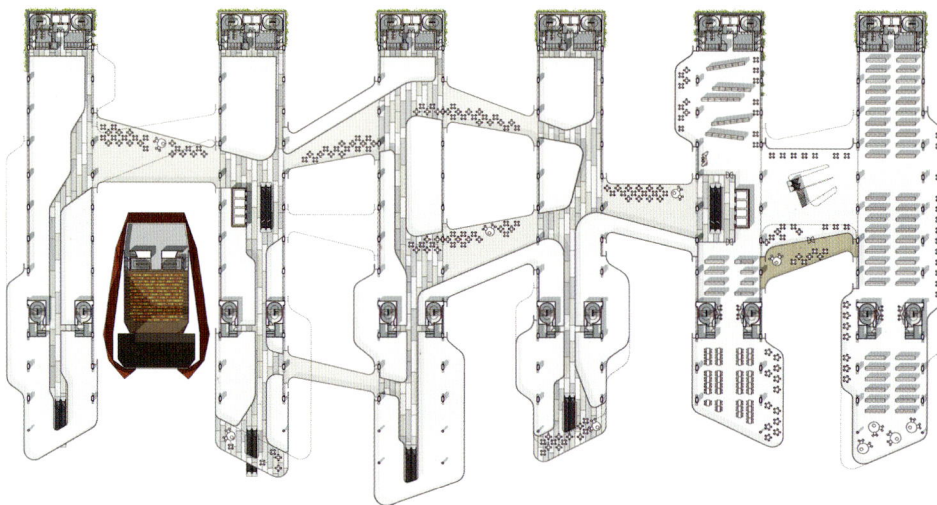

Ⓝ 10 20 50 m

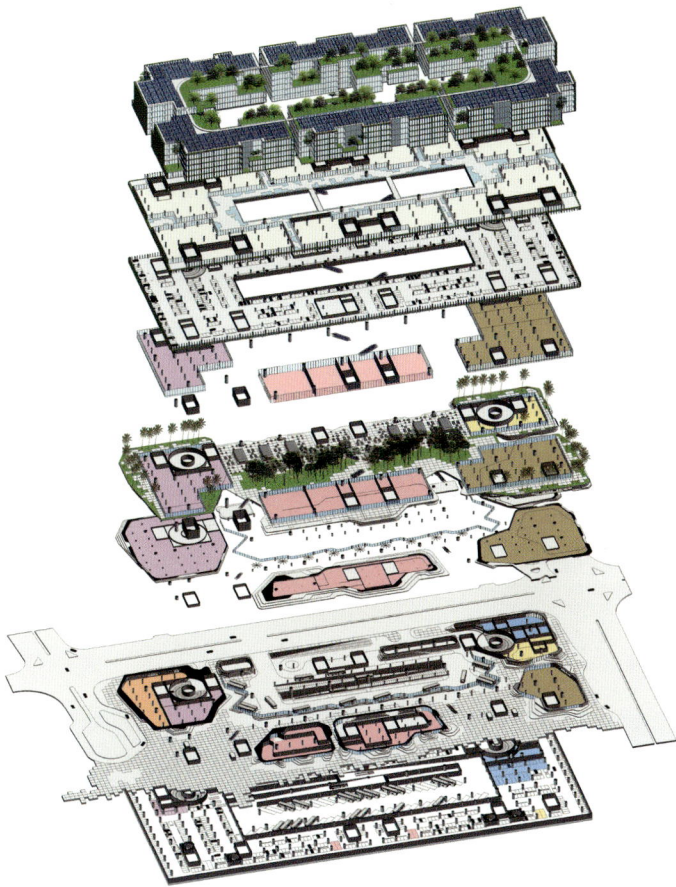

KAMPUNG ADMIRALTY

SINGAPORE, 2013—17

Shortly after being passed over for the Tampines and Punggol competitions, WOHA entered another one, for a mixed-use project in northern Singapore, but this time they won the commission, and another prototype could be built and evaluated. The competition brief had called for a development with four distinct programmatic components — elderly housing, healthcare facilities, a community hub and a shopping centre — and as with their Tampines proposal, WOHA integrated each of those components into one structure, and if not exactly a 'city within a city', it was unquestionably a town within a city. Kampung Admiralty[1] (2013—17), an eleven-storey complex commissioned by the Housing and Development Board, contains an underground car park and shopping centre, and a large open-air community space on the ground floor with a mezzanine-level food court below two floors of medical facilities, surmounted by two eight-storey towers of apartments for elderly citizens. These stratified components are all visually interconnected by layers of landscaping, by a central lightwell that floods the lower floors with daylight, and by an expansive and luxuriant rooftop parkland that descends as a set of terraced gardens over three levels to playgrounds and recreation areas on the sixth floor. Aside from the organic profusion on its roof, Kampung Admiralty is a relatively humble piece of architecture. The commitment to programmatic integration and widespread user-friendliness had overridden any inclination towards architectonic indulgence, and WOHA were more than content to let the landscape define the building, to provide a readily identifiable image of sustainability.

1   *Kampung* is the Malay word for 'village' and is commonly used in Singapore to describe small community settlements.

PERURI GREEN
JAKARTA, 2012 (SCHEME)

The Peruri Green scheme for the southern edge of central Jakarta was a resolutely modernist complex of five slab-block towers rising above a shopping mall and car park podium. The configuration was highly reminiscent of the Rockefeller Center in New York City, or it would have been if that complex were completely cloaked by vines, studded by trees, and carved apart to stimulate airflow. Reflecting the ambition to consolidate Jakarta's urban sprawl, this project had a much larger scale and density than WOHA's contemporaneous schemes in Singapore, but the principles remained the same. It had much in common with the community proposals for Tampines and Punggol, and given its size and scale, it would have been quite a landmark — one with a wonderful 'green' aesthetic expression.

> " The configuration of Peruri Green was highly reminiscent of the Rockefeller Center in New York City, or it would have been if that complex were completely cloaked by vines, studded by trees, and carved apart to stimulate airflow.

← Five towers are screened by vines growing on aluminium lattice. The extensive public gardens at street level include a mosque roofed by a glass-bottomed reflection pool.

TROPICAL URBAN BUSINESS PARK
PENANG, 2014 (SCHEME)

Proposed for a site near Penang Airport, the Tropical Urban Business Park marked a reversion to the robust expression of structure that had characterized The Met, SkyVille @ Dawson and the School of the Arts in particular. As with those buildings, the parti of sociability and sustainability was unambiguously displayed by seemingly over-scaled inhabited walls, which segmented and shielded a sequence of massive internal spaces. As another reiteration of WOHA's strategy of stratification, three apartment blocks and one office tower were placed upon a podium whose roof served as a second ground level: a broad communal area for residents and office workers. Four terraced atria descended five floors from the podium roof to the 'real' street level of the city, and all the spaces and towers were sheltered by a huge 'floating' roof plane, which was occupied by a public sky-park.

←
The city-within-a-city development created its own micro-environment of shaded spaces and public parks.

↗
An exploded axonometric shows the apartment blocks 'sandwiched' between the fifth-floor communal level and the rooftop parkland.

PATRA MANDALA PARK
JAKARTA, 2015 (SCHEME)

↑
Patra Mandala
Park. Jakarta,
Indonesia, 2015
(scheme).

→
Sky Forest
City Tower.
Singapore, 2015
(scheme).

With their scheme for Penang, WOHA had demonstrably shifted gears and were striving for a more complex resolution of macro-architecture: the building could be seen as a city in itself, never mind a city within a city. The medium-rise volumetric had been 'blown up' to a decisively larger, almost intimidating scale that couldn't really be taken much further, and WOHA's next proposals would revert to more definitively high-rise forms and spatial arrangements. The process of Macro-Architecture Micro-Urbanism was to intensify, and as flagged by several schemes designed in 2014 and 2015, the next phase of big-picture thinking would see the inevitable conjunction of their community proposals with their sky city typology. The Oasia Downtown hotel (2011–16) was nearly complete, and the clearly articulated structural strategies of that hyper-conspicuous tower had armed WOHA with a fresh template for sustainable, sociable high-rise construction. Several proposals designed in quick succession – the Vertical Stacked City (2014) in Shenzhen, the Sky Forest City Tower competition entry (2015) in Singapore, and the Patra Mandala Park apartment scheme (2015) in Jakarta – all inserted extensive liveability components into towers with an emphatically expressed verticality.

SKY FOREST CITY TOWER
SINGAPORE, 2015 (SCHEME)

> **The process of Macro-Architecture Micro-Urbanism was to intensify, and as flagged by several schemes designed in 2014 and 2015, the next phase of big-picture thinking would see the inevitable conjunction of their community proposals with their sky city typology.**

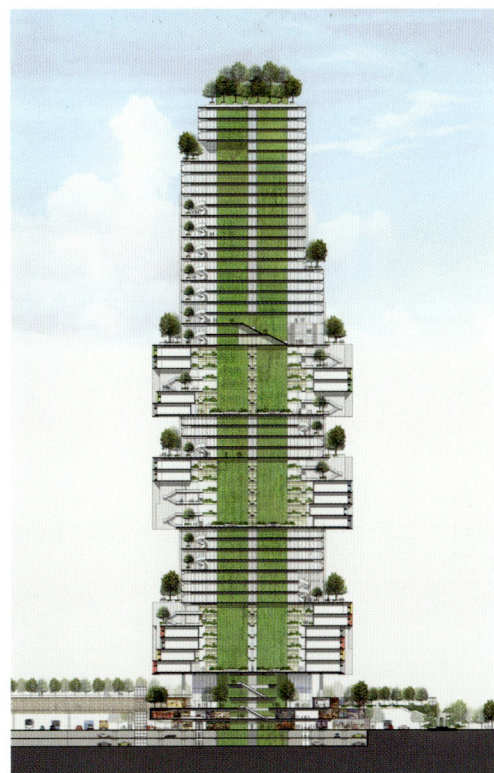

↑
Vertical Stacked City. Shenzhen, China, 2014 (scheme).

←
Vertical Stacked City. Section.

VERTICAL STACKED CITY
SHENZHEN, 2014 (SCHEME)

20 50 100 m

SELF-SUFFICIENT CITY

JAKARTA, 2014 (SCHEME)

With a very broad geographical footprint, WOHA's most comprehensive Macro–Architecture Micro–Urbanism proposal represented the ultimate 'suburb of the future', and it went through several iterations before it was eventually tagged the Self-Sufficient City. Initially submitted as a competition entry in 2013 for the new town of Tengah in northwest Singapore and revised a year later for a proposed development in northern Jakarta, the scheme to house 210,000 residents was a heroic conception of a multi-layered city-as-landscape, wherein the macro-scaled environment would have a micro-scaled domestic ambience. The 'city' would be completely autonomous and self-reliant, and one does not know whether such a utopian undertaking will ever be constructed, anywhere, but WOHA realized that the 2013 competition was an opportunity to articulate a parti for mega-scale development, from which they could extract elements and fundamental strategies for future use.

The renderings of the Self-Sufficient City show a dreamily idealistic environment for living in the tropics, where WOHA had indeed envisaged a city that performs like a rainforest. In more prosaic terms, the megastructural collection of buildings was constructed with four layers, as a three-dimensional matrix rather than a two-dimensional grid. The Rooftop Canopy layer was both protective and productive, sheltering the buildings and public spaces while providing solar energy and food from 'sky farms'. The Residential and Workplace layer contained twelve floors of naturally lit and ventilated apartments, placed in blocks that tapered down to their base in order to minimize their footprint. The Parkland layer comprised a new undulating landscape that restored natural biodiversity, while the Transportation and Services layer — weaving across and below the parkland — contained service networks and a mass-transit railway. WOHA made all the calculations for sustainability and

self-sufficiency, estimating that three square kilometres of photovoltaic panels could generate 350,000 megawatt hours of energy per year, which would exceed the projected requirements for residents and services. The daily waste of 679 tonnes would be either recycled or converted into 104,000 megawatt hours of biomass energy per year, while a hydroponic system on the sky farms would enable the requisite daily production of 55,000 kilograms of vegetables.

"The 'city' would be completely autonomous and self-reliant, and one does not know whether such a utopian undertaking will ever be constructed, anywhere, but WOHA realized that the 2013 competition was an opportunity to articulate a parti for mega-scale development, from which they could extract elements and fundamental strategies for future use.

←
The apartment blocks are surrounded by and partially enclose large tracts of re-wilded rainforest.

As it happened, WOHA did not have to wait for long to implement several of the Self-Sufficient City's key strategies, as they were commissioned in 2017 to provide a masterplan for the Punggol Digital District. Currently under construction on a flatland site in northeast Singapore, this new precinct was envisaged by the government as an autonomous, completely integrated development, built on a blank slate as a prototype for ongoing technology-led economic growth. WOHA designed all but one of the ten buildings, and the scheme as a whole utilized the Self-Sufficient City's fundamental parti of layering (stratification) at a macro scale. In terms of infrastructure, logistics, transportation and community, the development is self-sufficient, or at least self-reliant, and – crucially – WOHA were able to enact a policy of re-wilding, whereby 50% of the site's surface would be unapologetically natural: a genuinely green environment and, literally, a wilderness. This simple equation was subsequently taken by WOHA to the largest scale with their Fifty-Fifty City proposal of late 2020, which visualized a 'half human, half nature' reconstruction of an extensive and soon-to-be-outdated brownfield zone in central Singapore. The key intention of this proposal was the regeneration of the city, and by extension, the regeneration of the planet. Given that it was conceived during an ominously unsettling global pandemic, the idealization of a happy, healthy and harmonious city was especially timely and – one hopes – more than auspicious.

SELF-SUFFICIENT CITY
JAKARTA, 2014 (SCHEME)

↑
The newly designed land-scape activates social activity as well as restoring natural biodiversity.

←
The entire complex is roofed by a solar canopy comprised of photovoltaic panels that can generate all the site's energy requirements.

←
Site plan, showing the organic nature of the human-made topography and the permeable grids of the apartment groupings.

→
The solar canopy shades the urban farmland and sky parks on the roofs of the apartment blocks.

Building for the World

A Second Decade of Public Architecture

Although the curiously unforeseen global recession of 2008 knocked most of the economies in the developed world off-kilter, Singapore and much of Asia got off relatively lightly (and WOHA were not affected as badly as they had feared). Still, there was a universal 'pause and rethink' moment in architectural practice. In retrospect, it can be seen that sustainability had become architecture's tipping point, and WOHA's desire for genuine innovation would be increasingly appreciated and widely respected, now that the implications of climate change were shaping the underlying parti of any thinking architect's work. Wong Mun Summ and Richard Hassell had been frustrated, albeit philosophically, with regard to the lack of attention previously paid to their innovations in the cause of sustainability, but the wind was changing. As the second decade of the century progressed, WOHA's ideas and schemes were now being assimilated into the mainstream of global architectural discourse.

Singapore had been undergoing a remarkable transformation, at least in terms of its urban morphology, right from the moment in 2006 that 'licence to build' was approved for a huge swathe of reclaimed land to the east of the business district. Singapore had been obliged to reassert itself at a time when other cities were showing signs of challenging its regional pre-eminence, and an assemblage of conscientiously iconic structures – mostly designed by foreign architects – would be erected in order to reboot the global city brand on the shores of the newly created Marina Bay. At the same time, a smattering of highly photogenic and widely publicized buildings sprung up all across the island to designs by eminent foreigners,[1] but unlike the preceding exercise in world city creation (instigated in 1975), it could be gauged that the government was now actively encouraging a degree of participation by local architects, not least as an expression of their avowed intention to create the 'world's greenest city'.

1 The list of well-known foreign architects who designed significant (landmark) buildings in Singapore from 2006 is quite formidable: Toyo Ito, Michael Graves, Moshe Safdie, Foster and Partners, Daniel Libeskind, Wilkinson Eyre, UN Studio, Buro Ole Scheeren, Jean Nouvel, Zaha Hadid, Studio Milou, Richard Meier, Ingenhoven, and Thomas Heatherwick.

WOHA were to provide Singapore with a pair of highly conspicuous hotel developments that would vie for attention with any of the landmarks designed by esteemed foreigners. However, the outward appearances of Parkroyal on Pickering (2007–13) and Oasia Downtown (2011–16) were not dictated by the government's desires for a global city, but by WOHA's aspirations for a green city. While promoting a resolutely localized contextual and environmental agenda, the two buildings were startling and ingeniously crafted architectural objects, their consummately organic façades looked completely different, and they quickly became 'icons' and Instagrammable symbols of Singapore. When seen in light of the long-enshrined policy of inviting world-class (foreign) architects to shape and define the city, these elucidations of WOHA's visions of verdant tropicality as a form of civic splendour represented a remarkable triumph.

↑
Oasia Downtown. Singapore, 2011—16.

→
Parkroyal on Pickering. Singapore, 2007—13.

> "
> Sustainability had become architecture's tipping point, and WOHA's desire for genuine innovation would be increasingly appreciated and widely respected, now that the implications of climate change were shaping the underlying parti of any thinking architect's work.

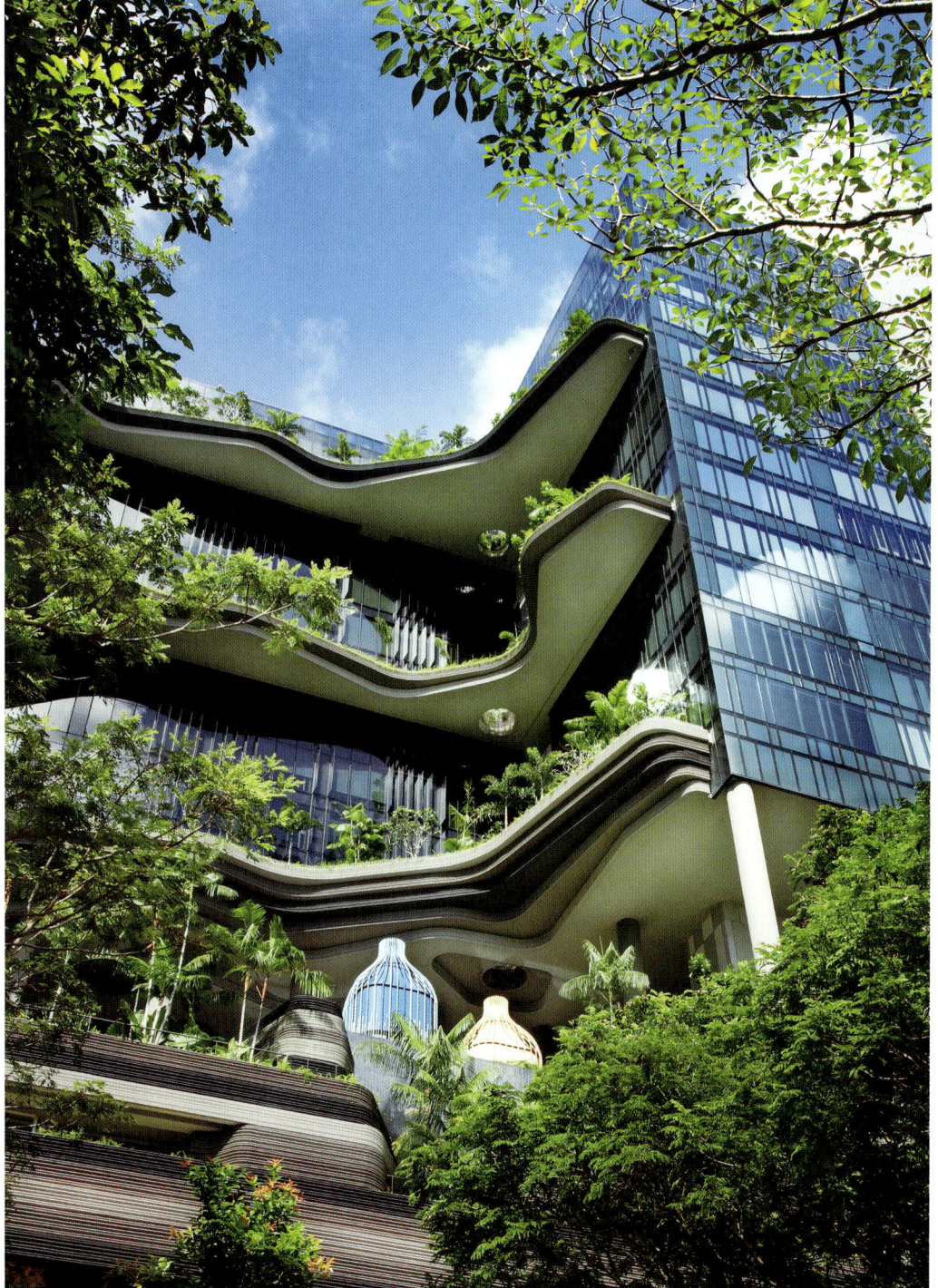

A sequence of adaptive reuse projects that fundamentally addressed the concerns of community and
precinct renewal had begun back in 2001, and a decade
later WOHA could claim to have regenerated many
areas of inner-city Singapore. Two further commissions would soon extend that sequence (which remains
ongoing), and by using quirky architectural forms
and unexpected juxtapositions, these quite singular
projects were specifically intended to enliven and
refresh their immediate neighbourhoods.

SPACE ASIA HUB

BRAS BASAH, SINGAPORE,
2009—11

**The Space Asia Hub redevelop-
ment comprised the restoration
of a 19th-century villa and a
double-fronted shophouse,
now linked by a three-storey
orthogonal volume concocted
from the gutted structure of
an existing utilitarian building. Crisply detailed in black
steel with plate glass, this new
centrepiece was a minimalist,
modernist, Miesian tribute
which, in its reticence, drew
attention to the Rococo orna-
mentation of its period-piece
bookends. Befitting a high-
end furniture showroom, the
interior design of the conjoined
structure was dazzling, with
a counterpoint provided by a
robust structural framework.
The external architecture of
the new ensemble was treated
tenderly, ensuring that the
conserved buildings took the
limelight and restored a semblance of nostalgic ambience
to a precinct that had sadly lost
its charms.**

↑
The steel and
glass frame of
the retrofitted
structure is
flanked by the
restored shop-
houses and villa.

←
As an illusory
device, mirrored
steel was used
for the ceilings
and mullions in
the structur-
ally minimalist
double-height
entry volume.

←
'Black cloud'
light fittings can
be seen in the
new office block
rising above
the restored
shophouses.

→
A footbridge
that connects
co-workers in
the adjoining
building forms
part of the
project's quirky
proportions.

↓
A vertical public
garden was
created on
the laneway
frontage, sharing
a triangular
geometry with
the fenestration
of the entry
volume.

48 NORTH CANAL ROAD
SINGAPORE, 2009—12

In Singapore's city centre, the transformation of a small site at **48 North Canal Road**
comprised the incorporation of two Moderne-
style shophouses into a new nine-storey
office building with a consciously convoluted
architectural expression. WOHA have always
taken great delight in coaxing awkward-
looking forms and proportions into a
configuration that somehow manages to
appear neatly composed, and the discordantly angled planes and geometries of this
copper-clad building certainly demonstrated
their skill at such artifice. One might observe
that such a composition could only have been
possible on a site as unprepossessing as this,
where the building was crammed into a space
that offered absolutely nothing in terms of
contextual reference. Capricious architectural
expression aside, an honourable legacy of this
development was the reinvigoration of the
two laneways that bound the site, as WOHA
had supplied a pocket park, an origami-style
tunnelled pathway and vertical shards of
vegetation for public pleasure and delight.

"The architectural expression results from the articulation of the methods for passive environmental control, with an artfully composed profusion of brightly coloured sunscreening devices wrapping across the façades of the orthogonal modernist structures.

GOODWOOD RESIDENCE

SINGAPORE, 2006—13

Well away from the back lanes of the inner city, Goodwood Residence is the only upmarket condominium that WOHA have designed and built in Singapore; an odd circumstance for a successful local practice, and one that reflects their avowed preference to work in public, rather than private. At this stage in their careers, Wong and Hassell did confess that discussions held with the developers for exclusive properties were '... *generally unproductive... we were pulling in different directions and they just weren't interested in our ideas and our objectives*'. By ideas and objectives, they were referring to sustainability, but WOHA did receive an opportunity to implement their strategies at the level of residential luxury on a flat site at the foot of Goodwood Hill, a beguiling colonial-era neighbourhood where Tudor-style bungalows reside within the lawns and beneath the trees of a tamed tropical landscape. WOHA effectively extended that harmonious and environmentally sustainable parti by placing a broad communal lawn between two cross-ventilated twelve-storey blocks with an L-shaped plan. As with the colonial bungalows, the architectural expression results from the articulation of the methods for passive environmental control, with an artfully composed profusion of brightly coloured sunscreening devices wrapping across the façades of the orthogonal modernist structures. However, the project could only be glimpsed from the street, and although thoroughly enjoyed by the residents, the tropicalized aesthetic pleasures of the façade articulation and landscaping were hidden from the gaze of the public at large, which was an anomalous position for such civic-minded architects.

←
Looking to the central courtyard through the rods of the adjustable metal screens enclosing the apartment balconies.

→
The Park. The
street elevations
of the seven-
storey podium
were inspired by
traditional Indian
architectural
forms.

THE PARK
MUMBAI, 2012—

The Park, a mega-scaled apartment complex in
the central Worli district, has six seventy-storey
towers containing 4,000 apartments rising
above a seven-storey car park podium. The
design potential of the 4.5-hectare podium
intrigued WOHA, and they contrived to combine the geologically inspired stratifications of
the Parkroyal at Pickering hotel with elevations
derived directly from Indian architectural motifs.
Spread across the podium roof, a vast park for
the residents contains a cricket pitch, ornamental gardens, tennis courts and swimming pools.
The design strategies and external expression for
the towers were subjected to several re-designs
before construction began, but WOHA were able
to screen several elevations with a perforated
metal skin and develop variations of the New
Cuffe Parade pinwheel plan.

NEW CUFFE PARADE
MUMBAI, 2010—

WOHA's first two commissions
in India were for residential
projects in Mumbai, and even
though Wong and Hassell had
never been inclined to take
a backward step, '... everything is a learning curve for us,
we always want to try something new and different'. The
magnitude of the complexities
presented was quite extraordinary. Both projects had a size
and scale that were unprecedented and, as it turned out,
so were the complications and
challenges endured throughout
the (still ongoing) processes of
design and construction.

When WOHA began
work on the New Cuffe Parade
residential complex, it was
calculated that with 4,400
apartments contained within
nine towers, the development
would actually be the largest
ever built, anywhere in the
world. As the site was close to
Mumbai's airport, the heights
of the proposed towers had
to be reduced, and WOHA's

romantically disposed
site-planning — inspired by
Indian textile patterns — was
replaced by an orthogonal
grid with ten towers that had
a pinwheel plan to facilitate cross-ventilation. After
another assessment of height
regulations, the towers were
shortened again and are now
under construction. Despite
the shortening processes, the
towers — ornamented by jali-
style screens — retain WOHA's
original design intentions, and
most significantly for such a
large complex, a pinwheel plan
enabled the use of shear walls
surrounding a central void,
which formed a more efficient
construction method than using
the smaller lift core for support. The grand design gesture
was the site-wide landscaping,
which formed a communal
garden that took great delight
in referencing a variety of
traditional Indian pleasure
gardens, pavilions and
colonnades.

↑
New Cuffe
Parade. The
towers rise
above a plea-
sure garden
landscape with
chhatri pavil-
ions, arcaded
walkways and
ornamental
ventilation
shafts.

→
The Park.
Podium roof
plan.

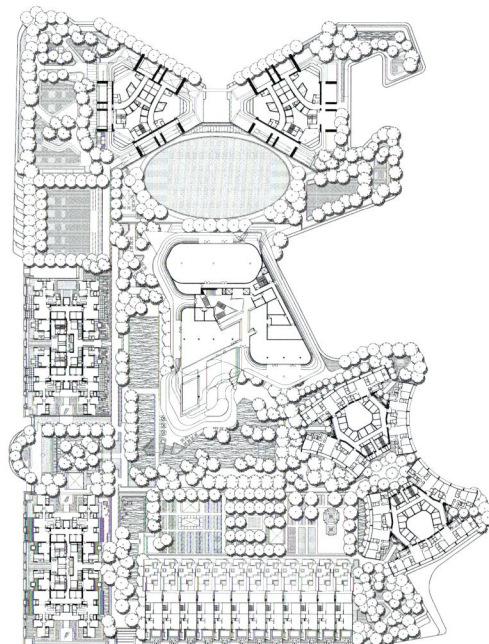

(N) | 20   50   100 m

CAPITAMALL TIANFU

CHENGDU, 2008—15

The CapitaMall Tianfu, a very large commercial, retail and residential complex to the south of Chengdu's city centre, was WOHA's first urban project in China, and it was located in a flat, *tabula rasa* precinct with no identifiable context, apart from a collection of similarly scaled buildings all under construction. As the programmatic configuration was quite conventional — com-

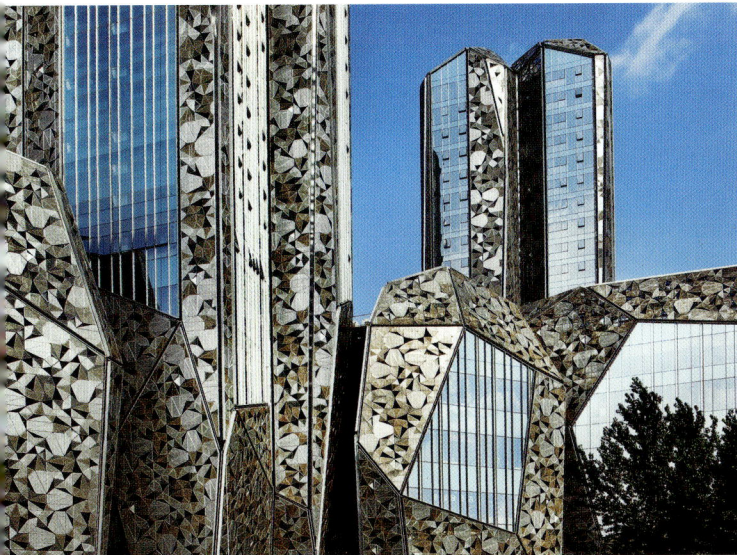

↑ CapitaMall Tianfu. Gleaming panels of perforated aluminium serve as an environmental filtration screen.

mercial and residential towers placed above a retail podium — WOHA turned their attention to the architectural expression, and their primary intention was to somehow alter the perception of a rather stocky and unwieldy collection of forms. They assumed that the surrounding buildings would be neutral in appearance, although the forms might play a few games, and decided to devise a representational composition that would be most notable for its decorative skin. The large blocks were sculpted to represent a rock formation, a set of huge boulders clad in faceted panels of copper-coloured perforated aluminium, and the façades shimmer and sparkle no matter what the weather conditions.

The mathematically-derived geometric patterning of the panels — contained within tilting shards of extremely irregular proportions — relieves and camouflages the bulk of the complex, which now appears as a deftly composed assemblage with a quasi-geological monumentality.

↑ The Grove. Vines grow from a lattice framework, each apartment has a private garden, and cantilevered sky gardens extend from the common areas on every fourth level.

THE GROVE

GUANGZHOU, CHINA, 2010—15

With cantilevered sky gardens, a great wall of vines and a large landscaped communal area, The Grove apartment development formed an extension of the ideas displayed at Newton Suites (2003—07) and Goodwood Residence (2006—13) in Singapore, and with magnificent views of nearby forested hills, it provided a thoroughly greened living environment. The sixteen-storey apartment block had a C-shaped plan, and both the individual apartments and the building's mass were perforated and opened up to catch the winds and provide cross-ventilation. When completed, the condominium stood as something of an outlier in an area of Guangzhou ripe for regeneration, and WOHA were providing a template for environmental awareness on the fringes of a mega-city where the frenzied rate of development will soon be required to acknowledge the virtues of sustainable construction.

↖
The apartments
are veiled with
ornamental
screens, which
soften the
severity of
the overall
composition.

→
Looking from
the street entry
to the clearly
articulated and
over-scaled
external
framework of
the tower.

HUAKU SKY GARDEN
TAIPEI, 2010—17

In a purely architectonic sense, the Huaku Sky
Garden is one of WOHA's best buildings, with
an abstracted external framework powerfully
articulated in light-grey granite. The explicit
reference is to the rectangular asymmetry of
traditional Chinese joinery, and the thirty-storey
apartment tower rises above a congested low-
rise neighbourhood with a formidable presence
that completely redefines a large area of Taipei.
The architecture is not responding to the existing urban morphology; it is instead providing a
new identity, and in the context of Taipei, that is
no bad thing. Ringed by mountains, the city has a
beautiful setting, but its waterways and low hills
are squeezed tight by a sprawling urban mass
bereft of character and cohesion. The stand-up
screen appearance of the tower was enhanced
by a zoning requirement that prevented a rectangular floor plan on the triangular site, which
meant that half the volume had to step back on
plan, giving the structure an additional depth
of dimension. The structural loads were carried
by perimeter columns, so the apartments are
column-free and cross-ventilated, and each
has a crossover section with double-height
sky gardens. Atypically, the tower's orthogonal expression is not obfuscated by greenery,
but the building is unmistakably WOHA, and
the lower levels are wrapped by cloaks of vines.

> **"**
> The explicit reference is to the rectangular asymmetry of traditional Chinese joinery, and the thirty-storey apartment tower rises above a congested low-rise neighbourhood with a formidable presence that completely redefines a large area of Taipei.

← Viewed from the Yan Ming mountain range, the tower has a strikingly elegant presence in the context of Taipei's undistinguished urbanity.

'As of 2020, over fifty new projects in Taichung have been closely modelled on our design for Sky Green.'

—WOHA

← The apartment complex introduces vertical landscaping to the heart of the city with the provision of sun-filled aerial gardens.

→ The two towers are wrapped by common sky gardens, reflected in the mirrored glazing.

↘ Typical floor plan.

SKY GREEN
TAICHUNG, 2014—19

The Sky Green apartment complex in the city of Taichung was notable because it was not an experimental prototype. Instead, the development was something of a virtuoso exercise in which WOHA could — with alacrity — demonstrate their principles for sustainable sky-city living. Wong and Hassell had been invited to Taichung in 2012 by the city government and Feng Chia University to present and exhibit their strategies for sustainable architecture, and were subsequently commissioned to design the Sky Green tower: '*After we spoke in Taichung and exhibited our work, the authorities revised their city planning regulations to enable buildings like ours.*' The parti of the project, which consists of two twenty-six-storey towers, was thus an encyclopedic implementation of all WOHA's strategies and devices — sky villages, sky gardens, sky terraces, ledges and recesses for sun-shading, green walls, cantilevered balconies, cross-ventilated apartments, breezeways, voids for vertical ventilation — and it had quite an impact: '*As of 2020, over fifty new projects in Taichung have been closely modelled on our design for Sky Green.*' Interestingly, but not surprisingly, the completed structure looks like the consummate WOHA building, and when seen in that light, one can observe that it is probably the closest that they will ever come to realizing the programmatic purity of their Duxton Plain prototype of 2001.

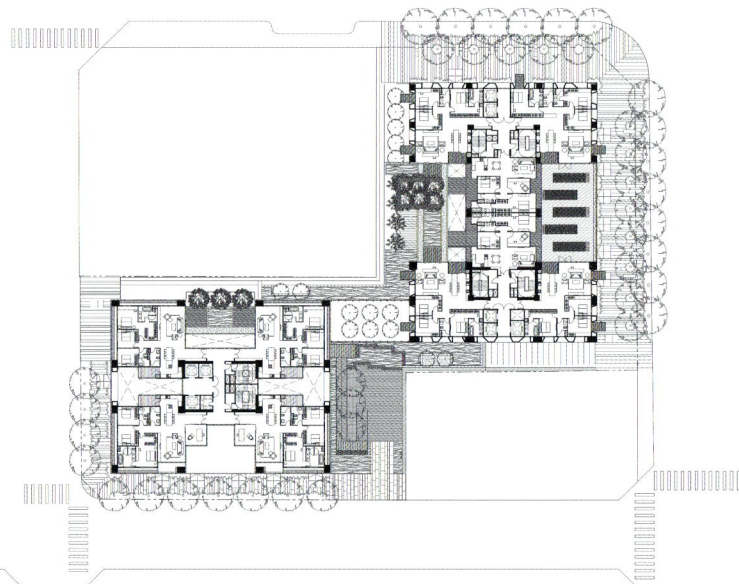

Ⓝ ⌊__5___10_____20 m

CROWNE PLAZA HOTEL EXTENSION

CHANGI AIRPORT, SINGAPORE, 2013—16

WOHA's familial engagement with the city of Singapore was to continue, almost as if it were the work of a separate practice — one that revitalized neighbourhoods and communities and focused on micro-morphology. With the extension to their own Crowne Plaza Hotel at Changi Airport, WOHA reprised the sprightly spirit that distinguished the appearance of the original hotel, again providing a sparkle and a human scale to a typologically repetitive, hyper-functional built environment. Due to its landscaping rather than its terminals and car parks, the land-side area of Singapore's airport is far more attractive than most of its international counterparts, and WOHA designed the hotel buildings as architecture to be seen in tropical parkland; an act of urban softening with an ecological twist. However, in terms of providing a prototype, the construction method employed for the extension was of particular interest to the architects. The components (the guest rooms) of the ten-storey building had been assembled in Shanghai in a process known as PPVC (prefabricated prefinished volumetric construction), and WOHA were quick to realize the potential of this development, observing it to be the 'logical next step in the evolution of construction'. After the guest room modules had been shipped to the site from China, they were stacked atop one another over a period of three weeks — a process that may have taken a year with a con-

↑
WOHA's original hotel can be seen to the left of the extension, which is screened by vertical strips of aluminium mesh.

→
The supporting piers are clad with panels of corten steel.

ventional method of construction — thus greatly reducing inconvenience and obstruction in a highly trafficked location. Perversely, and as a very WOHA-style paradox, the completed building exuded craftsmanship and featured decorative detailing, both inside and out. Precisely crumpled aluminium panels

screen the two end façades, grids of mullions with flowering plants frame the two lengthy guest room elevations, while the striated stone walls of the access road and the Richard Serra-like sculpting of the corten steel supports in the undercroft provide unexpected tectonic and topographic delight.

↑
View from
the entry to
the central
administration
building. WOHA
created a luxu–
riant community
environment
in a previously
undistinguished
setting.

←
A ramped
timber amphi–
theatre steps
down between
building blocks
that were
retained and
modified.

ENABLING VILLAGE
REDHILL, SINGAPORE, 2014—16

**Described by WOHA as 'a
demonstration of heartland[1]
rejuvenation and community
building', the Enabling Village
was created with the adaptive reuse of the Bukit Merah
Vocational Institute, a gated
site with a set of architecturally undistinguished buildings
that 'did not contribute to the
neighbourhood'. The specific
intention of the design and
planning was to provide a
relaxed and caring, yet stimulating environment for people
with disabilities: one that
would integrate companionably
with the community at large.
The entry building was overlaid with screens of colourful
battens and surrounded by
extensive ponds and gardens
that contained timber cabanas.
A variety of idiosyncratic artefacts and artworks — upturned
shipping containers as shelters,
large concrete pipes as places
for contemplation, and animal
kingdom murals — provide
all the outdoor spaces with**

**a cheerful ambience, which
extends throughout the internal
educational areas, theatres and
retail outlets. Most equitably
for a programme of rejuvenation and community building,
the crafted structures and
biophilic landscaping are not
dissimilar to those of WOHA's
Alila Villas Uluwatu resort
(2003—09) in Bali, and one
might note that the Enabling
Village's cabanas appear to
have been 'borrowed' from
that upmarket enclave. The
concept of designing a 'resort
for people with disabilities'
in the respectful and mutually supportive heartlands
of Singapore was more than
appropriate, and the project
formed a 'sociability' twinset
with WOHA's village for the
elderly at Kampung Admiralty
(2013—17).**

1   Approximately 90% of Singapore's
residents live in what is fondly referred to
as the 'heartlands', an interlinked series
of twenty–two new towns that stretch
across the island as conurbations of
medium– to high–rise apartment blocks.

← The landscaping and communal areas have a splendidly informal ad hoc ambience, with upended shipping containers providing shelter in the herb gardens.

→ Large concrete pipes were inserted below the amphitheatre, to be used as contemplative spaces or quiet meeting places.

↓ Timber cabanas are scattered throughout the lush and languid tropical landscape of the village.

"The specific intention of the design and planning was to provide a relaxed and caring, yet stimulating environment for people with disabilities: one that would integrate companionably with the community at large.

↘ Section.

2   5   10 m

← The amphi-theatre and gardens appear as an urban oasis, raised above one of Orchard Road's busiest intersections.

↓ Bird's-eye view showing the slopes of vegetation descending to Orchard Road.

DESIGN ORCHARD

ORCHARD, SINGAPORE, 2016—19

In a markedly different urban context from the Enabling Village, this development on a corner site in Singapore's internationally revered retail precinct formed another exercise in rejuvenation and community building. WOHA did not design a building so much as build an 'oasis', carpeting the terraced roof of a low-rise volume with a luxuriant patch of greenery in the shape of a small public park and amphitheatre, accessed by a short flight of stairs on the street corner. The shell of the volume is neatly composed, with an off-form concrete wall punctured by porthole windows on the Cairnhill Road elevation, while full-height glazing on Orchard Road reveals the 'co-working incubation and retail spaces for young designers' contained within. For the architects, however, the structure was essentially devised to provide a very pleasurable hanging garden in the heart of the city. With waves of tropical plants cascading down the gentle slopes — from and around a collection of giant terracotta pots — WOHA had quietly inserted a diminutive piece of biophilia into their greater 'green city' jigsaw puzzle.

The terraces serve as a popular informal meeting and relaxation area in the heart of the city.

↑
Four distinct
outdoor
environments
are framed
by massive
vine–clad
columns and an
extended right–
angled strip
of unadorned
masonry.

PAN PACIFIC ORCHARD

ORCHARD, SINGAPORE, 2015—

Currently under construction, the Pan Pacific Orchard hotel forms a variation of the strategies and structures that informed the Oasia Downtown hotel tower (2011—16), where guest rooms contained within L–shaped blocks overlook large landscaped public areas, high in the sky and exposed to the elements on two sides. The Pan Pacific design actually extends the already capacious parameters of that prototype, with four stacked volumes (atria) whose spaces are more demonstrative than the architecture, so that the residual sense of enclosure felt in the three sky parks of Oasia Downtown has been even further diminished. The twenty–three–storey tower has an emphatic expression on its eastern elevation, with the only visible struc–tural element presenting itself as a continuous right–angled S–shaped strip. The two huge cylindrical columns on the corners of this façade will be completely shrouded in greenery, and the vision takes WOHA's architecture one step closer to relegating form in favour of foliage.

↑
The topographic podium extends the scale and demeanour of the remaining 19th-century buildings, including the Customs House at right.

←
Viewed across the Brisbane River, the tower has an open core that serves as a vertical breezeway with communal sky gardens.

443 QUEEN STREET

BRISBANE, 2014—

WOHA's only previous excursion to Australia, for The Hyde apartments (2005—10) in Sydney, had produced a building that was quite conservative in appearance. The architects' innate modes of expression had been fundamentally formed by responding to a tropical climate, but Sydney has temperate weather, it can get quite cold, and structural permeability is not really desirable. On the other hand, Brisbane, 900 kilometres to the north, has a climate that lends itself to a degree of tropical expression: '*Apartments can open out to a benign climate, they can be permeable and naturally ventilated, so we could design a passive-energy low-technology building.*' 443 Queen Street — currently under construction on the banks of the Brisbane River — is immediately recognizable as a tropically inflected WOHA tower, replete with sky gardens, breezeways and pulled-apart cross-ventilated blocks, set above a topographic podium. Located in the central business district, the site is flanked by a variety of towers without much semblance of their subtropical genius loci, and it is intriguing to note that WOHA's only contextual obligation was to respect the adjoining Customs House, built in 1889 with a neoclassical form that derived directly from the colonial-era public buildings of tropical Asia. On both the street-front and the waterfront, the colonnade beneath WOHA's sculpted podium (as handed down from their Parkroyal on Pickering hotel) unaffectedly extends the scale and rhythms of the pilasters and columns adorning the Customs House, thus reinforcing an elemental and nicely nostalgic sense of place.

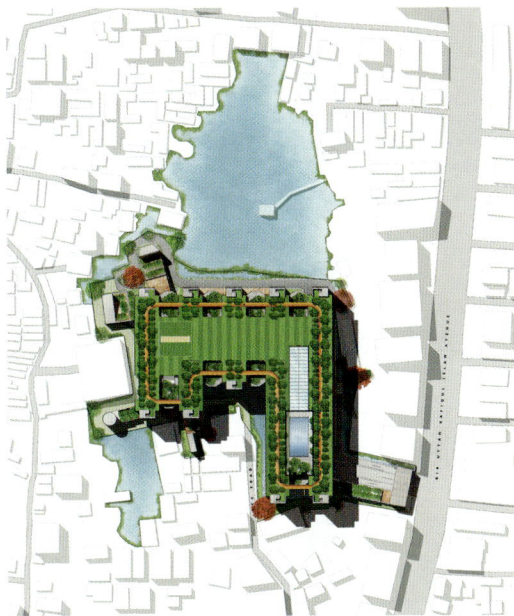

← Site plan.

→ The univer-
sity campus
is seamlessly
integrated with
the wetlands
created by the
remediation of a
highly polluted
swamp.

↓ Sections.

(N) └─ 20 50   100 m

BRAC UNIVERSITY

DHAKA, 2012—

The diversity of WOHA's architecture, both programmatically
and demographically, was now
quite extreme, even though
Wong and Hassell rightly
insist that their strategies,
and indeed their aesthetics,
remained consistent. At the
same time as the 443 Queen
Street apartments were being
built for comfortably well-
off Australians, the BRAC

University campus in Dhaka
was being completed to facilitate the further education of
young Bangladeshis, as part
of a programme of 'self-
empowerment' instituted
by the Bangladesh Rural
Advancement Committee.
Located on a flooded and
highly polluted swamp, which
is now being thoroughly remediated as an integral part of

the development, the building itself appears to be a vast
structure. As with the School
of the Arts (2005—10), it was
one of WOHA's exceptionally
voluminous, very spacious
buildings. The BRAC campus
did not only borrow its scale
from the School of the Arts,
but reiterated that building's

open-ended arrangement of
breezeways, atria, layered
ground planes and one-room-
thick classroom blocks, so that
the entire structure could be
naturally ventilated and socially
integrated. Nine levels of
academia, housed in five linear
blocks, are raised above a four-
level-high sequence of open
public spaces, which form an
extension of the newly regenerated aquatic landscape.
The BRAC campus also echoed
the formal expression of the
School of the Arts; it was clear
that for this particular project,
WOHA's overriding intention
was to supply a proven formula
for sustainability and sociability, and as the BRAC campus
was so large, they were
amplifying the earlier building's
programmatic virtues in a
context far removed from
downtown Singapore. Dhaka
is one of the world's most
congested and impoverished
mega-cities, and WOHA were
in a position where their architecture could provide residents
with a new degree of amenity,
while conscientiously enacting a process of sustainable
urban rehabilitation. They were
well aware that projects such
as this might have a sub-
stantial impact, well beyond
Bangladesh, in the urban environments that most required
big-picture thinking.

└─ 10 20   50 m

"

**Dhaka is one of
the world's most
congested and impov-
erished mega-cities,
and WOHA were in a
position where their
architecture could
provide residents
with a new degree
of amenity, while
conscientiously
enacting a process
of sustainable urban
rehabilitation.**

NS SQUARE

MARINA BAY, SINGAPORE, 2020—

Held on 9 August every year to mark the anniversary of independence in 1965, the National Day Parade is central to Singapore's collective psyche and sense of national identity. The celebration was held variously at the Padang, the National Stadium and several decentralized sites before it was formally relocated in 2007 to the northern edge of the newly operational Marina Bay, to a floating platform that would also serve as a year-round stage for other functions and events. The Marina Bay development was a bravura exercise in global city positioning as much as anything else, and the shores of the central lake were lined with a collection of iconic structures. Marina Bay Sands, Gardens by the Bay, the Helix Bridge, the Esplanade Theatre, and assorted hotels and office towers: they were all designed by eminent foreign architects on a masterplan originally drawn up by IM Pei, and in such august company, the rudimentary construction of the floating platform and its grandstand looked increasingly forlorn. However, the concept was a good one and the vista from the grandstand, looking over the parade ground and the bay to the sights of downtown Singapore, was irresistible. In 2020, WOHA won the competition to completely re-design the site of that floating platform and grandstand, which would now be named NS Square.

WOHA's winning scheme appears, at first glance, to be a curiously anti-iconic non-landmark, but in the context of such glittering — and occasionally over-designed — architecture, the thinking made an awful lot of sense. There are no two ways about it, when you view Marina Bay in its totality, the location is over-developed and visually discordant (much like all recently erected cityscapes) and the buildings are crammed together in a manner that diminishes their individual impact. WOHA's first move was to reconfigure the rectangular platform as a 'red dot' (an appellation used by Singaporeans to depict their nation's diminutive geographical position) and then to formulate a grand-stand[1] that manages not to draw attention to itself: *'We were deconstructing the stadium as a type. Stadiums are not built in the centre of cities anymore, they're usually surrounded by car parks in a wasteland, so they need to be show-off structures ... but we did the opposite.'* WOHA were deconstructing a typology, but they were firmly responding to the overall city plan. At the hinge between several downtown precincts, the site is critical to Singapore's current and future development, and WOHA's imprint will need to be taken into account by any subsequent scheme. The bright red dot will incontrovertibly serve as the focus, the bullseye, for all further planning moves.

1   The grandstand was designed in collaboration with Populous, an architectural practice that specializes in stadiums.

↖ Sited at the northeast corner of Marina Bay, the stadium and parade ground occupy a crucial position in Singapore's ongoing urban development. The 'red dot' of the parade ground (shown here with an SG logo) is intended as the fulcrum for any further planning moves.

SINGAPORE PAVILION
EXPO 2020, DUBAI, 2018—2020

Section and first-floor plan.

Erected for Expo in Dubai (currently delayed by the global pandemic), the Singapore Pavilion was designed as a microcosm of Singapore, or at least of WOHA's vision for Singapore. Like many such pavilions, the building looks like an architectural model built at a 1:1 scale, and the programmatic practicalities are subsumed by the inherently idealistic fantasies needed to make an Expo interesting. There are, of course, many contradictions with sustainability at events like an Expo, but WOHA wanted to use the opportunity to devise and construct a working prototype that might encourage subsequent (fully sustainable) developments in the Middle East, and could serve as an advocacy tool for policy direction. WOHA's pavilion is green, green, green, which is of course quite a statement in the parched environment

of the Arabian desert, and it achieves net zero energy by drawing water from the ground and passing it through a solar canopy desalination system in order to irrigate the verdant planting, which festoons the interior and exterior. The simple orthogonal structure has a marketplace on the top floor, placed above three permeable double-storey cones whose walls and ceilings form a continuous carpet of creepers. Air-conditioning is only used in the basement, and a consummate process of dry misting maintains a comfortable microclimate throughout the pavilion, which is traversed via sets of spiralling walk-ways. WOHA were at pains here to include every one of their Garden City Mega City strategies to present a complete exposition of their principles at work, only here in Dubai it was a garden city in a desert city.

Section and first-floor plan.

Garden City Mega City

Rethinking Cities for the Age of Global Warming

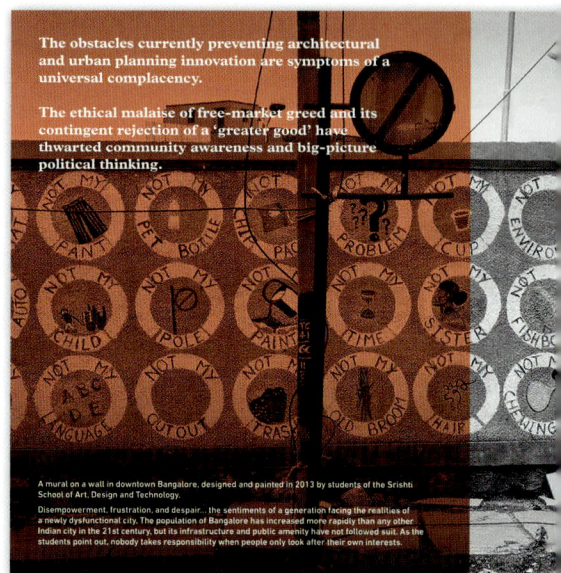

The obstacles currently preventing architectural and urban planning innovation are symptoms of a universal complacency.

The ethical malaise of free-market greed and its contingent rejection of a 'greater good' have thwarted community awareness and big-picture political thinking.

A mural on a wall in downtown Bangalore, designed and painted in 2013 by students of the Srishti School of Art, Design and Technology.
Disempowerment, frustration, and despair... the sentiments of a generation facing the realities of a newly dysfunctional city. The population of Bangalore has increased more rapidly than any other Indian city in the 21st century, but its infrastructure and public amenity have not followed suit. As the students point out, nobody takes responsibility when people only look after their own interests.

A fundamental premise of architectural communication is that nobody pays much attention to it, apart from other architects. Architecture has long been considered by its practitioners and its critics to be an intellectualized aesthetic, and most of its discourse continues to be extremely esoteric, not to mention arcane. Architecture has thus been marginalized in popular culture, which has possibly gratified its adherents, but it has also been effectively excluded from analysis and commentary at the level one might describe as influential. Most mainstream architectural publicity has focused on the design of private houses, which has little tangible import in the field of world affairs, and the attention paid to luxury lifestyles is intrinsically counterproductive in terms of maintaining a sustainable existence.

A newspaper columnist, television presenter or public intellectual can speak of an eminent artist, actor, chef, sportsperson or film director – David Hockney, Meryl Streep, Jamie Oliver, Serena Williams, Steven Spielberg – without the need for further explanation, but should they mention Richard Rogers or even Le Corbusier, befuddlement may well ensue. And this is a perplexing circumstance, given that architecture and town planning have so much more of a tangible impact on our temporal existence than any artform or popular entertainment. And architecture is, to state the obvious, a very visible artform, and while it may not always be popular, it is universally understood. Contemporary architecture is taken for granted, as infrastructure, while in a cultural and even an intellectual sense, architecture mostly appears to be a thing of the past, not of the present, never mind the future.

As Wong Mun Summ and Richard Hassell are insistent that architecture and town planning hold the key to urban remediation and environmental salvation, the lack of widespread attention paid to architecture is not perplexing so much as challenging. It was late in 2014, after twenty years in practice, when Wong and Hassell came to the realization that they would need to do more, in terms of communication, if their proposals for 21st-century architecture and urban planning were to have a quantifiable impact.

WOHA had won many international awards, several sizeable books had been published on their work, they had participated in group and solo exhibitions, and their every building was guaranteed a feature in design magazines and on blog sites, but no matter how radical the innovations, it did seem to them that their architecture and their ideas had become commodified, reduced to images for consumption rather than tools for advocacy. The audience, the demographic, remained the same, each new building was seen as just another WOHA building and the why (the reason) had been replaced by the what (the photographic publicity). At one level – by focusing on the why rather than the what – WOHA wanted to reboot their message to the architectural constituency, and at a much broader level, they considered that they were obliged to communicate with the world that lay beyond the architectural compounds, to insert architecture and urban planning into sociological discourse at large. Their subsequent treatise, their manifesto on the crisis facing Asia in the 21st century,

* Only 2% of the planet's land area is urbanized, but that 2% consumes 80% of our energy, most of which is fossil-fuelled. In the age of global warming, the relentless growth of mega-cities is destroying our planet.

'Seeing the problems of 21st-century urbanism laid out so clearly and comprehensively, from their roots in global inequality to the lived reality of the Global South, was riveting. Why had no one done this before? Why did WOHA see what their Western peers couldn't?'

—Daniel Brook

'Unsociable and Unsustainable', *n+1 magazine*, 5 December 2016.

The innumerable varia[t]
Corbusier's template h
the suburbs of Asian m

The size of the mega cities and the scale of their problems have not yet resonated in global centres of design and power... in the architectural associations and economic forums of the 'old world'.

Contemporary architectural and social theorising has not yet focused upon the very new world of mega city Asia, which will be the story of the 21st century.

Mumbai has a population of approximately 25 million, over half of whom live in slums, which have a density estimated at 300,000 people per km². The Dharavi district (pictured) is located close to the city centre, and comprised of makeshift shelters wedged between dilapidated apartment blocks. Although Dharavi has one million residents, it is geographically constrained, and at least four other Mumbai slum districts now have a greater population. With up to 300 families arriving every day from rural India, the proportion of slum-dwellers in Mumbai continues to increase, and rehabilitation projects have not been able to curtail the spread of the settlements.

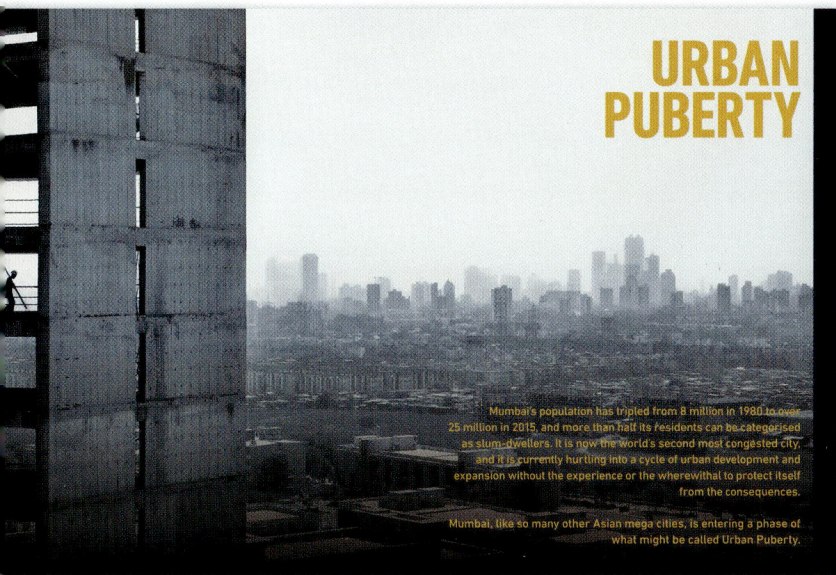

URBAN PUBERTY

Mumbai's population has tripled from 8 million in 1980 to over 25 million in 2015, and more than half its residents can be categorised as slum-dwellers. It is now the world's second most congested city, and it is currently hurtling into a cycle of urban development and expansion without the experience or the wherewithal to protect itself from the consequences.

Mumbai, like so many other Asian mega cities, is entering a phase of what might be called Urban Puberty.

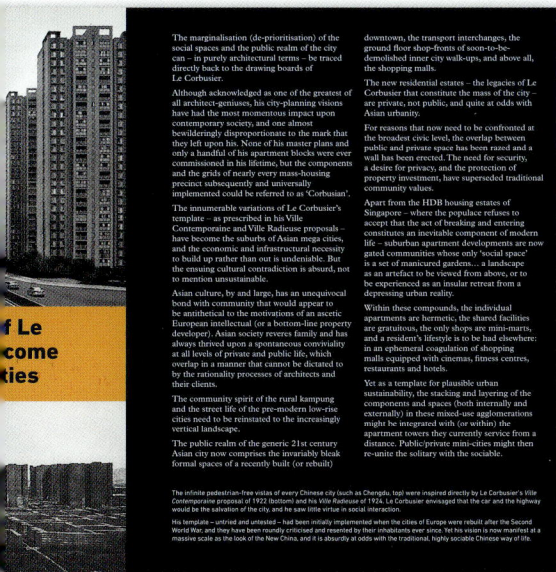

The marginalisation (de-prioritisation) of the social spaces and the public realm of the city can – in purely architectural terms – be traced directly back to the drawing boards of Le Corbusier.

Although acknowledged as one of the greatest of all architect-geniuses, his city-planning visions have had the most momentous impact upon contemporary society, and one almost bewilderingly disproportionate to the mark that they left upon his. None of his master plans and only a handful of his apartment blocks were ever commissioned in his lifetime, but the components and the grids of nearly every mass-housing precinct subsequently and universally implemented could be referred to as 'Corbusian'.

The innumerable variations of Le Corbusier's template – as prescribed in his Ville Contemporaine and Ville Radieuse proposals – have become the suburbs of Asian mega cities, and the economic and infrastructural necessity to build up rather than out is undeniable. But the ensuing cultural contradiction is absurd, not to mention unsustainable.

Asian culture, by and large, has an unequivocal bond with community that would appear to be antithetical to the motivations of an ascetic European intellectual (or a bottom-line property developer). Asian society reveres family and has always thrived upon a spontaneous conviviality at all levels of private and public life, which overlap in a manner that cannot be dictated to by the rationality processes of architects and their clients.

The community spirit of the rural kampung and the street life of the pre-modern low-rise cities need to be reinstated to the increasingly vertical landscape.

The public realm of the generic 21st century Asian city now comprises the invariably bleak formal spaces of a recently built (or rebuilt) downtown, the transport interchanges, the ground floor shop-fronts of soon-to-be-demolished inner city walk-ups, and above all, the shopping malls.

The new residential estates – the legacies of Le Corbusier that constitute the mass of the city – are private, not public, and quite at odds with Asian urbanity.

For reasons that now need to be confronted at the broadest civic level, the overlap between public and private space has been razed and a wall has been erected. The need for security, a desire for privacy, and the protection of property investment, have superseded traditional community values.

Apart from the HDB housing estates of Singapore – where the populace refuses to accept that the act of breaking and entering constitutes an inevitable component of modern life – suburban apartment developments are now gated communities whose only 'social space' is a set of manicured gardens... a landscape as an artefact to be viewed from above, or to be experienced as an insular retreat from a depressing urban reality.

Within these compounds, the individual apartments are hermetic, the shared facilities are gratuitous, the only shops are mini-marts, and a resident's lifestyle is to be had elsewhere: in an ephemeral coagulation of shopping malls equipped with cinemas, fitness centres, restaurants and hotels.

Yet as a template for plausible urban sustainability, the stacking and layering of the components and spaces (both internally and externally) in these mixed-use agglomerations might be integrated with (or within) the apartment towers they currently service from a distance. Public/private mini-cities might then re-unite the solitary with the sociable.

The infinite pedestrian-free vistas of every Chinese city (such as Chengdu, top) were inspired directly by Le Corbusier's Ville Contemporaine proposal of 1922 (bottom) and his Ville Radieuse of 1924. Le Corbusier envisaged that the car and the highway would be the salvation of the city, and he saw little virtue in social interaction.

His template – untried and untested – had been initially implemented when the cities of Europe were rebuilt after the Second World War, and they have been roundly criticised and resented by their inhabitants ever since. Yet his vision is now manifest at a massive scale as the look of the New China, and it is absurdly at odds with the traditional, highly sociable Chinese way of life.

✳ Most of the mega-cities are located in the tropics, where the climate is very hot and occasionally very wet, and all design and construction must be specifically attuned to local conditions.

was entitled *Garden City Mega City*. It was published in 2016 as a book with two parts – one devoted to the problems, the other dedicated to the solutions – and it was both a call to arms and a detailed manual for sustainable city planning.

Garden City Mega City looked to the past to identify precedents. It saw the responsibilities of urban design and its architectural components as a continuum in the history of civilization, and as the title suggests, it specifically wished to re-invoke the spirit of the early 20th-century garden city. This was counterintuitive, as the essential tenet of the garden city was the provision of an escape from the insufferable cities rather than a plan to improve them, but a century later, WOHA simply updated the logic and proposed that mega-cities should be transformed into garden cities. There would now be no need to flee to leafy commuter suburbs, not that many residents could actually do so in 21st-century Asia.

The original garden city was a direct response to the Industrial Revolution, which had spawned an agglomeration of overcrowded and unsanitary cities across Great Britain and parts of Europe and North America in the 19th century, and this was the demographic and societal precedent for Asia's extraordinary rate of urbanization in the early 21st century. The ensuing problems were identical – poverty, disease, alienation, housing, pollution, transportation and infrastructure – but they were now compounded and complicated by the manifestations of climate change. During the 20th century, the rolling out of suburbs full of bungalows led to the environmental desecrations of urban sprawl, while the serried ranks of segregated housing blocks built all over the world had wantonly separated citizens from their community. WOHA prosaically suggested that urban planners combine the best of both those planning typologies and discard the worst, which is what they had actually done with many of their schemes. Their phrase 'high-density high-amenity' neatly encapsulated the desired outcome, and the delights of the garden city were thus incorporated within the high-rise housing blocks of the mega-city, replete with a sense of community, a reconnection with nature and a reduced rate of energy consumption.

LAYERING CITIES

Multiple Ground Levels

Both... And...

High-Density High-Amenity

Cities Within Cities

Sky Villages

Domesticated Megastructures

Inverted Skyline

Over the last two centuries – as towns became cities and cities became mega cities – land has been taken for granted, as an infinite horizontal site for building, farming and mining. But the land has run out. It is now a limited commodity and a precious resource, yet it is still being exploited, and eco-systems are being destroyed, possibly forever. That cannot continue.

The accelerating expansion of the mega cities is killing the land they require to survive. Due to the decline in quality of available land – as cities spread out over the farms that had always sustained them – crop production has fallen sharply, non-renewable energy supplies have dwindled, and transportation costs have increased. The vicious cycles of urban degradation now extend to the hinterlands of the cities and the countryside beyond, and they are all contributing to the exponential rise of global warming.

Waves of building construction, transport infrastructure, and industrial development have blithely obliterated the vegetation and despoiled the waterways that had been the reasons for settlement in the first place. This comprehensive subsumption of large tracts of land – often the most fertile and resourceful in their region – has been completely unsustainable, both environmentally and socially.

Re-planning cities – vertically, not horizontally – is the only option left for mega city survival. As well as reclaiming, restoring, and re-energising our existing land, new land must be created. The use of land needs to be intensified by layering urban (and rural) environments – residential, recreational, commercial, agricultural, and infrastructural – above and below the existing ground level of the city. With a substantial increase in acreage and conduciveness, nature will take its own course, and revitalised eco-systems can serve to remediate the blighted landscapes of the mega cities.

In the face of widely acknowledged malfunction, massive cities are still being constructed in accordance with a rigidly enforced, yet blatantly outdated and inappropriate planning template. The extraordinary recent growth of these cities is unprecedented, and WOHA are calling for a correlative response by architects and planners... for research and proposition and experimentation,

and for a swift all-encompassing rethink of an entrenched city-building template.

WOHA's seven strategies for Layering Cities – illustrated by built projects and proposed schemes – derive from their first-hand experiences, from their empirical studies of mega city problems and mega city possibilities.

By visualising a city in terms of layers – as a three-dimensional matrix, rather than a two-dimensional grid – the challenge of averting the social and environmental dysfunction of the mega cities can be confronted, and problems can be resolved. WOHA's strategies can be adapted and applied at varying scales and in various places... from buildings to towns to cities, from country to country, from continent to continent, and from one climatic zone to another.

The various components of the Kampung Admiralty development are stacked and layered within a single building. Markets, shops, plazas, health-care facilities and a rooftop park are integrated, not segregated.

KAMPUNG ADMIRALTY 2013 SINGAPORE

Macro Architecture Micro Urbanism

PLANTING CITIES

Screens of Green

Sky Gardens

Sky Parks

Topographic Architecture

Garden City Mega City had to be taken seriously because WOHA had reached a point where they were able to use a now-sizeable array of designed and built prototypes as exemplars. They were not relying upon renderings of hopeful but unsubstantiated schemes and proposals, as they could collate and communicate their strategies and principles by holding up their completed buildings as proof. This was not architecture as theory, this was architecture as practice, and WOHA's built projects could demonstrate what a building actually does, rather than what it might do or should do.

'*Garden City Mega City was a form of self-analysis on all our projects, and it confirmed that we had been doing the same things over and over again. Inherent patterns emerged in different building forms and typologies.*'

WOHA's self-analysis of their projects was codified and presented in *Garden City Mega City* as a set of principles that could be employed to construct the 'ideal' sustainable city of the future. Three overarching categories – Layering Cities, Planting Cities and Breathing Cities – were broken down into specific strategies that had already been implemented and/or proposed at various scales, such as Multiple Ground Levels, Sky Villages, Screens of Green and Vertical Breezeways. All were illustrated by WOHA's schemes and buildings, and crucially, the self-analysis was then presented in a chapter titled 'Rating Cities', which examined selected WOHA projects for their performance and their value to the city as a whole.

With little modification, the cold-climate architecture of Europe and North America has recently proliferated in tropical cities, where its environmental incompatibility can only be offset by the use of large amounts of energy for cooling.

'In what can be seen as a return to the thinking that existed before the advent of the automobile and the apparently unlimited supply of fossil-fuel energy, WOHA have been re-imagining mega-cities as 21st-century garden cities: dense and vertical, yet sociable and sustainable.'

—WOHA

LAYERING CITIES

Replanning cities — vertically, not horizontally — may be the only option left for mega-city survival. As well as reclaiming, restoring and re-energizing our existing land, new land must be created. The use of land needs to be intensified by layering urban environments — residential, recreational, commercial, agricultural and infrastructural — above the existing ground level of the city.

PLANTING CITIES

The biodiversity of the mega-cities and their surrounding regions is dwindling quickly. Wildlife habitats and ecosystems are being obliterated, and for residents the loss is personal as well as environmental. The density of the cities does not permit the reallocation of land for parks, so the sites for re-greening must be found above ground level.

BREATHING CITIES

Tropical architecture has always relied on the perforation of a building's exterior, allowing light and air to penetrate the internal spaces in a process that would now be described as passive (non-energy reliant). Passive design on the largest possible scale would be extraordinarily beneficial both to the environment and the quality of life in the city.

RATING CITIES

Developments are currently assessed for their economic and spatial efficiency, but WOHA's five measurements are conducted on behalf of a city's residents, rather than its property developers. Sociable architecture and sustainable cities have become 21st-century priorities, and building developments need to be rated in terms of their contribution to society and the environment, as well as their economic viability.

In the age of global warming, the glass-box central-core model for building design is fundamentally inappropriate for a tropical environment, but planning regulations have enshrined that typology, and alternatives have been effectively excluded.

PARKROYAL ON PICKERING 2007 SINGAPORE

BREATHING CITIES

Tropical Community Spaces

Horizontal Breezeways

Breezeway Atria

Breezeway Courtyards

Vertical Breezeways

Breezeway Towers

One Unit Thick

The archetypal modernist model for high-rise climate cities of the United States. The towers – all of which can trace their lineage to the initial proposals of Mies van der Rohe – were expediently engineered to maximise the ratio of a building's volume to its surface area by using non load-bearing curtain walls.

With large floor-plates that spread from a central core, these hermetically-sealed apartment towers and office blocks, which rely upon comprehensive artificial ventilation, have proliferated across the globe and account for nearly half the world's energy demands.

By and large, architects have paid little heed to the local climate or context of tropical Asia, which is home to many of the world's largest and most rapidly growing cities, and most of the buildings are neither sustainable nor appropriate. Responsible climatic design has been marginalised – excluded from the conversation – by developers and planning authorities in favour of curtain-walled towers that ostensibly symbolise affluence and aspiration.

Tropical architecture has always relied upon the perforation of a building's exterior, allowing light and air to penetrate the internal spaces in a process that would now be described as passive (non energy-reliant) design. That basic principle has not been superseded, and it can be applied at every scale… to puncture and open out a room, an apartment, a building, a precinct, and a city, so that they can 'breathe' without the aid of artificially induced ventilation.

In the age of global warming and the growth of the tropical mega cities, such large-scale passive design would be extraordinarily beneficial to both the environment and the quality of lifestyle. The two go hand in hand after all, and the sooner that urban planners and developers embrace the requirement for sustainable design and construction, the sooner the cities can function in a contextually appropriate manner.

As crucial as the environmental and social prerequisites for the 21st century mega-cities of tropical Asia also need to deploy an identity that does not take its cue from the century cities of North America. As we see it by WOHA, that identity may well be found a result of re-applying the fundamental traditional principles of tropical architecture to the new tropical mega cities.

RATING CITIES

The strategies proposed by WOHA must be assessed within a very big picture. There is only one priority, and that is the holistic planning of the city.

An individual innovation can only be deemed successful if it serves as a fundamental component of a system that performs better than ever before.

A self-sufficient building or a micro-sustainability solution will be of little value if the surrounding city collapses. And if something catastrophic happens to a mega city, the ramifications will be global.

Observing that contemporary masterplans continue to presume that outdated components will be inserted within an unsustainable urban grid, WOHA are instead designing projects that will function successfully in a genuinely self-sufficient city. WOHA think of their prototypes as components for a fully sustainable future city.

In the same way that developing countries and new generations recently leapfrogged technologies (as an example, the traditional method of shouting across a street was replaced directly by mobile phones, because telephone landlines had never been installed), they should now overlook the inefficient modernist city plans of the 20th century in favour of building Garden Cities for the 21st century.

20th century cities were planned as collections of segregated components, which were measured in terms of their economic productivity. The value of buildings was assessed only by capital cost efficiency – building plot ratios, net to gross floor values, and surface to volume ratios – rather than their overall contribution to the city as components within a self-sufficient system.

Cities must now be made of, by and for people… they need to be more than vast agglomerations of inanimate stand-alone financial equations. Sociable architecture and sustainable cities have now become the 21st century priorities, and building developments need to be assessed in terms of their contribution to social and environmental sustainability, as well as their economic viability.

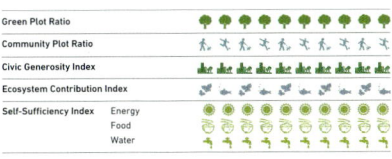

Developments are currently assessed and rated in terms of their economic and spatial efficiency, but WOHA's five measurements are conducted on behalf of a city's residents, rather than its property developers. Six WOHA projects, designed between 2003 and 2014, have been evaluated on the following pages.

It must be stressed that the benefits of social and ecological sustainability should immediately be factored into any property investment formula in the 21st century, as tangible improvements to the quality of life – for a city and its residents – will dramatically increase a development's value.

High density must equate with high amenity.

Green Plot Ratio

Community Plot Ratio

Civic Generosity Index

Ecosystem Contribution Index

Self-Sufficiency Index

A detailed explanation of the data used to calculate each of the five measurements can be found in the Rating Cities appendix (pages 204–209).

SCHOOL OF THE ARTS 2005 SINGAPORE

→ **GREEN PLOT RATIO**
The amount of landscaped surface compared to a development's site area.

→ **COMMUNITY PLOT RATIO**
The amount of community space allocated within a development's site area.

→ **CIVIC GENEROSITY INDEX**
The extent to which a development encourages and facilitates the public life of the city.

→ **ECOSYSTEM CONTRIBUTION INDEX**
The degree to which a development supplements a city's ecosystem.

→ **SELF-SUFFICIENCY INDEX**
The capacity of a development to provide its own energy, water and food.

RATING CITIES

Sociable architecture and sustainable cities have now become the 21st century priorities, and building developments need to be assessed in terms of their contribution to social and environmental sustainability, as well as their economic viability.

The following data is used to calculate each of WOHA's five measurements, which were devised to assess the social and ecological performance of high-density buildings or precincts.

	Energy
Green Plot Ratio	
Community Plot Ratio	
Civic Generosity Index	
Ecosystem Contribution Index	
Self-Sufficiency Index	Food
	Water

Green Plot Ratio

The amount of landscaped surfaces compared to a development's site area.

The measurement includes all new and preserved vegetation, vertical and horizontal landscaping, water features, lawns and trees, raised planters, and urban farms.

All buildings need to encourage bio-diversity, reduce the urban heat island effect, provide shade and cooling, improve air quality, soften the harshness of the cityscape, restore wildlife habitats, and re-connect people with nature.

1 – Horizontal Green (Public)
The amount of surface area with landscape coverage of at least fifty percent, which is accessible to the public and/or all the building's occupants.

2 – Horizontal Green (Private)
The surface area of private sky gardens with landscape coverage of at least fifty percent.

3 – Horizontal Green (Inaccessible)
The surface area of landscape only accessed for maintenance.

4 – Vertical Green
The surface area of external and internal façade greenery, and vertical farm systems.

5 – Horizontal Blue (Public)
The surface area of both natural and constructed water bodies, which is accessible to the public and/or all the building's occupants.

6 – Horizontal Blue (Private)
The surface area of private sky gardens with water features and/or pools.

7 – Vertical Blue
The surface area of vertical water features, such as waterfalls.

The sum of these surface areas is then compared with the development's site area to establish its Green Plot Ratio.

Community Plot Ratio

The amount of community space allocated within a development's site area.

The measurement includes fully public areas, semi-private communal spaces, care centres, libraries, restaurants, cafés, and community centres.

The amenity of an urban precinct is largely determined by the quantity and quality of its community spaces. The buildings should encourage human interaction and facilitate social gatherings. Human scale, accessibility, and inclusivity, are crucial to the success of community integration.

1 – Community Space
The amount of surface area occupied by socially interactive space, which is accessible to the public and/or all the building's occupants.

This amount of surface area is then compared with the development's site area to establish its Community Plot Ratio.

Civic Generosity Index

The extent to which a development encourages and facilitates the public life of a city.

The index rates the value of a development's public attributes, such as urban connections, shared relaxation areas, sheltered walkways, gardens, and artworks.

In a sociable city, buildings should be judged by their 'human' characteristics… are they friendly, generous, and accommodating?

1 – Ground level shelter, services and amenities
2 – Ground level accessibility and activity
3 – Visual pleasure provided by horizontal and vertical landscaping
4 – Public access to spaces and facilities within the building
5 – Spatial engagement and connection with an urban network

Satisfying each one of these criteria achieves a rating of twenty percent, so that satisfying each five achieves a rating of one hundred percent.

Ecosystem

The degree to which a development supplements a city's ecosystem.

The index rates connections between city's land and settings for naturespaces environmental

As land in cities building develops a city's land reverse the urbanisation caused by urban and developments fauna, as well as

20% – A development flying birds and

40% – A development plantings, species and insects.

60% – A development inter-connected Provision is made and insects.

80% – A development specifically designed throughout the city wildlife can liv

100% – A development and interconnected sanctuary with The maintenance account, as well rare species.

Parkroyal on Pickering
2007

COMPLETED 2013 – SINGAPORE

○ A five-storey **Topographic Architecture** podium clad with vegetation sits below a sixteen-storey 'E plan' hotel tower and an office tower.

○ **Sky Gardens** – framing the views from the guestrooms – are placed on curvaceous cantilevered shelves at every fourth floor of the hotel, creating a **Domesticated Megastructure**, which provides human scale in the high-rise context of Singapore's downtown.

○ A large **Multiple Ground Level** on the roof of the podium serves as an open-air **Tropical Community Space**, sheltered by the hotel tower above.

○ The high Green Plot Ratio and the amount of Civic Generosity provide downtown Singapore with a **High-Density High-Amenity** city block.

Green Plot Ratio	240%	
Community Plot Ratio	150%	
Civic Generosity Index	100%	
Ecosystem Contribution Index	80%	
Self-Sufficiency Index	Energy	1%
	Food	0%
	Water	65%

232–233

Prototypology

Multiple Ground Levels

Sky villages are layered as multiple ground levels at every eleventh floor within the SkyVille@Dawson public housing project. Communal terraces and gardens – on the 36th, 25th, and 14th levels – can be seen when looking down the voids between the apartment blocks.

SKYVILLE@DAWSON 2007 SINGAPORE

Garden City Mega City was to become a project in itself, and it travelled widely as a series of exhibitions and social media presentations that added new schemes and, eventually, new strategies to the mix, along with further documentation of completed buildings. The exhibitions in Venice and New York (2016), Mexico City (2017) and Austin, Texas (2018), used videos and drone footage to convey the realities of mega-city Asia as well as the liveability virtues of such WOHA buildings as The Met, Parkroyal on Pickering, SkyVille @ Dawson, Oasia Downtown and Kampung Admiralty. Wong and Hassell were invited to many and varied symposia to explain their urban living strategies: they were invited to walk through the streets of London with the city councillors and suggest ways to integrate greenery and biodiversity; they initiated student workshops throughout Asia; and the book could be found on the reading lists of urban planning and architecture courses across the globe.

High-Density High-Amenity

Replete with resort-style landscaping and a luxuriant swimming pool, the fifth-floor public areas of the Parkroyal on Pickering hotel are surrounded by the steel and glass architecture of Singapore's business district. The site-wide open-air space sits beneath the guest rooms, and provides a tantalising glimpse of what may become a preferred inner-city lifestyle.

PARKROYAL ON PICKERING 2007 SINGAPORE

✱ **A mandated compliance with environmental rating systems and the use of greenery-as-decoration are only temporary solutions. The building typologies need to be rethought in climatic terms, so that urban components can be opened out and connected to each other, rather than sealed in and separated.**

Breezeway Atria

Rising above the fifth-floor ground plane, a six-level atrium (below) within the School of the Arts provides a communal space for students, overlooked by the classroom blocks. Another, more public, atrium (left) sits beneath as the street-level entry to the school and a set of theatres.

SCHOOL OF THE ARTS 2005 SINGAPORE

Breezeway Atria can rise above Multiple Ground Levels as grand vertical volumes, which form three-dimensional 'shared' precincts within the perforated structure of a tropical tower. The atria facilitate constant cross-ventilation and natural light, whilst rejuvenating the lifestyle and social interaction of city residents.

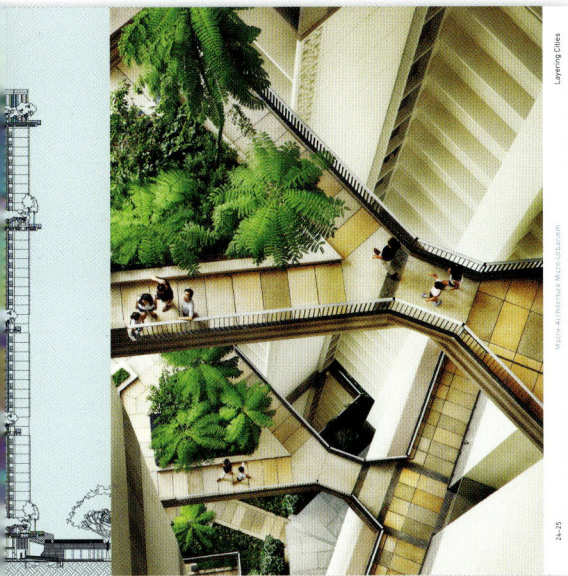

24–25

'Our follow-up to Garden City Mega City will not be at the building scale, it will be at the urban and masterplanning scale. We need to know the values of all the components that make up the city, so we are devising new rating indexes. We should be scoring how a building integrates with the systems of a city … energy, mobility, hydrology, biodiversity and so on. The health of our eco-systems is now critical, and we should be measuring that … it would be a civic assessment, rather than rating an individual building.'

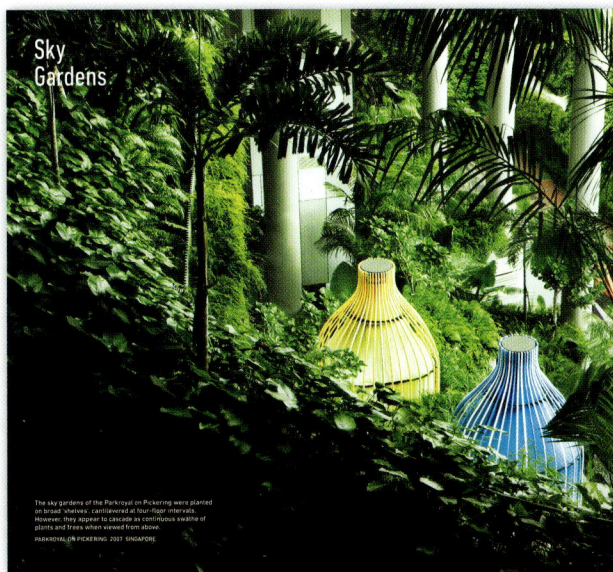

—WOHA

As anticipated, any tangible impact or progress at a bureaucratic level has been incremental – one step at a time – and WOHA have been persistent in their advocacy of the Rating Cities formulae in particular: 'We include the indexes and ratios in our submissions for new projects, proposing that they be used as the method for measuring the likely success of a building. All planning departments have their own values, which are often deeply entrenched, but we get a lot of comments and positive feedback … particularly with the Civic Generosity Index.' Invited to Taichung in 2012 for a talk by the city government and the university, WOHA's presentation (actually a huge exhibition in an aircraft hangar) was effectively a trial run for *Garden City Mega City*, and the principles and strategies were so well received that the local planning regulations were altered in order to enable the construction of the Sky Green apartment towers (2014–19). It is estimated that over fifty new developments in Taichung have been designed according to the principles laid down in *Garden City Mega City* and demonstrated by Sky Green, something of a 21st-century equivalent to the mass implementation of Le Corbusier's housing block template for the 20th century (only WOHA were advocating environmental sensitivity and social interaction, not constructional expediency and human isolation). In Australia, the city of Brisbane has incorporated versions of the *Garden City Mega City* strategies in their planning documents 'Buildings that Breathe' and 'A Design-Led City'.

WOHA now treat the principles of *Garden City Mega City* as intrinsic to all their commissioned work, and they are working on the next phase of the project as if it were an ongoing commission: *'Our follow-up to Garden City Mega City will not be at the building scale, it will be at the urban and masterplanning scale. We need to know the values of all the components that make up the city, so we are devising new rating indexes. We should be scoring how a building integrates with the systems of a city … energy, mobility, hydrology, biodiversity and so on. The health of our ecosystems is now critical, and we should be measuring that … it would be a civic assessment, rather than rating an individual building.'*

Sky Gardens

Sky Gardens can be placed at strategic levels in a high-rise tower, responding to the building's context, orientation, structure, and circulation zones...

The sky gardens of the Parkroyal on Pickering were planted on broad 'shelves', cantilevered at four-floor intervals. However, they appear to cascade as continuous swathe of plants and trees when viewed from above.
PARKROYAL ON PICKERING 2007 SINGAPORE

110–111

Vertical Breezeways

Both the Sky Forest City Tower and the Vertical Stacked City are ventilated by air rising through a hollow central core.

The core-as-breezeway of the Vertical Stacked City is not a continuous void, so it can function as either a horizontal or vertical breezeway, depending on the weather conditions in southern China.

In equatorial Singapore, however, the shaft of the Sky Forest City Tower has been closed to ensure a permanent updraft.

SKY FOREST CITY TOWER 2015 SINGAPORE (this page)
VERTICAL STACKED CITY (REVISED SCHEME) 2014 SHENZHEN, CHINA (right)

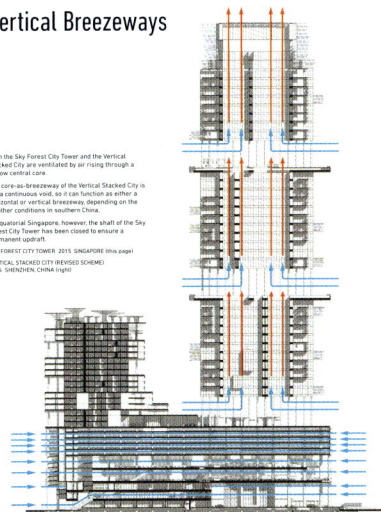

170–171

Scaling Up and Up

Designing Cities of the Future

'Architecture should be like sunshine from the blue sky and the breeze in spring, which will inspire minds, warm hearts, cultivate taste and clean up undesirable work styles.'

—President Xi Jinping, October 2014

With their 2001 entry for the Duxton Plain public housing competition in Singapore, WOHA had identified and flagged the social and environmental problems that were looming in Asian cities. They delivered a far-reaching solution and, as they anticipated, their scheme was not selected: '*It was considered too radical.*' WOHA had proposed nine forty-storey towers linked by horizontal layers that formed new ground levels in the sky, as village-like neighbourhoods with gardens and meeting places in the fresh air, which would be twenty or thirty or forty floors above the street. It was a pronouncement of WOHA's vision for a city of the future, highly sociable and highly sustainable. WOHA were ahead of their time, but in reality, the time wasn't yet ready for Duxton Plain. Six years later, however, a similar proposal on a similar scale was commissioned by the very same organization – the Housing and Development Board – and SkyVille @ Dawson was completed in 2015. Looking back, it is clear that this was the salient point: the time will come, sooner rather than later. Twenty years after Duxton Plain, and WOHA are back in the same position, but now the proposals are set in China.

Ever since the nation 'opened up' in the 1990s, China's urban construction landscape has been a confounding yet exhilarating phenomenon. Fantasies of a brave new world have proved irresistible to Western architects. They were granted opportunities to design at a super-scale, and most of the completed projects have been well received and widely publicized. Many of the buildings were essentially essays in emblematic form-making – landmark creation – but as the cityscapes consolidated, it became increasingly clear that the validity of the architectural expression needed to reflect the maturity of contemporary China. Realizing that a newly humanist agenda could be implemented with some magnitude in such a dynamic environment, WOHA have been singularly intent upon devising strategies for projects that did not present themselves as stand-alone architectural statements, but as schemes that focused upon civic and communal inclusiveness. WOHA's recent wave of proposals have all been massively-scaled, and they do not comprise a new direction for the practice so much as a broader trajectory. The thinking remains the same, traceable back to Duxton Plain in 2001, but the strategies and the scope have been scaled up and up. The magnitude of these schemes is breathtaking, and the big-picture urbanism – as mandated by the central government – is extraordinarily 'goal-oriented', yet once again WOHA's ideas appear too far-sighted: even though they did win several competitions, WOHA's proposals did not eventuate.

In terms of its urban restructuring, China has recently taken a great leap forward, the emphasis has been placed squarely on workplace productivity derived from communal cohesion and shared ambition, and the sustainable and sociable intentions have put the indecisions displayed in many Western nations to shame. As the nation proceeds with its ambitions for 21-st century modernity and global stature, China has set out to attract international 'talent' (as it is officially described) by enticing innovators, entrepreneurs and the like with a startling array of live/work/play environments: new urban paradigms for high density and high amenity, which ostensibly have the same planning, environmental and social objectives as those long-held by WOHA. A set of proposals made by WOHA in 2020 form a spectacular series of architectural forms and programmatic ideas, hyper-scaled stage-sets that coalesce in one's imagination as a kaleidoscopic visualization of a fabulous future. They are best viewed through the video animations that WOHA use for their presentations – *Westworld* meets Buck Rogers in a Garden City Mega City somewhere in China – where the virtual camera takes an endless journey through the sun-filled spaces of a radiant mini-city.

WOHA grasped this opportunity to reconfigure their earlier 'sky city' prototypes, now armed with a presumption that they could be built, and might be done so with a more intricate compositional and structural matrix than Duxton Plain, The Met and SkyVille @ Dawson. The viability of sustainable megastructures was now being taken seriously in China, and WOHA felt they had the latitude to push the boundaries further, designing sky cities with a man-

'A set of proposals for Chinese cities form a spectacular series of architectural forms and programmatic ideas … hyper-scaled stage-sets that coalesce in one's imagination as a kaleidoscopic visualization of a fabulous future.'

—WOHA

dated urbanist programme, and as they were located in contexts that provided a blank slate for architectural expression, WOHA's geometric configurations are quite startling. The computer-generated images of WOHA's mega-schemes are charmingly reminiscent of those of the Metabolists in the 1960s and the 'Metropolis of Tomorrow' charcoal drawings of Hugh Ferriss in the 1920s, yet they are of today. The futurist imaginings of the 20th century could only anticipate the advances in technology and the need for such high density and connectivity. In the relentlessly energetic expansion of 21st-century China, particularly in new cities like Shenzhen, the future that had been imagined has now arrived.

Two of the WOHA proposals were for Talent Cities – updated versions of convention centres – that provide an array of informal streets and market-places where entrepreneurs and venture capitalists can interact. The intention was communally motivated, with the Talent Cities offering accommodation and recreation areas as well as workspace. This was a 'Silicon Valley comes to the city' endeavour, which is very much in keeping with the urbane revitalizations seen over the last few decades in the hipster precincts of Beijing and Shanghai, and the possibilities now opening up are intriguing, to say the least. China's artistic and commercial sectors are intersecting, and they are motivated to assert a fresh spirit of entrepreneurial and cultural inclusivity. These two Talent City schemes reflect that sense of impending dynamism with a crackle of energy previously unseen, even in WOHA's most adventurous designs, possibly because paying dutiful respect to established societal or corporate preferences just does not seem appropriate to such imagining.

←
Young Talent City. Shenzhen, 2020 (scheme).

SHI BAN QIAO
HANGZHOU, 2019 (SCHEME)

The Shi Ban Qiao scheme emplaced an airy and skeletal Metabolist-style megastructure in the heart of Hangzhou's downtown, which is now being redeveloped to implement a much higher population density. Commercial and wider community facilities occupy the lower levels — which adjoin an old factory building — with housing and workspaces for 'talent' on the mid-levels. Running tracks, small parks and recreation areas were interspersed throughout the volumes, and the upper floors were allocated to resettlement housing, where residents are relocated in accordance with governmental policy. The structure was a leaner version of that proposed for Duxton Plain, and it incorporated similar social strategies, now attuned to Chinese culture. Meeting places — described by WOHA as 'mahjong cabanas' — protrude from the external walkways and overlook communal gardens laid out as horizontal villages with tea pavilions on four elevated levels, or decks, that extend from one corner of the site to the other. The minimal elegance of the mini-city was heightened by its elevation on slender columns, with the walkways, gardens and slab-blocks hovering above vast public spaces, which were opened up for all residents of the city. In the manner of SkyVille @ Dawson, the complex is crowned with sky parks that afford a view of Hangzhou's fabled West Lake.

←
Residents can walk from one corner of the complex to another on sky streets layered on every fifth level.

SHI BAN QIAO

HANGZHOU, 2019 (SCHEME)

← Viewed from a sky street, 'mahjong cabanas' protrude from the external corridors of the housing blocks.

→ With views to Hangzhou's West Lake, the rooftop is completely covered by lawns, gardens and groves of trees.

← The mixed–use complex is raised above commu–nity areas and public parkland, which includes restored indus–trial buildings.

→ Section.

10 20   50 m

> **"**
> Pedestrian linkages became the parti of the architecture, and WOHA refer to the project as the Escalating City. All vertical circulation is by means of escalator, ascent to the top floors only takes two minutes, and the only lifts in the five twenty-storey slab-blocks are there for emergencies.

YOUNG TALENT CITY

SHENZHEN, 2020 (SCHEME)

As opposed to a central setting in the ancient and long-revered city of Hangzhou, the site for the Young Talent City was located on the northern outskirts of the instant mega-city of Shenzhen. Once an insignificant township across the border from Hong Kong, Shenzhen was chosen in 1980 as the first of the Special Economic Zones (which would attempt to integrate capitalism with socialism). Its population has leapt from 68,000 to over 20 million in the space of forty years and its newfound global-city status is testament to China's embrace of global economics. Spreading through flatlands enclosed by low hills, the metropolitan area has an amorphous (some might say faceless) ambience, and communal identities have yet to arrive: the goal-oriented mega-city thus presents a *tabula rasa* setting for future city imagining.

The Young Talent City is planned to be the anchor for a district designated as an urban hub, sited on both sides of a street above an MRT railway station. WOHA took this 'constraint' as the cue, or excuse, to institute a network of horizontal walkways between slab-blocks on either side of the road, so that all connections took place within the building, not on external footpaths. From that point, pedestrian linkages became the parti of the architecture, and WOHA refer to the project as the Escalating City. All vertical circulation is by means of escalator, ascent to the top floors only takes two minutes, and the only lifts in the five twenty-storey slab-blocks are there for emergencies. Horizontal circulation between the blocks takes place on various datum levels, and the interconnecting walkways serve as sky streets, sky parks and outdoor meeting places. The complex has three strata of usage, with administration and formal amenities on the lower levels; workspaces, offices, and informal entrepreneurial areas on the mid-levels; and cheap rental accommodation and recreation areas on the upper floors.

The entire structure has an exuberant presence, with cherry-red footbridges slashing in and out of the five parallel slabs, which are adorned by curving yellow balconies and sky gardens, and the expression is that of a bolted-together assemblage rather than a monumental edifice. Although neat and slender, the slab-block forms are essentially reiterations of those used throughout the world (and China in particular) since the mid-20th century, and the entrenched industry-standard methods of construction are crucial to the viability of WOHA's approach. The radical thinking is to be found in the deconstruction and opening-out of such conventional high-rise structures, utilizing their fundamental sturdiness as the supporting framework for systems of sustainability. The value of the systems is to be found in the relationships and connections between the parts, not necessarily in the parts themselves.

← The sky bridges that cross over the street between the blocks are used as informal meeting and recreation areas.

→ The complex is comprised of a matrix of horizontal and diagonal circulation routes that traverse and overlap with the workspaces and communal amenities.

↓ The five slab–blocks serve as the structural framework for a multiplicity of external spaces layered throughout the height of the complex.

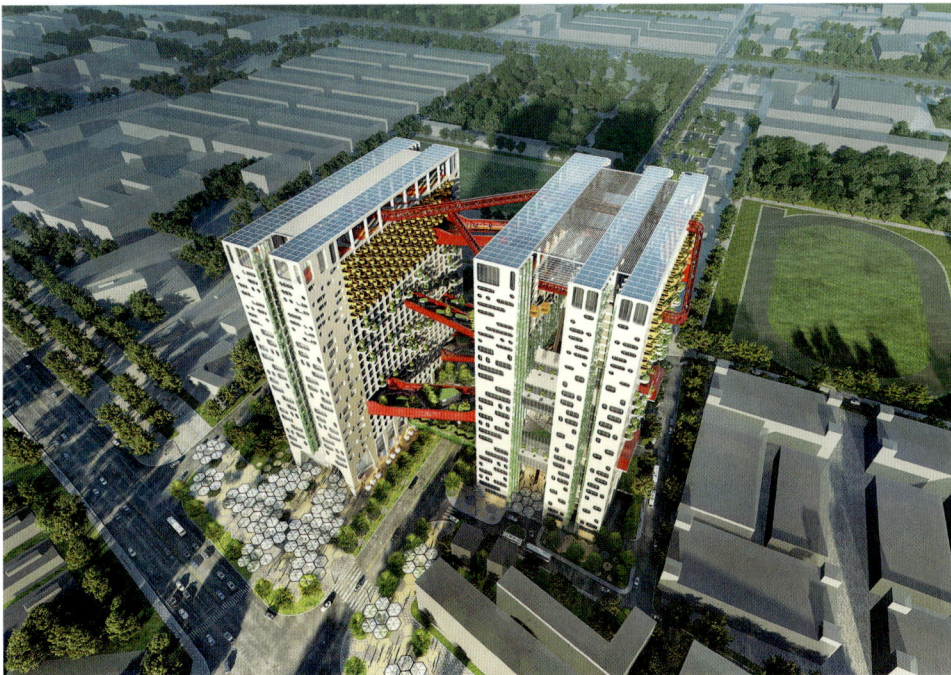

"

The scheme for the Qingpu Complex was a grand conflation of several typological forms well known to students of architecture, and it will surely be reprised one day (presumably in China) as a hyper-scaled rendition of classical and modernist city-making principles.

QINGPU COMPLEX

SHANGHAI, 2019 (SCHEME)

On a site in the western districts of Shanghai, near the domestic airport and China's largest convention centre, WOHA were invited to submit a proposal for a 'gourmet paradise', a huge market and restaurant complex to be supplied by domestic and international producers. This foodie mecca on a rectangular site would be combined with housing, and WOHA reverted to the split-level parti that initially surfaced with the School of the Arts (2005—10), where the academic levels were placed above the public areas on a new ground level, so that the structure had two clearly separated strata. The scheme for the Qingpu Complex was a grand conflation of several typological forms well known to students of architecture, and it will surely be reprised one day (presumably in China) as a hyper-scaled rendition of classical and modernist city-making principles. A series of vaulted halls on an orthogonal grid contain the markets, shops, cafés and restaurants, and they open out to the

↑
A winter view of the large internal park on the sixth level.

→
The market and restaurant complex is contained within a series of vaulted halls that open out to a lake formed by a broadening of the local canals.

streets and an adjoining canal beneath the flaring canopy of a site-wide ground plane on the sixth level. Ten floors of apartments rise from this level as slab-blocks, forming a continuous ring of perimeter housing that encloses multi-layered public gardens. This internal park was comprised of a wonderful arrangement of landscaped terraces — with a distinctly Chinese composition when seen on plan — that look down into the market areas through a deep canyon, and WOHA were revisiting an

idea first unveiled with the Punggol Community Park Station proposal of 2013. These communal pleasure gardens have a wide urban connection, as the set of waterways at the base of the canyon forms an extension of Shanghai's capillary of small canals. All services and access roads were diverted to the basement, so the complex was completely walkable as an autonomous entity: a notion that was quite antithetical to the urban grain of China's established cities, which have always been

considered as a network of small, manageable components. Featuring such readily apparent formal references as Roman vaulting, 19th-century galleria arcades, high-modernist perimeter block housing, and 20th-century curvilinear expressionism — not to mention traditional Chinese water gardens — the scheme was bold and captivating: with more than a hint of bravado, it integrated a new way of urban thinking with a monumental piece of architectonic form-making.

SHENZHEN OCT

SHENZHEN, 2019 (SCHEME)

The Shenzhen OCT proposal has a cluster of three linked towers as its central component, which appears to have been designed as a giant waterfall with splashing cascades tumbling down from thirty levels of landscaped terraces. Aside from its aesthetic and biophilic qualities, this huge aquatic installation was designed as a vertical remediation system to cleanse the highly polluted Shenzhen Bay, and — as if in the Iguazu Falls — the water descends layer by layer to re-enter the natural ecological system in a newly purified state. The complex can be seen as a recalibration of the topographic architecture of WOHA's Parkroyal on Pickering hotel (2007—13) on a much larger scale, with similar — only more dramatic — vistas looking up and down the central void. The smaller adjoining towers all contribute to the site-wide water-cleansing process.

↑
As a filtration and remediation system for Shenzhen Bay, water cascades down the terraced sky gardens that cloak the three towers.

←
The central atrium presents a monumental elaboration of WOHA's topographic architecture.

> **"**
> **Both complexes were envisaged as vertical remediation systems to cleanse Shenzhen Bay. Water drawn from the bay descends layer by layer to re-enter the natural environment in a newly purified state.**

VANKE HEADQUARTERS

SHENZHEN, 2019 (SCHEME)

As with the scheme for the OCT complex, the proposal for Vanke's corporate headquarters was envisaged as part of a Shenzhen Bay water-cleansing programme, and it presented a rather eccentric response to its downtown location, with an external carapace of deliberately generic architecture shielding a luxuriantly landscaped work environment. Again, the essential parti was a monumental extrapolation of the principles displayed at Parkroyal on Pickering, with layers and layers of planted terraces creating a vast vertical park, which contains running tracks, swimming pools and informal meeting areas.

↑
The sheer street elevations serve as a shield for resplendent vertical gardens.

→
An abundance of sky gardens and sky parks are layered throughout the complex. The buildings rise as mountains with waterfalls.

VANKE YUN CITY

SHENZHEN, 2014—19

One of WOHA's Chinese mega-projects has actually been built (or nearly built) in the shape of three conjoined office towers on the outskirts of Shenzhen, and it first saw light in 2014 as the Vertical Stacked City, a proposal that underwent many revisions before getting the go-ahead as Vanke Yun City. Rising to sixty floors, the structure was completed in 2019, but the huge internal spaces — which were the essential parti — still await completion, and they may be waiting a while, as the complex will now not function as a multi-use agglomeration of tenancies, which had been the intention. In the original proposal, the Vertical Stacked City was envisaged as a capacious single tower with three clusters of 'villages' layered as aerial neighbour-hoods between stacks of corporate office floors. The villages protruded in three bands from the glazed building envelope as haphaz-ardly arranged clumps of live/work/play pods, and this compositional device was retained in a different form, with four layers of smoothly detailed extrusions now poking through the

The exterior has a dichotomous appearance, with clusters of glazed work-spaces poking through the ribbed façades of the towers.

→ Section showing the gardens and terraces layered within the atrium, which rises the full height of the building.

← The aesthetic expression can be seen as a response to the context of new cities like Shenzhen, where the only reference points are other high-rise towers.

sheer elevations of a building mass that appears to be a single tower. WOHA say that the joy will be found inside the structure, where the three towers will enclose huge green vertical gardens, whenever they are completed. In elemental terms, this organic typology is the formal opposite of the Oasia Downtown hotel (2011—16), where the gardens formed the external elevations, and WOHA refer to the intended space as 'the paradise within'. However, the external demeanour is curious and compelling on its own terms, rising above a broad plain of newly built and anonymously gridded commercial towers. Its expression is very unusual: it appears from different vantage points as a completely different building, and it doesn't look like WOHA were the architects. A case of new aesthetics arising out of new circumstances and an alien context. A possible comparison might be the occasional building by Rem Koolhaas: architecture that doesn't reveal the hand of the designer, yet looks strangely assured and contextually correct, but it's hard to say exactly why.

Regenerating Cities

PUNGGOL DIGITAL DISTRICT
SINGAPORE, 2017—

F ollowing on from their earlier (c.2000) civic-minded projects, WOHA embarked upon a course in which they conceived of their architecture in terms of its urbanity – its contribution to city-making – and they would later refer to and codify the process as Macro-Architecture Micro-Urbanism. With the completion of The Met in 2009 and the School of the Arts in 2010, they had pragmatically provided new templates for construction in tropical Asian cities: The Met was a never-before-seen model for a residential sky city, and the School of the Arts was a monumental and elemental demonstration of how methods for passive sustainability could be implemented without compromise in an institutional building. Several subsequent prototypes – Parkroyal on Pickering, SkyVille @ Dawson, Oasia Downtown and Kampung Admiralty – were designed and built with urban sustainability strategies that were more or less interchangeable and they made a significant impact upon their specific typology in an increasingly globalized context. They were highly principled pieces of architecture that had done their utmost to integrate with and potentially improve their context, but they were standalone buildings, plugged into a pre-existing urban network. WOHA understood that their underlying methodology had reached the point where they were obliged to extend their ideas beyond the limits of an individual structure: they wanted to reshape the networks and systems of a city.

↑
Section showing the layers of above-ground circulation routes and below-ground transportation networks.

Constantly striving to overcome the island's geographic and demographic constraints, Singapore has been distinguished by its transformative schemes for city-building ever since it attained independence in 1965. To date, the Housing and Development Board has overseen the construction of twenty-three satellite towns — linked in a molecular fashion by expressways and a highly efficient public transport network — which now accommodate nearly 90% of the population in high-rise apartments envied by the residents of all other Asian countries. Singapore's airport and container port have long been global hubs; the financial, technological and education sectors maintain top-of-the-table rankings; a comprehensive environmental initiative saw to it that the city was assessed as Asia's greenest by 2016; and a premium has always been placed on the commissioning of iconic

(and periodically innovative) architecture. To one degree or another, this big-picture mindset has suited WOHA very well, and those Singaporean strands of ambition intertwined with their own to define the scope of a masterplan commissioned and approved in 2017.

WOHA's vision for the Punggol Digital District evolved from their Self-Sufficient City scheme, a 2013 competition entry for the new town of Tengah, which had proposed a multi-layered and resolutely sustainable integration of buildings and landscape on a swathe of underutilized and gently forested country in western Singapore. On the northeast edge of the island, the Punggol site offered a similar tabula rasa prospect, and WOHA's masterplan prescribed that as much of the existing forest should be retained as possible, and that all outdoor areas should undergo a process of re-wilding. This compre-

> **The development was explicitly not determined by aesthetic and architectonic expression; it is instead a conscientiously futuristic piece of macro-scale architecture-as-urbanism, one where the programme for integrating environmental, infrastructural and social systems formed the parti.**

hensive (and uncompromising) environmental initiative had been made possible by a policy of 'no roads' in the densely occupied central zone, which was a key move, and one that would go on to direct the logistical framework of the entire development. Delivery, service and transportation vehicles could only enter that central square kilometre at basement level, thus establishing an underground service layer that was then extended — with the use of self-driving vehicles — throughout the rest of the site. With heavy vehicle traffic kept to a minimum, the parkland and thoroughfares of the entire precinct could thus be claimed by pedestrians and wildlife as their own preserve.

Much like the talent hubs in China, the Punggol Digital District is intended to form an environment where students, graduates and industry professionals could mingle in order to 'sustain Singapore's long-term economic growth by bringing good jobs and social amenities closer to residents' (as proclaimed in a government press release). To that end — to facilitate the mingling — the development comprises both a digital-economy business park and a campus of the Singapore Institute of Technology, and their facilities, projects and people would effectively be shared. Arrivals from the underground MRT station emerge to an abundantly tree-lined boulevard and a vista of parkland and forest, framed by terraces and sky gardens on the lower levels and layers of the buildings. This integration of the natural and built environments was made with community, commerce and ecology in mind, providing extremely pleasant and very sociable spaces in order to stimulate the desired entrepreneurial outcomes, while conserving and regenerating the native landscape of Punggol. The development was explicitly not determined by aesthetic and architectonic expression; it is instead a conscientiously futuristic piece of macro-scale architecture-as-urbanism, one where the programme for integrating environmental, infrastructural and social systems formed the parti. WOHA were now designing as city planners: *'The large-scale problems we're facing can only be solved if we address problems at a city level. We can't do it one building at a time ... it is necessary to always look at the big picture.'*

↑
Much of the campus is comprised of layered landscapes that provide shelter and generate airflow.

→
Communal tropical gardens are found on different levels throughout the campus.

> Intrigued by how the possibilities opened up when vehicles and services were diverted underground at Punggol, WOHA identified urban mobility as the key required to unlock the 21st-century planning puzzle: how to satisfy the two seemingly unreconcilable prerequisites for a truly sustainable city, one which called for a re-wilded natural environment on the one hand and high-density high-amenity on the other.

THE FIFTY-FIFTY CITY
SINGAPORE, 2020 (SCHEME)

WOHA's next step in their process of Macro-Architecture Micro-Urbanism was of such a scale that it could now be referred to as Macro-Urbanism. Their Fifty-Fifty City proposal of 2020 aimed to comprehensively regenerate a huge swathe of inner-city brownfield Singapore as a consummately naturalized environment, and the systems of the city were all that mattered now: '*When architectural prototypes have been resolved ... systems can be the field of creativity.*' Intrigued by how the possibilities opened up when vehicles and services were diverted underground at Punggol, WOHA identified urban mobility as the key required to unlock the 21st-century planning puzzle: how to satisfy the two seemingly unreconcilable prerequisites for a truly sustainable city, one that called for a re-wilded natural environment on the one hand and high-density high-amenity on the other. In an ideal city, the rehabilitation of the natural world would coexist with the continual scaling-up of urban development, but the networks of mobility quite simply prevent any

chance of broad-ranging reciprocity, never mind harmony. Streets, roads, railways, cars, trucks, buses, trains: all invasive, polluting and dangerous, but — as things stand — cities cannot function without vehicular transport.

The Fifty-Fifty City took as its location a six-square-kilometre patch of Singapore, on the edge of the city centre and currently occupied by industrial estates nearing the end of their useful lifespans. Before the spread of the modern city, the setting was one of a gentle flat plain interspersed by languid waterways, but the ecosystems were disrupted by the processes of land reclamation and ultimately despoiled by industrial waste and pollution. Proximity to the downtown meant that high-rise mixed-use redevelopment would be inevitable, and as the natural environment was ripe for remediation, the precinct presented an ideal opportunity to serve as the site for an exercise in sustainable coexistence: 50% of the land surface would host extremely high-density settlement, while its other half would be re-wilded, in order to revert to nature.

WOHA surmised that the site had the capacity to constitute another central business district, and the proposed scheme linked large collections of towers with varying heights on an organically inflected plan that paid more heed to the landscaping and the water than to Singapore's existing city grid. (As seen in the renderings, the modelling for the building forms was pointedly generic and amorphous, indicating that attention should be focused on the public realm.) Traditional vehicular functions at street level were relocated underground, to form a subterranean network for transportation, deliveries and services: one that could not interfere with or intervene in the outdoor environment. Roads would now be greenways where people could travel through landscaped precincts and

natural wilderness on foot, by bicycle or by sharing small driverless vehicles to connect with city-wide transport in the usual manner, at underground rail and bus interchanges. At basement level, all the buildings and tower clusters would be interconnected by conduit roadways and occasional railways, which — unencumbered by physical and logistical impediments at ground level — would be indisputably more efficient (and cheaper to build and maintain): 'If all buildings and developments are connected at an underground level, we can open up the ground level to create parks, and we can leave areas undeveloped ... on a continuous ground plane where nature can run its course.'

The Fifty-Fifty City was predicated on the notion — inherent to the cause of true sustainability — that 50% of the planet must be reserved for nature,[1] and WOHA were here proposing that the process should begin at home, in the cities. At first impression, such visions of the future feel too outlandish, too idealistic and far too difficult to implement, but the forms and networks of cities have always been created by incremental yet decisive transformations, invariably motivated by the requirements for transportation. Removing land-hungry and organically dead systems of mobility from the surface of the earth — precinct by precinct — is no more than yet another transitional reaction to the ways and needs of the times. Facing up to the potential ramifications of global warming has become an imperative, and if city planners can be encouraged to act in an effective firefighting role, the integration of high density with environmental regeneration will be crucial: in fact, it will be essential.

1   In his book *Half Earth: Our Planet's Fight for Life*, Edward O. Wilson — one of the world's most respected biologists — states that we must 'dedicate fully half the surface of the earth to nature'. WOHA see this as a fundamental planning principle — one that must be adopted at any scale.

↑
50% of the site area is reserved for nature, with the other half occupied by high-density high-amenity towers.

←
With all transportation, deliveries and services located underground, the landscape between the towers comprises greenways and waterways rather than roads.

→
Throughout the Fifty-Fifty City, the ground level has been regenerated as a natural environment and reclaimed by the community at large.

Converge + Connect + Intersect. The Form Axiom

NIRMAL KISHNANI, PhD
SCHOOL OF DESIGN AND ENVIRONMENT
NATIONAL UNIVERSITY OF SINGAPORE

> Designers – with strategic arrangements of space, system and surface – can favour flows and exchanges that are life-sustaining. Good design, by this definition, is many systems fitted together within a form that promotes reciprocity within a wider system-of-systems.

In an episode of the HBO science-fiction series *Westworld* (season 3, 2020), the Oasia Downtown hotel has a cameo. Singapore is home to a handful of cutting-edge buildings, of which the Oasia hotel is, quite possibly, the most allegorical. The precision of its engineered form — orthogonal shape, gauze-like skin, relentless colour — surrenders to random patches of green, an ebb and flow of metal and foliage enacted in slow motion. Interestingly, this dialectic of human-made and natural is also the premise of *Westworld*, in which form — human form — blurs the line between living and constructed.

Alongside its popular appeal, Oasia Downtown fits neatly into a discourse on nature and architecture, which has had a long history. The *organic functionalists* of 19th-century Europe, for instance, took an interest in morphologies in nature, as discussed by evolutionary biologists, and asked what these might teach architects about the indivisibility of form and function.[1] The same question was later stripped of etymology by modernists, who expunged nature as a reference. The pendulum swung back in the last quarter of the 20th century, when proximity to living systems was found to improve human wellbeing. The term *biophilic design* described the inclusion of natural elements and attributes at the drawing board. Further along the road, *biomimicry* was coined to describe lessons learned from biological structures and processes, and subsequently applied to buildings and their systems.

Today, climate change, species extinction and (of late) pandemics are the new 'natural' imperatives: global in scale and terrifying in impact. In response, the *ecomodernists* call for an outright rescue of nature.[2] The binary of the human-made and the

1   David J. Adams, 'The Form–Function Relationship in Architecture and Nature: Organic and Inorganic Functionalism', in *Architecture, Sculpture, and Painting of the First Goetheanum: The Collected Works of Rudolf Steiner*, Steiner Books, 2017.

2   John Asafu-Adjaye, et al., *An Ecomodernist Manifesto* (2015), www.ecomodernism.org.

natural must be refuted, they say. Were the two to act in partnership, the argument goes, planetary systems could once again thrive. If not, there would be systemic collapse, with the extinction of much life on earth, including our own species.

In this quest for partnerships, form is finding a new purpose. Form-making — which, for some time, has been an act of object shaping — is reclaimed by those who see it as something more. Both human-made and natural worlds are complex interconnected systems that rely on the same biotic and abiotic flows. It follows that designers — with strategic arrangements of space, system and surface — can favour flows and exchanges that are life-sustaining. Good design, by this definition, is many systems fitted together within a form that promotes reciprocity within a wider system-of-systems.[3]

Take the Oasia hotel; like many WOHA buildings, it wants to be good. A tall commercial tower, over 190 metres high, it is situated in a dense urban area and wrapped in vegetation that may seem, on the surface, like greenery for its own sake. That it alters its urban condition, however — becoming a biophilic trigger for an entire neighbourhood, and a habitat for birds and small animals — gives pause for thought.[4] Here, the meaning of function expands: form-making becomes the synthesis of many goals, and a way of bringing nature into the everyday.

To understand this ambition and, more generally, the WOHA position on form, it is necessary to trace the lineage of ideas. The 1980s saw a convergence of several strands of thinking in Asia: the search for identity, an interest in environmental performance, and new theories on tropical urbanism. It was against this canvas that Wong Mun Summ and Richard Hassell, some 4,000 kilometres apart, began their journey at two schools of architecture.

Three Perspectives On Form

... as Poetics of Place

At the start of the 1980s, designers were invested in the polemics of place and identity: architecture as a statement of *where* and *why*. Critical Regionalism, a movement revived by American historian Lewis Mumford and championed by Asian theorists, celebrated the specifics of a locale, its economy, culture and climate.[5] This was in part a postcolonial assertion of autonomy, and in part a rejection of the universalism propagated by the International Style. Some of the most renowned Regionalists of the period were Balkrishna Doshi (India), Geoffrey Bawa (Sri Lanka) and Glenn Murcutt (Australia).

A subset of this movement was Tropical Regionalism. Singapore architect Tay Kheng Soon was one of the first to discuss tropicality as a quest for a form language that included big sheltering roofs and permeable walls; an approach that, he argued, was rooted in contemporary urban reality.[6] At the other end of the spectrum, Singapore-based Australian architect Kerry Hill courted the vernacular — thatched roofs, local materials and fluidity of indoor-outdoor spaces — expressed, at the time, through resorts and private homes. In both positions, climate was the common denominator. Poetics of place would be conveyed through porosity to air and light, and an arrangement of shade, shadow and shelter.

From the start of their careers, Wong and Hassell were drawn to Regionalists like Bawa and the Argentinian architect Emilio Ambasz, who presented new viewpoints on architecture and landscape. They also spent four formative years in Hill's office, working on resorts in pristine natural settings. Once they had set up WOHA, the pitched roof, as a form device, would be jettisoned, no longer deemed necessary as a signpost of place. The romanticism of tropical gardens would give way to a perspective on nature as ecosystem.

The typology of the private residence, which formed the bulk of their work in the 1990s, would eventually prove too small for big ideas. 1 Moulmein Rise (Singapore, 1999—2003), a twenty-eight-storey residential tower with fifty apartments, was WOHA's breakout project; the first to present a take on tropicality for an urban setting. The tectonics of an uncluttered orthogonal tower, layered with micro-details of windows and brise-soleils, projected climate intelligence *and* compositional intricacy. This would become a trademark of the firm's style, seen later in Newton Suites (Singapore, 2003—07), The Met (Bangkok, 2003—09) and Oasia Downtown (Singapore, 2011—16).

... as Evidence-Based Performance

The oil crises of the 1970s forced a rethink of energy consumption. In Asia, buildings were deemed a liability because of their growing reliance on air-conditioning, and research focused on the envelope: a pathway for energy flows that contributed to cooling loads.[7] However, the journal papers and statutory codes that emerged on this at the time did not alter upstream design

3   Nirmal Kishnani, 'Form, a Structure of Relations', in *Ecopuncture: Transforming Architecture and Urbanism in Asia*, FuturArc, 2019, pp. 76—85.

4   Philip Oldfield, 'What Would a Heat-Proof City Look Like?' in the *Guardian*, 15 August 2018, https://www. theguardian.com/ cities/2018/ aug/15/what-heat-proofcity-look-like. 'We've almost created, in some ways, the notion of a huge tree in the city,' says Wong Mun Summ. '[It's] a device in the city that really supports a thriving ecosystem three-dimensionally in a very dense environment.'

5   Léa-Catherine Szacka and Véronique Patteeuw, 'Critical Regionalism for Our Time', in *The Architectural Review*, 22 November 2019, https://www. architectural-review.com/essays/ critical-regionalism-for-our-time/10045392.

6   Tay Kheng Soon, 'The Architectural Aesthetics of Tropicality', in *Line, Edge and Shade: The Search for a Design Language in Tropical Asia*, Robert Powell, Page One, 1997, pp. 40—45.

7   Jeyasingh, Vijayalaxmi, 'Concept of Overall Thermal Transfer Value (OTTV) in Design of Building Envelope to Achieve Energy Efficiency', in *International Journal of Thermal and Environmental Engineering*, 1(2), December 2010, https://www. researchgate. net/publication/267862613_ Concept_of_Overall_Thermal_ Transfer_Value_ OTTV_in_Design_ of_Building_Envelope_to_Achieve_ Energy_Efficiency.

thinking. Thermal gains could be managed by tweaking windows and curtain walls further along in the design process. This approach to performance — as a downstream optimization of parts or subsystems — would persist for decades, well into the age of green buildings that was to come.

In the 1980s, the Malaysian architect Ken Yeang was the first to adopt a stance on the *wholeness* of form, imagined at the start of the process and connected to *evidence-based performance*. His bioclimatic model was in part feature-based (sun-shades, sky courts and greenery), and in part rule-based (geometry, orientation and placement of cores).

Wong and Hassell shared the intuitions of Yeang and his inclinations towards passive design. They too resisted design-as-optimization, concerned that simulations could become a rabbit hole of incrementalism. Both would come to see building-integrated vegetation as a pivot to ecological thinking. Their positions on form, however, could not be more different.

WOHA's early experiments were spurred on by quixotic clients who sometimes asked for *'a breeze in a particular room at a particular time of day'*. The specificity of the request, a kind of environmental functionalism, led to a broader search for tectonic rules. Here, rooms would be elevated to emancipate the ground, and living spaces were pathways for natural ventilation, called breezeways.[8] The building would be an agglomeration of catchers and conduits which, unlike Yeang's exuberant display of protuberances and voids, were restrained within a modernist language.

As the size of projects grew, WOHA's ideas jumped in scale. The School of the Arts (Singapore, 2005—10) and BRAC University (Bangladesh, 2012—), for instance, embody form strategies that were conceived in early WOHA houses. Each is a composition of elevated blocks separated by breezeways, with public space below and airflow above, channelled through a deep floor plate.

... as Urban Structure

Cities in Asia expanded and densified in the 1980s, obliging the Tropicalists to turn their attention to urbanism. The Kampong Bugis Development Guide Plan (Singapore, 1989) was the culmination of ideas on the tropical city that could be traced back to the 1960s, when the author Tay Kheng Soon designed the People's Park Complex (Singapore, 1967—70) with his partner at the time, William Lim. The principles of plan-

ning included mixed-use programming, a bid to reverse rigid zoning, and two-tiered pedestrian movement — what Tay called '3-D planning'. The urban block would be organized around a web of sheltered public spaces (arcades, streets, squares) and linked to high-speed mobility networks such as train lines.[9] In the Kampong Bugis Plan, urban form also mimicked a 'forest', with heavy planting and biodiversity.[10]

The Bugis Plan, though never built, shaped the conversation on tropical cities. The other influence, from Wong and Hassell's vantage point, was a shift in real-time Singapore planning. By the 1990s, the Garden City vision had led to widespread greening. Vegetation, for its size and prevalence, had become an urban system. The Park Connector Network, initiated in 1995, sought to correct fragmentation by introducing pathways for the movement of people and fauna.[11] A decade later, Singapore's Active, Beautiful, Clean Waters Programme (2007) called for the transformation of hard-edged stormwater systems into naturalized streams that expand public space, improve urban hydrology and create room for biodiversity.[12] By the time the Nature Conservation Masterplan was announced in 2015, vehicular roads were being redesigned as *natureways*, to aid the movement of wildlife.[13] Developers were encouraged to see rooftop gardens as biodiversity habitats.[14]

WOHA's proposal for the Duxton Plain public housing competition (2001) was the first to explore intersecting systems and three-dimensional planning: 1,800 apartments would be grouped into nine towers, acting as urban columns that support a network of *streets* and *squares* on every fifth floor. Elevated community decks connected to public space below, and by extension, the neighbourhood. These interrupted the towers vertically, subdividing the whole into smaller social clusters or *villages*. Breezeways cut through the built form, both vertically and horizontally. Similar to the Bugis Plan, the goals here were sociability and liveability, i.e. how people interact with each other, and how spatial structure affects quality of life.

The firm's second watershed project came twelve years later: a residential estate for 210,000 people on a 730-hectare site in Jakarta, Indonesia. By now, WOHA's position on urbanism included *generative* systems, such as food farms and solar canopies, and ecology. Buildings were conjoined into grid-like megastructures. The ground was a datum for pedestrians and cyclists, and for

8   Patrick Bingham-Hall, *Garden City Mega City: Rethinking Cities for the Age of Global Warming*, Pesaro Publishing, 2016, pp. 146—83.

9   Liane Lefaivre and Bruno Stagno, 'The Suppression and Rethinking of Regionalism and Tropicalism after 1945', in *Tropical Architecture: Critical Regionalism in the Age of Globalization*, Alexander Tzonis, Liane Lefaivre and Bruno Stagno, eds, Wiley and Sons, 2001, p. 46.

10   Tay Kheng Soon, 'Rethinking the City in the Tropics: The Tropical City Concept', in *Tropical Architecture: Critical Regionalism in the Age of Globalization*, Alexander Tzonis, Liane Lefaivre and Bruno Stagno, eds, Wiley and Sons, 2001, p. 272.

11   Stephanie Yeow, 'A Garden City's Green Veins', in *The Straits Times*, 27 November 2017, http://www.straitstimes.com/singapore/a-garden-citys-green-veins.

12   Khoo Teng Chye and Valerie Chew, eds, *The Active, Beautiful, Clean Waters Programme: Water as an Environmental Asset* (Singapore, Centre for Liveable Cities, 2017), https://www.clc.gov.sg/docs/default-source/urban-systems-studies/rb172978-mnd-abc-water.pdf.

13   'Greening Singapore So Wildlife Can Return', in *The Straits Times*, 7 June 2018, www.straitstimes.com/sites/default/files/attachments/2018/06/07/st_20180607_nature07_4041868.pdf.

14   *Design Guides to Promote Biodiversity on Roof Gardens: CS E12:2017*, Centre for Urban Greenery & Ecology, National Parks Board, 2017, https://www.nparks.gov.sg/skyrisegreenery/news-and-resources/guidelines.

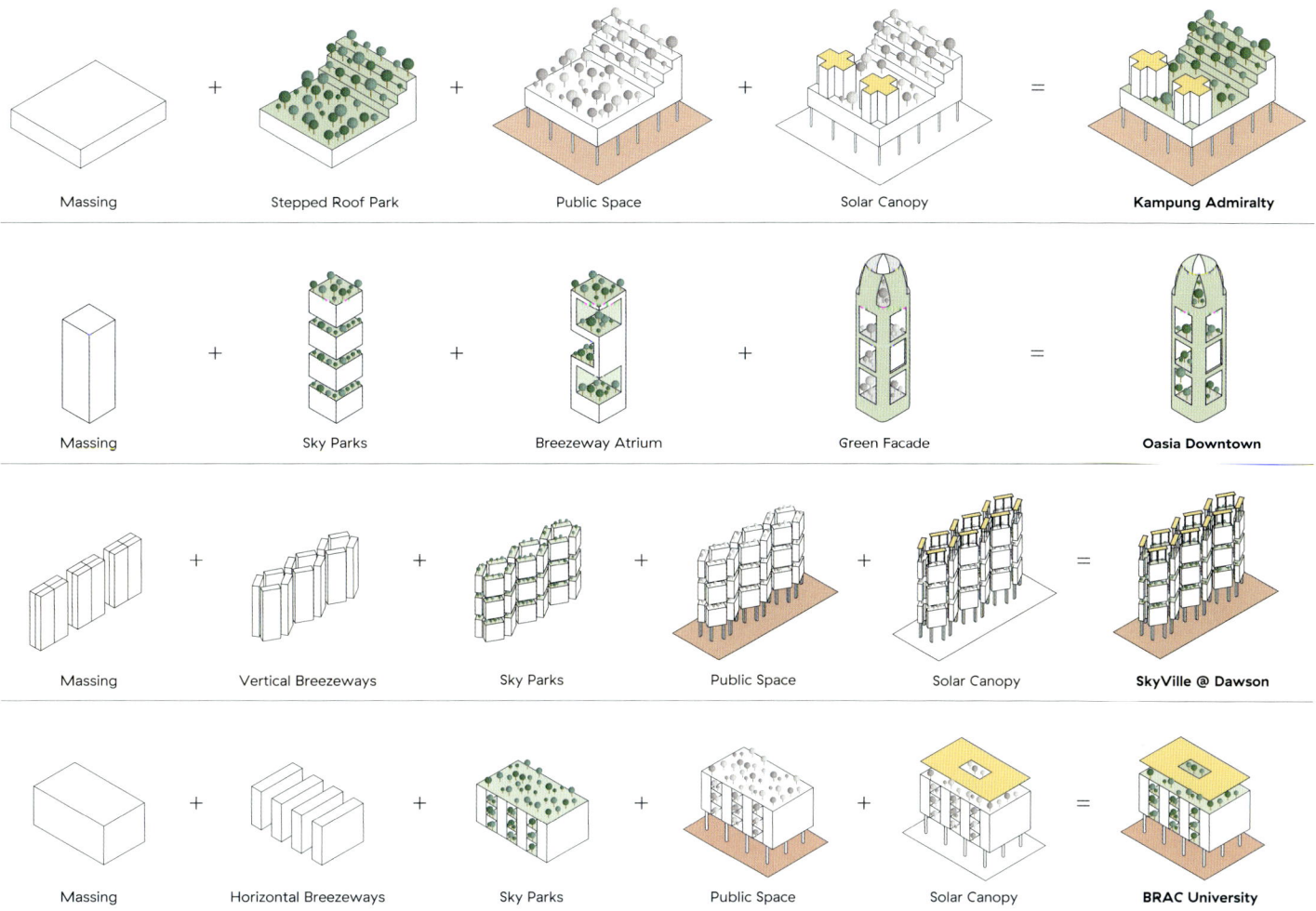

| Massing | + | Stepped Roof Park | + | Public Space | + | Solar Canopy | = | **Kampung Admiralty** |

| Massing | + | Sky Parks | + | Breezeway Atrium | + | Green Facade | = | **Oasia Downtown** |

| Massing | + | Vertical Breezeways | + | Sky Parks | + | Public Space | + | Solar Canopy | = | **SkyVille @ Dawson** |

| Massing | + | Horizontal Breezeways | + | Sky Parks | + | Public Space | + | Solar Canopy | = | **BRAC University** |

the movement of non–human species. It was a radical rethink of building typology in the service of urban morphology, and a reframing of hard urbanism to include soft socio–ecological systems.

Connecting Systems, Bridging Scales

In the book, *Garden City Mega City: Rethinking Cities for the Age of Global Warming* (2016), Wong and Hassell explain their work as a response to the bigness of climate change and urbanization.[15] Form is key to this extrapolation. It is elaborated as features and attributes, summarized as a toolkit of strategies that reduces dependency on fossil fuels and strives for a spirit of generosity. Actions at the building scale, replicated and upsized, would be key to outcomes at the urban scale. The stacking of mixed–use programmes, for instance, creates room for social, productive and ecological processes. It connects ground to roof and, when repeated and linked across buildings, becomes a scaffold for three–dimensional communities. In the WOHA body of work, there are sub–themes to this multi–scalar approach: the role of nature, the significance of semi–outdoor spaces, and the contiguity of systemic flows.

Second Nature

Australian theorist Leon van Schaik called the WOHA style the 'new ugly' for its seemingly dissonant composition of natural forms and patterns, expressed as hills, grottoes or terraces.[16] Nature in a WOHA building is also present as vegetation, nested deep in the fabric of the architecture.

Newton Suites (Singapore, 2003–07), a thirty–six–storey condominium, has a vegetated feature wall that's the same height as the tower. Its green plot ratio (surface area of greenery relative to site) is 130%.[17] In Parkroyal on Pickering (Singapore, 2007–13), which has a ratio of 240%, the building as a whole was conceived as a receptacle for verdant terraces. A few years later, the Oasia Downtown hotel reached a ratio of 1,110% with vast planted façades and three lush atria.

By the time Kampung Admiralty (Singapore, 2013–17) — a mid–rise community project in a high–density residential area — was completed, WOHA had moved from quantity to performance. With a green plot ratio of 110%, its vegetation is linked to water flows within small constructed ecosystems that mimic nature, and rainwater is drawn by gravity through planter beds and bioswales

↑
Form postulate.
Source: Author.

15 Patrick Bingham–Hall, *Garden City Mega City: Rethinking Cities for the Age of Global Warming*, Pesaro Publishing, 2016, pp. 7–6, 12–75.

16 Leon Van Schaik, *Practical Poetics in Architecture*, John Wiley and Sons, 2015, p. 224.

17 Ong Boon Lay, A. Ho and David Ho Kim Lim, *Green Plot Ratio – Past, Present & Future* (2012), https://www.researchgate.net/publication/236634754_Green_Plot_Ratio_-_Past_Present_Future.

that absorb and clean. The water is then collected in a central rain garden, pumped out for irrigation or filtered down to the biotope and eco-pond in the plaza on the ground. The roof, which resembles a plateau and terraced hill, is a social space that is natural in all ways: analogue, elements and process.

A survey in 2018 found that 88% of people surveyed in or near the Oasia Downtown tower were enthusiastic about its appearance, stating that it contributed positively to the quality of the city centre.[18] The building is home to birds and climbing animals, accounting for half the species found in nearby green patches. In the same audit, Kampung Admiralty did even better. Its green roof holds a remarkable diversity of species, fifty in total, far exceeding patches of green in the neighbourhood.[19] Since it opened, it has become a thriving social nexus.

What is noteworthy about the transition from Newton Suites to Kampung Admiralty is the underlying paradigm shift: from nature-inspired forms that benefit a few, to nature-based solutions for the good of many. What happens in and on a building is tethered to urban and ecological systems that lie outside its site and shell.

Third Space

The third space connects indoor with outdoor. Ken Yeang and the Regionalists saw these semi-outdoor spaces as key to the goals of energy use, indoor comfort and social engagement. The work of WOHA, aiming for the same, reveals a rich taxonomy of third spaces that does more than mediate and mitigate. It generates new spatial possibilities.

Here, form is contoured to facilitate flows of air and light; what is referred to as *breathing* architecture.[20] It offers internal shade through the arrangement of multiple blocks. Greenery and water are deployed as moderators of temperature and humidity, and the space is connected to amenities and programmes in ways that make it socially vibrant.

In a study of four WOHA buildings — Kampung Admiralty, Oasia Downtown, the School of the Arts and SkyVille @ Dawson — onsite measurements of semi-outdoor spaces revealed a microclimate.[21] Air temperatures were 1.4 to 2.3°C cooler than outside. Air moved at an average 0.86 metres per second, sometimes as high as 2.26 metres per second, even when wind speeds were low. Likelihood of thermal comfort (PMV 0 to +1) was estimated at 98%.

To gauge sociability, residents of SkyVille @ Dawson were surveyed along with their neighbours in SkyTerrace @ Dawson.[22] Both developments are about the same size, built at the same time, and are home to a near identical demographic mix. In terms of form, however, they differ significantly. SkyVille has five shaded sky decks, tucked within a vertically connected void. SkyTerrace, designed by another architect, has six communal decks, attached externally to the towers. Not surprisingly, the decks of SkyVille were cooler than those in SkyTerrace. Some 250 visitors were counted over a period of seven days in the former, and in the same week, the figure was only 60 in the latter. SkyVille residents said they knew an average of 10.2 neighbours, compared with 7.5 in SkyTerrace. Self-reported energy use in the apartments was 17% lower in SkyVille than in SkyTerrace. It was estimated that if SkyVille's form were adopted in all future public housing in Singapore, savings could amount to SGD$153 million per year and CO_2-eq emissions would contract by 300,000 t.[23]

Fourth Dimension

Three-dimensional planning has long been touted as a response to the challenge of density, a way of extracting more per unit of land without compromising urban quality. SkyVille @ Dawson, for instance, has twelve vertical villages, each serving some eighty apartments. Separated by communal decks, this segmentation reduces the perceived bigness of a development that is forty-six storeys high with close to a thousand units. SkyVille takes its cue from the Duxton Plain competition entry, which had the same form-logic. It, too, sought a relatable community size, one that feels like a mid-density neighbourhood with walk-up apartments.

In recent urban proposals, WOHA's three-dimensional approach has shifted towards what Tay Kheng Soon called the fourth dimension: a temporal axis of flows.[24] In Tay's proposal for Kampong Bugis, this was discussed mainly as the movement of people. In WOHA's proposal for the Jakarta residential estate, this includes biotic and abiotic exchanges. Water, for instance, was channelled through the buildings, aided by mechanical systems. It moved onto detention and filtration systems within constructed landscapes, and then connects to urban infrastructure and natural water bodies.

This idea matured in the Punggol Digital District (Singapore, 2017—) with the sinking of roads and transit lines to free the ground for walking and cycling. The terrain here aspires to be part of social, ecological

18 Anuj Jain, *Final Report: OASIA Downtown Biodiversity & Social Audit*, 26 April 2018.

19 Heather Banerd, 'Urban Greening and Architectural Form: A Bird's Eye View', in *FuturArc*, 61, July–August 2018, pp. 69—71.

20 Patrick Bingham-Hall, *Garden City Mega City: Rethinking Cities for the Age of Global Warming*, Pesaro Publishing, 2016, pp. 146—93.

21 Juan Gamero-Salinas, Nirmal Kishnani, Aurora Monge-Barrio, Jesus López-Fidalgo and Ana Sánchez-Ostiz, 'The Influence of Building Form Variables on the Environmental Performance of Semi-Outdoor Spaces. A Study in Mid-Rise and High-Rise Buildings of Singapore', in *Energy and Buildings*, 230, 1 January 2021, p. 110544.

22 Juan Carlos Gamero-Salinas, Nirmal Kishnani, Aurora Monge-Barrio, Bhavya Gandhi, Megha Bilgi and Ana Sánchez-Ostiz, 'The Influence of Building Form on Energy Use, Thermal Comfort and Social Interaction: A Post-Occupancy Comparison of Two High-Rise Residential Buildings in Singapore', paper presented at the Passive Low Energy Architecture (PLEA) 2020 conference, A Coruña, Spain, 1–3 September 2020.

23 Energy Authority Market (EMA), Singapore Energy Statistics 2019, https://www.ema.gov.sg/Singapore-Energy-Statistics-2019/.

24 Liane Lefairve and Bruno Stagno, 'The Suppression and Rethinking of Regionalism and Tropicalism After 1945', in *Tropical Architecture: Critical Regionalism in the Age of Globalization*, Alexander Tzonis, Liane Lefairve and Bruno Stagno, eds, Wiley and Sons, 2001, p. 46. 'Two dimensional planning on the horizontal should give way to planning in four dimensions, introducing the element of vertical (buildings in height) and the element of time (in transportation and programming of areas).'

and hydrological flows at the regional scale. When completed, the buildings, waterways and parks will contribute to network capacity in northern Singapore.

A Bigger Canvas

WOHA's journey from small to big to bigger has been a metaphorical stretching of the canvas. This is a *de facto* exploration of scale: how form changes and new systems emerge when boundary conditions are altered.

Seeking a bigger framework has also led the firm to positions on design norms. Newton Suites was the first tall building in Singapore to exceed a green plot ratio of 100%, an achievement that resulted in a subsequent change in building regulations. WOHA's 'Generosity Index' is a framework for decision-making meant to counter green checklists, allowing stakeholders to think in multi-scalar ways, aided by metrics.[25] Wong and Hassell's involvement in studio-based research at the National University of Singapore set out to show how Singapore can be substantially self-sufficient if all buildings were aligned with targets for the city as a whole, generating energy, water and food, and thereby augmenting urban infrastructure.

This bridging of scales — building, neighbourhood, city — is contingent on new ideas on form. This represents a continuation of design thinking that dates back to the 1960s, when better buildings were a step towards better cities. The Jakarta Masterplan was ostensibly many SkyVilles: the linking of individual buildings opened the door to new urban forms such as the *inverted skyline*, a sectional parti of connected roofs and freed ground.

In the WOHA oeuvre, form-making — the many acts of convergence, connection and intersection — is the purposeful arrangement of parts leading to a desired state of the whole. At one end of the scale is the question of how a building performs, how it is positioned as a system nested within wider systems. At the other end, they zoom out to understand systemic wholes (city, territory, planet), to ask what they need and how a new insertion might serve the greater good. A building like Oasia Downtown engages both scales. It is at once architecture and urbanism, an act of speculation and appropriation, polemic and performance. To Wong and Hassell, this is neither environmental determinism nor poetic optimism. It is reimagining the future at a key moment in the life of the planet.

Actions at the building scale, replicated and upsized, are key to outcomes at the urban scale. The stacking of mixed-use programmes, for instance, creates room for social, productive and ecological processes. It connects ground to roof and, when repeated and linked across buildings, becomes a scaffold for three-dimensional communities.

"

25 Patrick Bingham-Hall, *Garden City Mega City: Rethinking Cities for the Age of Global Warming*, Pesaro Publishing, 2016, pp. 194—205.

Buildings that Bloom, Cities that Regenerate and Flourish

TIMOTHY BEATLEY
TERESA HEINZ PROFESSOR OF SUSTAINABLE COMMUNITIES, URBAN AND ENVIRONMENTAL PLANNING
UNIVERSITY OF VIRGINIA, USA

> **WOHA's architecture is remarkable for the ways in which plants, greenery and nature are used as central organizing elements. Nature is not hidden or obscured; it is highly visible and ever-present, to be enjoyed by occupants, visitors and the public at large. This architecture is driven by the magic of the experience as much as by taking steps to achieving environmental targets.**

If there are any silver linings from the global pandemic that we find ourselves in, they include a greater appreciation for the importance of nature in our lives. Spending time in gardens and parks, watching and listening to birds … people have found ways to enjoy nature when the rest of their lives seem to have changed for the worse.

Nature is a constant in our lives, which has been remarkably reassuring. When everything else feels chaotic, we can still count on the dawn chorus of birdsong, the coos and whisperings of mourning doves and the chirping of cicadas, the evening breeze, and the wafting clouds we know are oblivious to human vagaries.

Perhaps we forget that access to nature is something we designed into our cities and communities. We intentionally planted trees, established parks and protected waterfronts as essential points of renewal and sustenance. These are the places where we come together to picnic and stroll, to protest, to grieve and to celebrate the phases of life. The global pandemic has made it even more clear that the design for and inclusion of nature must extend beyond the usual methods and places, and the wonderful work of WOHA demonstrates that these sustaining experiences of nature can and must be included everywhere in the city.

Nature Heals and Inspires, and So Can 'Natureful' Buildings

In 2013 I helped to launch the Biophilic Cities Network, which now comprises twenty-three cities — including Singapore — that embrace the goal of placing nature at the centre of our urban lives. This movement and design philosophy are inspired by the idea of biophilia: the belief that humans have an innate attrac-

tion to and love for the natural world. As we have co-evolved with nature over millennia, it is totally logical that we should be attracted to spaces and places that have richer natural qualities. We know intuitively that nature makes us feel better and improves the quality of our lives. A growing body of research validates this intuition, and the evidence is compelling: we are happier, healthier and smarter when surrounded by nature.[1]

As our patterns of settlement march inexorably towards cities, we are in urgent need of a new model of urbanism, one that I believe must place connections with the natural world at the centre, and we have been calling them Biophilic Cities. Singapore has been a leader in this global movement, and WOHA's designs have been particularly convincing, advocating the benefits and beauty of a nature-centred world.

Overcoming Plant Blindness

Botanists often speak of *plant blindness*, the observation that when people think of nature they tend first to think of animals.[2] Yes, we need architecture that thinks about flora as well as fauna, but there appears to be another kind of plant blindness: the tendency to forget about plants when designing the built environment. When seen in this light, it is hard to overstate how unusual WOHA's buildings are. A recent multi-country survey of office workspaces discovered that nearly half the respondents did not have access to natural light, and nearly 60% worked in offices without plants or greenery.[3]

WOHA's architecture is remarkable for the ways in which plants, greenery and nature are used as central organizing elements. Nature is not hidden or obscured; it is highly visible and ever-present, to be enjoyed by occupants, visitors and the public

1 See Jie Jin, et al., 'Effects of Biophilic Indoor Environment on Stress and Anxiety Recovery,' in *Environment International*, 136, March 2020.

2 Christine Ro, 'Why Plant Blindness Matters,' BBC, 28 April 2020, https://www.bbc.com/future/article/20190425-plant-blindness-what-we-lose-with-nature-deficit-disorder.

3 'Human Spaces: The Global Impact of Biophilic Design in the Workplace', 2015, https://greenplantsforgreenbuildings.org/wp-content/uploads/2015/08/Human-Spaces-Report-Bio-philic-Global_Impact_Biophilic_Design.pdf.

at large. This architecture is driven by the magic of the experience as much as by taking steps to achieving environmental targets. Nature seems to occupy every space, from the hanging plants that soften the edges to the sky terraces that provide unexpected glimpses of nature. Although green rooftops and living walls have become common in recent years, we do not really expect buildings to bloom. When I approached the Parkroyal on Pickering hotel for the first time, I turned a corner and there it was, a totally unexpected and thoroughly delightful green vision. The building held out the possibility that an urban structure could be more natural than artificial. Where does the natural world end and the building begin? The bird's-eye views of the sky terraces and garden ledges of the hotel have now become iconic images, synonymous with biophilic design and biophilic cities.

Rights to the 'Natureful' City

Nature is not evenly distributed in our cities: it is often seen as something expendable, as an afterthought, and even in the greenest of our cities access is often inequitable, with lower-income residents less likely to enjoy the benefits provided by nature. WOHA show that nature can and should be shared by everybody — that it's not just for leafy gated

↑ 'When I approached the Parkroyal on Pickering hotel for the first time, I turned a corner and there it was, a totally unexpected and thoroughly delightful green vision.'

communities, but for social housing and the new public spaces, streets and plazas of the city.

Outdoor Living in Hot Cities

Within the fabric of our increasingly vertical cities, there is a growing desire for outdoor spaces where one can escape from the insularity of the workplace, the apartment or the enclosed room. WOHA's Oasia Downtown hotel contains open-air sky terraces on four levels, including the twelfth-floor reception area, and it is an exhilarating feeling to experience such breezy outdoor spaces, high in the sky at the heart of a vibrant city. The open-air fifth floor of the Parkroyal on Pickering hotel is an incredibly busy place that hosts a variety of activities, from jogging and swimming to eating, socializing and stargazing, and I was able to (discreetly) watch a beautiful wedding unfold, as a memorable ceremony with the city as its backdrop.

The standard approach to designing a new office tower or hotel is to enclose and air-condition as much space as possible, but WOHA strive to minimize the artificial energy load (and one might note that such an approach is well-suited to reducing the risk of infection in a pandemic). As a recent report from the International Energy Agency predicts a more than three-fold increase in global energy consumption connected to space cooling, the dilemma of how to live in an ever hotter world without such reliance on air-conditioning has become critical: maximizing natural ventilation and creating naturally cooled and shaded outdoor spaces have been priorities for WOHA.

I have a feeling that in the new reality of a post-pandemic world we will be looking for ways to spend more time outside, and that will mean a focus on designing sheltered and shaded outdoor spaces in buildings and cities.

Planting trees and greenery of all kinds will be key, as shading and evapotranspiration will be essential urban design elements in all cities of the future.

The approach of WOHA is now essential: the biophilic qualities of their wonderful buildings soften the density, they create uplifting and restorative urban environments, and they serve to reduce the stresses that come from living in cities. The lush open spaces of a building like Kampung Admiralty activate an outdoor culture at a neighborhood or district scale, and WOHA's design rep-

resents a fabulous method of creating a new environment in a hot tropical climate.

A Different Set of Metrics

It is now clear that we need to develop and apply different metrics to judge the success and desirability of new buildings and developments, and the city as a whole. Biophilic Cities are outdoor cities, places that can provide abundant opportunities for people to break free of their enclosed lifestyle, and metrics can guide their progress. How bird-friendly is a city? How would a bird judge this structure or this settlement? Can what is good for birds also be good for humans?

Economic or market values currently predominate as the measures of good real estate, but WOHA insist that buildings should offer something more, and they have applied alternative metrics in order to judge the success of their projects. In a profession where robust post-occupancy surveys are rare and where the long-term monitoring of the successes and failures of building projects is unusual, WOHA's attitude is refreshing indeed.

The Self-Sufficiency Index is a WOHA-applied metric, it's one that I really value, and it's one that will be needed as we begin to question and reform the 'metabolism'

↓
'If we were to perceive the project from above, like a bird, Kampung Admiralty might easily resemble what existed before Singapore's development.'

> **Maybe, just maybe, if we design biophilic buildings and neighbourhoods in a WOHA way, we can in a subtle yet potent manner reactivate our innate biophilic sensibilities. Such designs would then have a more powerful impact than the simple provision of delightful places to live and work.**
>
> "

and ecological footprints of cities. Energy, food and water are the key dimensions of this index: we urgently need buildings that produce as much or more energy than they need; we must design to use water sparingly, to recycle and reuse, in order to emulate the natural water cycle that existed before there was a city; and we require a commitment to supporting local food production and to finding ways to encourage farming in dense urban environments.

Restorative and Regenerative

Designing anything that simply treads water, that simply reinforces the status quo, is no longer acceptable. Given the severity of the multiple interlocking environmental problems that we are facing on a global scale, there is now an urgent need to commit to buildings and urban environments that actively do more than cause less harm, consume less energy and emit fewer pollutants. Every new structure should strive to move the needle forward — to improve, to repair and to recover what has been lost. New designs must produce more habitat than they destroy in construction, and they must generate more energy from renewable technologies than is consumed by the building and its occupants.

WOHA have set a standard for others to follow, and hopefully exceed, and they contend that every new or renovated structure provides an opportunity to 're-wild' a significant piece of the city. At Parkroyal on Pickering, the replacement of nature lost at ground level with nature in the vertical realm has occurred at a rate of more than two-to-one, and at Oasia Downtown, this green plot ratio is an impressive eleven-to-one. What would happen if we applied this standard to everything built in cities? Kampung Admiralty, a tropical forest masquerading as a building, is quite astonishing because it brings together many different uses and activities, and it adds so much to the life and vitality of the surrounding district. If we were to perceive the project from above, like a bird, Kampung Admiralty might easily resemble what existed before Singapore's development.

Overcoming the Barriers to a Different Design Ethic

The significant obstacles to realizing a new vision of biophilic cities need to be confronted, and the reactions and resistance to WOHA's designs are indicative of larger challenges that lie ahead. The cost of biophilic design elements, and of their ongoing maintenance and

upkeep, is frequently mentioned by sceptics and it is a valid concern. However, the market response to developments like Parkroyal on Pickering demonstrates that profits follow nature, as the hotel was able to double its room rates as a consequence of the building's 'natureful' qualities. Other obstacles have more to do with prevailing notions of aesthetics and beauty, and WOHA have had much feedback from architects who are uneasy about the sense of 'messiness' that comes from using nature. The unkempt, woolly look of Oasis Downtown will not appeal to everyone, but I believe this is changing, and I am optimistic that more people — and cities — will embrace the intrinsic wildness of such biophilic structures in the future.

As we ponder what needs to be done to effectively address the global challenges of climate change and biodiversity loss, I believe that working to bolster and cultivate our sense of compassion will be key. Care and concern for otters and hornbills, and all the living organisms with which we share the planet — including *Homo sapiens* — will depend on breaking out of our own narrow, self-interested, human-centred frame of reference, and biophilic design and planning is an essential step in this direction.

Emerging evidence suggests that having nature around us will make us better human beings. In the presence of nature, we are more likely to be more generous, more cooperative and more creative, and we are more likely to care about the plight of humans and non-humans alike. When we occupy the 'natureful' buildings and neighbourhoods of the future, they might in turn help us to consider the plight of the larger natural world.

Maybe, just maybe, if we design biophilic buildings and neighbourhoods in a WOHA way, we can in a subtle yet potent manner reactivate our innate biophilic sensibilities. Such designs would then have a more powerful impact than the simple provision of delightful places to live and work. Whether taking personal action to protect others in a pandemic, or mobilizing collective efforts to preserve global biodiversity, a nature-infused urban life may create the conditions for the compassion and moral imagination that we need to think and act beyond narrow self-interest. That would be a very good result indeed.

Projects

St Mary of the Angels

BUKIT BATOK, SINGAPORE, 1999—2003

In 1998, WOHA were asked by the Franciscan order of the Roman Catholic church to look at a friary that required renovation, and they were struck by the potential of the spacious hilltop site in suburban Bukit Batok, 14 kilometres northwest of Singapore's city centre. WOHA took the initiative and drew up a masterplan for a comprehensive redevelopment of the entire site, which as it transpired was timely, as applications for the friary were increasing and the role of the church in the local community was becoming increasingly prominent. The masterplan proposed the construction of a new church, monastery, columbarium and car park, along with the renovation of the existing friary and the retention of the parish centre.

As observed, the site presented an opportunity to come up with something special – it was relatively unencumbered and unconstrained – and the project reveals many of the principles and strategies that would underpin WOHA's architecture and planning from then on. The fundamental intention of the revamp was to instil a sense of shared amenity and public pride that would extend to the neighbourhood's social networks, and the design was not driven by formal expression so much as by notions of community. This observation might seem contrary to the first-time visitor, as one is struck – immediately and forcibly – by the tectonic finesse of the architecture, but WOHA were here exhibiting, on the largest scale to date, that their parti was almost intuitively informed by an awareness of all the many and varied factors that might contextualize and define a place, socially and environmentally. The identification of a building's parti is inherently prone to misleading rhetoric on the part of the architect or their client, but if one simply acknowledges the parti as 'the reason for the design', then WOHA were operating beyond the confines of formal architecture.

→
The church and chapel viewed from the west, with the external community and congregational area in the foreground.

The plan was centred around a community space, which is both internal and external, as the large glazed doors of the church's totally transparent great west window open out to what should really be called a piazza, creating a conjoined area to be used for public as well as congregational activities. The piazza, partially shielded by the broad cantilevered extension of the church's roof, continues up as a set of gently inclined landscaped gardens on the roof of a subterranean columbarium, glimpsed through square skylights in the lawns. The buildings are all linked by walkways and colonnades, which provide an outdoor setting for the ritual processions and celebrations that usually take place inside the church. The statuettes and etched tablets that embellish the colonnades provide a Franciscan touch of piety and humility, and the entire architectural ensemble is engagingly rustic yet sharply detailed, composed as a tableau of medieval modernism.

WOHA were responsible for all the joinery and craft, and the completed project (which remains in perfect condition) formed a showcase for future reference, a remarkable assertion of a broad range of design skills: *'We designed everything ... the architecture, the interiors, the lighting, the landscape. It was the perfect project for us at that time.'* The grand orthogonal volume of the church constitutes a sumptuous piece of modernist interior design with a curiously appropriate Scandinavian flavour, overseen by a hovering Christ in bronze (designed by Teguh Ostenrik) and illuminated by a giant cruciform skylight

WOHA: NEW FORMS OF SUSTAINABLE ARCHITECTURE

and serried rows of ethereally slender lamps. The cruciform also defines the exterior of the adjoining chapel, which doubles as a campanile and forms a delightful piece of decorative architecture in its own right, clad in walls of translucent onyx. The lower-level columbarium has a formal elegance and sumptuousness of detail whose dignified Italianate solemnity is leavened and tropicalized by the quality of the sunlight passing through square-framed oculi and the warm breezes that flow through gaps in the cranked walls.

As the practice did not go on to specialize in religious buildings, the legacy of St Mary of the Angels should only be measured in programmatic terms, and the project must be regarded as the moment when WOHA demonstrated that

they were intent upon thinking beyond the constraints of a particular typology. As they recall, 'community was the key thing', but so many other priorities were also in play, and so they would remain. St Mary's was an exercise in site planning at an urban scale, in sustainable naturally ventilated construction, in ecological integration, in spatial connectivity and, of course, in architectonic surety. Twenty years later, WOHA would state (in reference to the Punggol Digital District) that formal architectural innovation was now less of a concern than the efficiency and viability of the city and its systems, but they could only make such an observation knowing that their ability to design at a civic scale — with a focus on popular public spaces — was very much in place, and that process began with St Mary of the Angels.

'There was a philosophical aspect to our design process, and we were very conscious of the Franciscan story. St Francis is now the patron saint of ecology; he was a rich man's son who left his wealth behind to preach ... out in the towns and countryside. We saw a parallel with aspects of Singapore's materialistic society, and we felt we should take the church out of an enclosed building into nature and the world at large.'

—WOHA

← The lighting standards, timber pews and all other fittings in the church were designed by WOHA.

→ The planning echoes the elegant orthogonal simplicity of postwar religious buildings in Northern Europe.

→ View from the altar to the west window. The suspended figure of Christ was designed by the Indonesian sculptor Teguh Ostenrik.

↑
With seating
provided for
contemplation,
each room in the
columbarium is
lit by a square
opening in the
gardens above.

→
View of the
central hallway
in the colum—
barium, which
sits beneath the
ramped gardens
to the west of
the church.

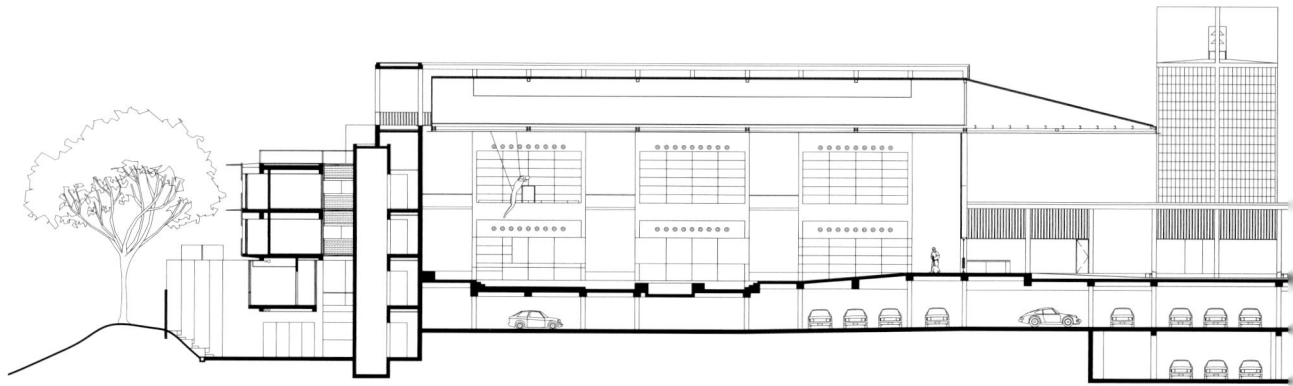

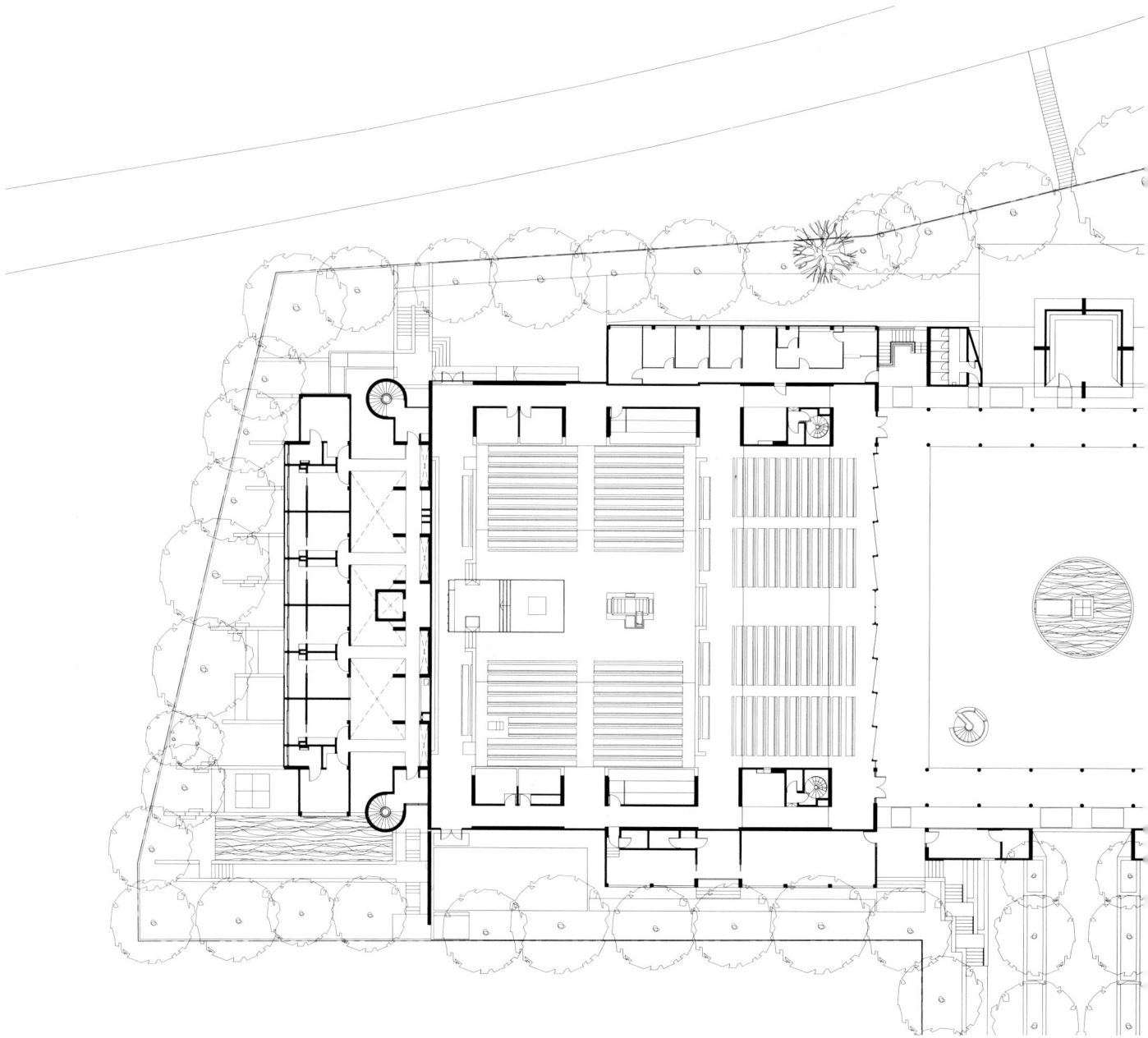

WOHA: NEW FORMS OF SUSTAINABLE ARCHITECTURE

Ⓝ └─────┴─────┴──────────┘
       5   10   20 m

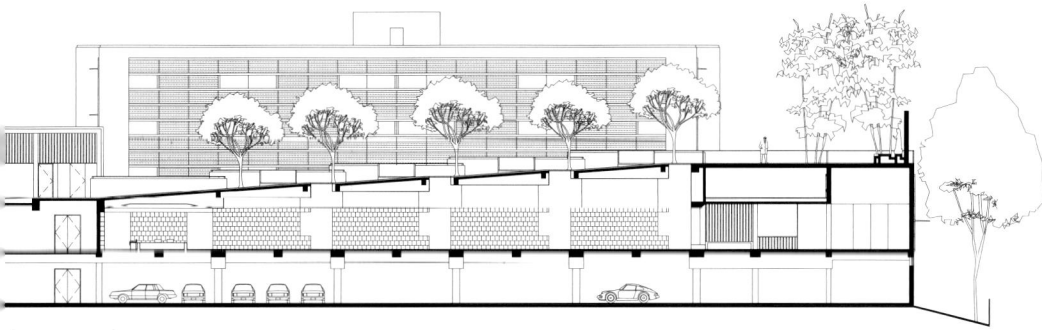

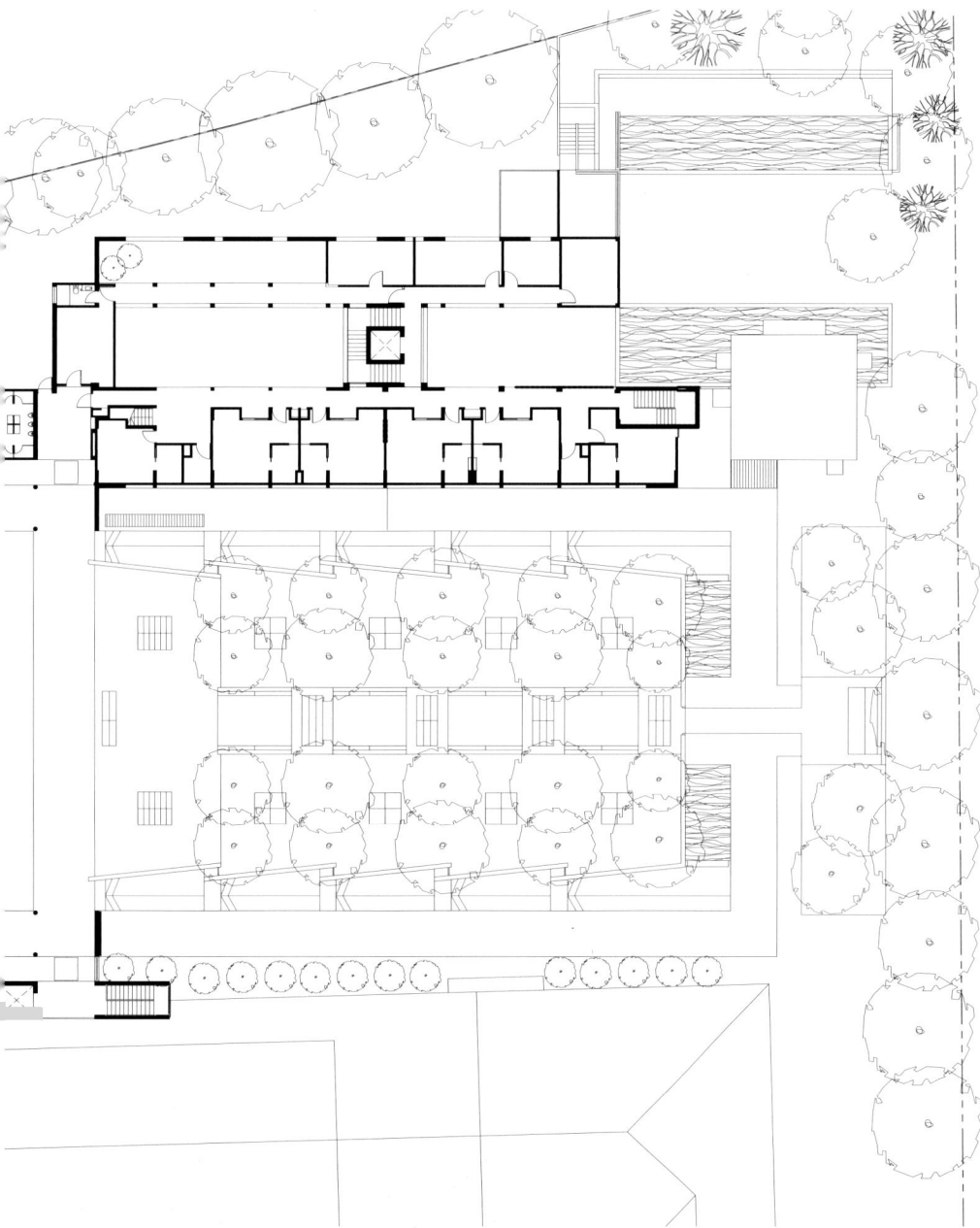

↑
Section.

←
Ground-floor plan.

↑
A timber altar in
the Chapel of the
Retreat, located
behind the
church for use
by parishioners.

↗
→
The chapel,
which also
serves as a bell–
tower, was clad
with translucent
panels of onyx.
The interior
fittings were
designed by
WOHA.

←
The form of
the crucifix was
used throughout
the buildings,
here seen on
the western
elevation of
the chapel.

→
The paved
courtyard,
used for both
community
and congrega—
tional events,
is partially
sheltered by
the slender
cantilevered roof
of the church.

1 Moulmein Rise

NOVENA, SINGAPORE, 1999—2003

Following victory in a limited competition for a condominium development, WOHA's first high-rise tower was built on a sloping corner site in Novena, five kilometres north of the city centre. Each of the other three entrants had proposed a set of medium-rise blocks with four units per floor, while WOHA submitted a scheme for a single slender high-rise tower with two units aligned on an elongated plan on each level, a layout that would take full advantage of the unobstructed views to the city and the sea, and thus appeal to potential occupants.

It was quite an indictment of the state of architecture in tropical Asia at the end of the 20th century to note that precious few innovations had taken place in the field of speculative housing design, which comprised the largest marketplace for property development. Air-conditioned apartments were sealed in by concrete and glass, and the typology was thus environmentally unsustainable and contextually inappropriate: the buildings were little more than derivatives of cold-climate towers built in Europe and America. WOHA were eager to address this vexatious, counterproductive circumstance. They were fully aware that a prototype for a sustainable tropical apartment tower was urgently required, and they got their chance in a salubrious pocket of Singapore. The design for 1 Moulmein Rise appeared to be a breakthrough (and it certainly constituted a prototype), but the bold new idea was very elementary: the façades were thought of in terms of vernacular form. Before the advent of air-conditioning, the roof and the external configurations constituted the basis for sustainable construction and comfortable living in hot and rainy climates, and WOHA reapplied this essentially low-rise schema to a modern urban condition. The tower's elevations were highly porous, and as every apartment occupied the width of the plan, each could have uninterrupted cross-ventilation.

→
The southern façade has a bipartite expression: the eastern apartments have irregularly spaced recessed windows, while those on the west are set back from horizontal ledges.

Continuous breezes flowed through the windows and openings on the north and south elevations, and the apartments were refreshingly comfortable. The cooling nature of an elevated lifestyle (air circulates more freely above the humid ground-level environment) had long been appreciated by residents of Singapore's public housing blocks, but WOHA's application of cross-ventilation within a single apartment had not been so explicitly prescribed before. To this end, one specific innovation was inspired by the traditional Indonesian longhouse, whose sheltered interiors were ventilated during rainstorms by breezes that flowed up and through fixed horizontal openings. WOHA dubbed their operable built-in-aluminium version the 'monsoon window' and it would be reprised most notably for

> **High-rise architecture would comprise much, if not most, of WOHA's work over the next twenty years, but the requirements and the intentions became increasingly complex and they would never design a tower quite so simply resolved and indisputably elegant as 1 Moulmein Rise.**

the SkyVille @ Dawson public housing project (2007—15).

As the tower was highly visible, the appearance of the building was a significant design consideration, and assuming that the zoning laws remained in place, it would never be hidden from view. WOHA treated the northern and southern façade designs as urban artworks — neatly restrained and coolly abstracted — deriving their expression from an adjustable system of standard components, and this strategy was subsequently used in variously scaled elevations and for neighbourhoods in masterplans. The southern façade has a vertically bipartite composition, which reflects the differing configurations of the twinned apartments on each floor, while a gleaming perforated silver skin on the northern elevation mutes external noise and conceals the secondary services and fire stairs.

High-rise architecture would comprise much, if not most, of WOHA's work over the next twenty years, but the requirements and the intentions became increasingly complex and they would never design a tower quite so simply resolved and indisputably elegant as 1 Moulmein Rise. Out of necessity, as the programmatic ambitions evolved to extend far beyond those of a private standalone apartment, the forms and appearance of all WOHA's ensuing projects expressed an increased complexity, but the straightforward strategies that directed this project remained intrinsic to the sustainability formula. WOHA were to use the phrase 'breathing architecture' as they went on to present their schemes to the world at large, and 1 Moulmein Rise remained the touchstone: an artfully composed, delicately assembled structure that had been simply conceived of as a machine for ventilation.

WOHA: NEW FORMS OF SUSTAINABLE ARCHITECTURE

150

←←
With only two apartments placed on each floor, the high-rise tower has a narrow footprint, freeing up the ground level for communal areas and a large swimming pool.

←
When viewed from the east and west, the tower appears incongruously slender. The narrow floor plate means that cross-ventilation within the apartments is constant.

→
As the tower could be seen from afar, the southern façade was considered as an urban artwork. This photo, taken in 2019, shows that it still asserts its presence on the skyline.

↘
West elevation.

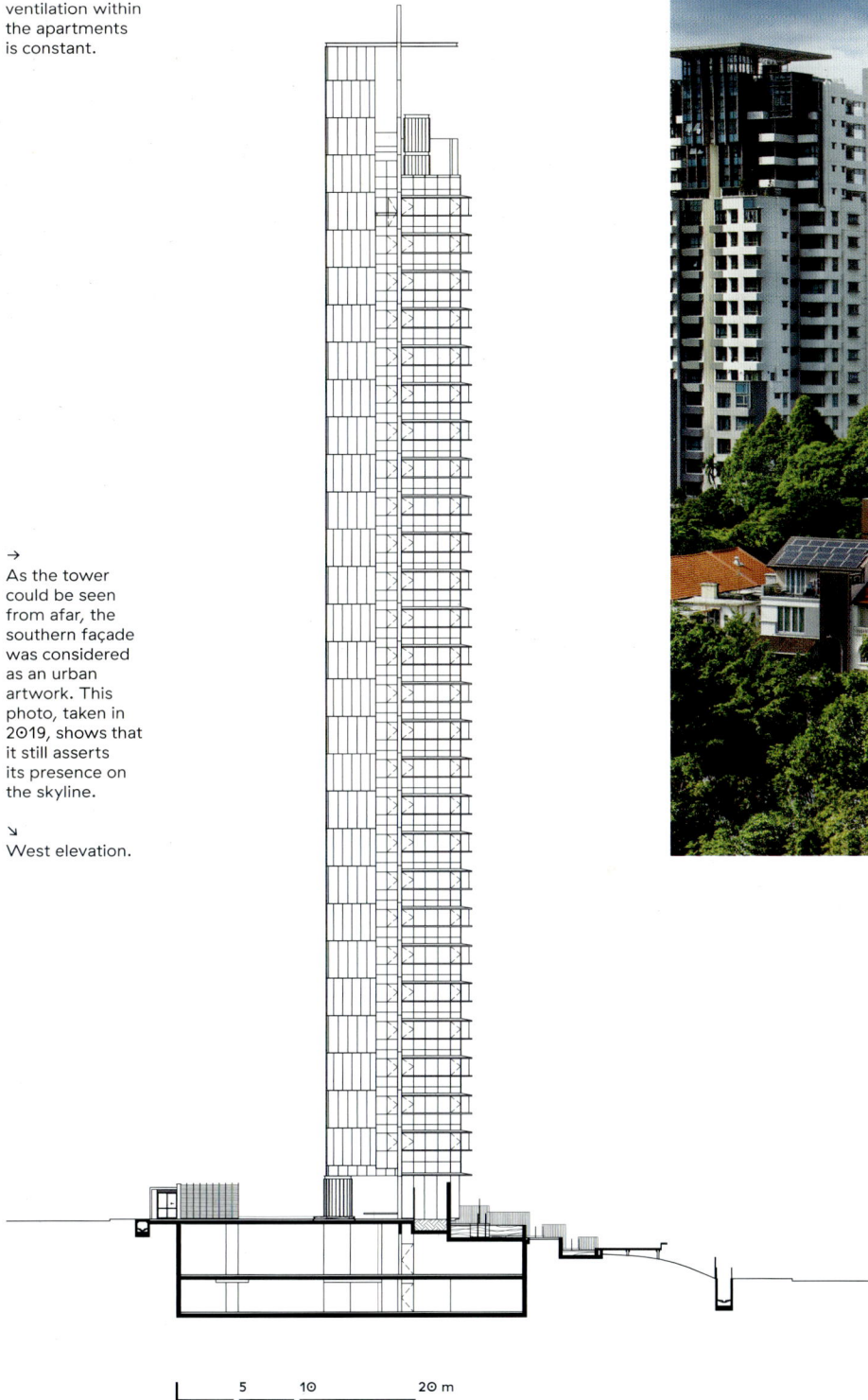

5   10   20 m

↑
A set of stepped and staggered swimming pools occupies the large site area to the south of the tower.

↗
An apartment in the western half of the tower showing operable windows recessed from the external horizontal ledges.

← Typical floor plan.

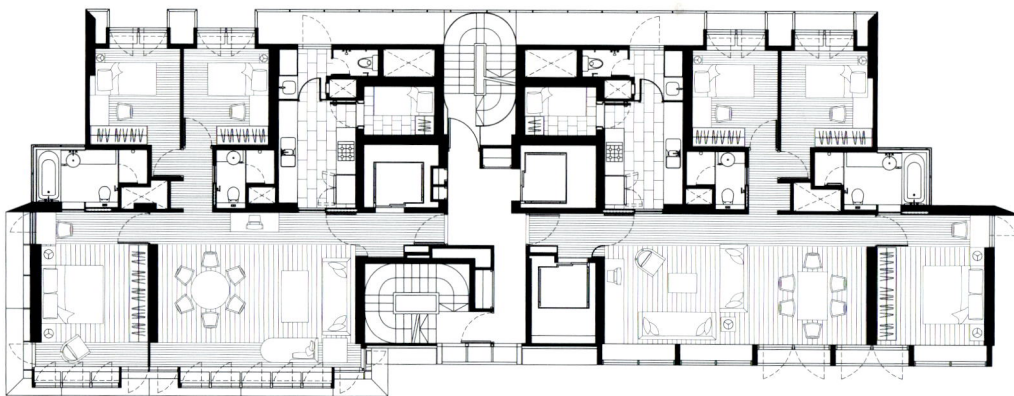

Ⓝ ┣━━ 5 1⊙ 2⊙ m

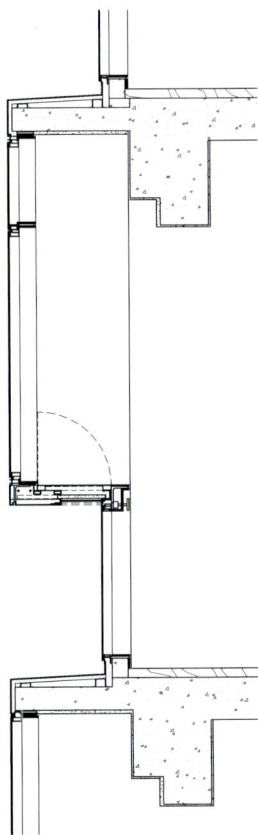

↑
Monsoon windows, set in ledges on the southern façade, allow breezes to enter the apartments during heavy downpours.

← Monsoon window section.

50   100   200 cm

←
The northern
façade is
sheathed by
a screen of
perforated
aluminium,
which shields
and conceals
the services
and fire stairs.

→
With extensive
views of the city
and the sea, the
outlook to the
south is maxi–
mized with strips
of sheltered
and screened
windows.

Bras Basah
MRT Station

SINGAPORE, 2000—08

Initially conceived as a clear-sighted solution to a thorny urban and infrastructural challenge, the Bras Basah station can now be appreciated as a wonderful architectural set-piece. Won in an international competition when WOHA were still relatively unknown, their scheme proposed that the vistas of one of Singapore's most cherished historic precincts could be retained by completely burying the station's structure and discreetly placing its entrances on the site's periphery. Having deftly resolved that overriding heritage design requirement, WOHA submerged the cavernous volumes of the station beneath a gently rippling reflection pool, which now nestles within the lawns surrounding Singapore Management University. Bathed in a dappled sunlight that changes intensity with the moods and vagaries of tropical weather patterns, the sunlit subterranean spaces have what can only be described as a cathedral-like quality; they are places from which one can gaze up to the heavens from the earth below.

> **To quietly glide through the stone-clad spaces is a breathtaking experience; it's a wonderful moment in time, and the volumetric geometries have more than a hint of the sublime.**

←
Escalators pass
through circular
struts alongside
a sloping wall
patterned by
sunlight shining
through the
water-covered
glass roof.

Enclosed by panelled walls of pale limestone, the central volume contains a pair of criss-crossing escalators that descend from the concourse between large cylindrical struts to a transfer level, where a shorter set of escalators continue to the platforms placed directly beneath Bras Basah Road. Daylight is bounced down to these depths from a tilted wall in that central void, a strategy previously utilized to illuminate the Shophouse at Emerald Hill, designed five years earlier. To quietly glide through the stone-clad spaces on the scissoring escalators is a breathtaking experience; it's a wonderful moment in time, and the volumetric geometries have more than a hint of the sublime. It is an orchestrated *promenade architecturale* — such as can be found in grandly scaled airport terminals — and given its location in the core of the city, the experience has added a new civic dimension to Singapore. The grimly vorticist passages of London's Underground stations have here been recast as exhilarating rather than claustrophobic, as Piranesi in sunshine, not in a dungeon.

WOHA's gesture of 'disappearance' ensured that the unimpeded views of the Cathedral of the Good Shepherd (1843—46) and the Singapore Arts Museum (1865—67) remained intact, and the refreshing micro-climate engendered by the reflection pool has instilled an ambience of tranquillity to the precinct. At a purely contextual level, WOHA were acting as landscape architects, and the rooftop water garden now serves as a forecourt to the historic buildings, bridged by two stainless-steel walkways from which one can gaze down into the voids of the station.

At ground level, the success of WOHA's urban beneficence was indisputable, but the city-integration strategies envisaged for the below-ground entry level were not realized. A gallery with a large revealing window at the concourse level was planned to serve as a visual extension of the Singapore Arts Museum, and a similarly reciprocal approach was proposed for the lower levels of the Singapore Management University, but the logistics of such integration proved to be too complex and the ambience of WOHA's grand space did not reach beyond its confines.

WOHA's frustration with what they saw as the denial of the station's greater value to the city is revealing. The subterranean architecture was audacious, the construction demonstrated much finesse, and the completed project was universally acclaimed, but WOHA were disappointed that it was essentially a piece of infrastructure built in isolation. They had achieved an aesthetic resolution to the site's contextual predicament, and by supplying a set of sun-filled spaces that illuminated the platforms placed deep beneath a roadway, they had overcome the major structural challenge contained within the brief, but WOHA had wanted to accomplish more. Their declared ambition had been to emulate the grand interiors of the 19th-century European stations, yet WOHA were also thinking about the complexity and connectivity of the city as a whole. They knew that no matter how wondrous, an isolated building could not add much in terms of broader urbanity, and from now on every project would be designed in a manner that attempted to break down the constraints of solitude.

↑
Looking up from
the subterra-
nean platforms
through a light-
scoop to the
concourse level.

←
Viewed from the crossover level, the cylindrical struts used to transfer earth-loads across the width of the void were arranged to pass between the pair of escalators.

↑
A view up
from the deep
platform level
shows the axial
symmetry of the
entire volume
and its elements.

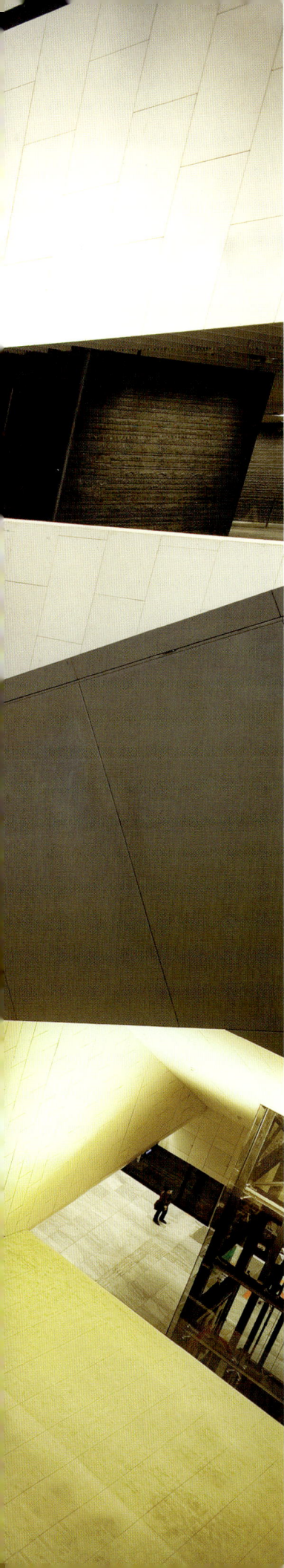

← In this view from the concourse level, the platforms can be glimpsed through the light–scoop at bottom right.

→ The muted colour palette reinforces the Piranesi–like experience of the monumental underground spaces.

↘ Section.

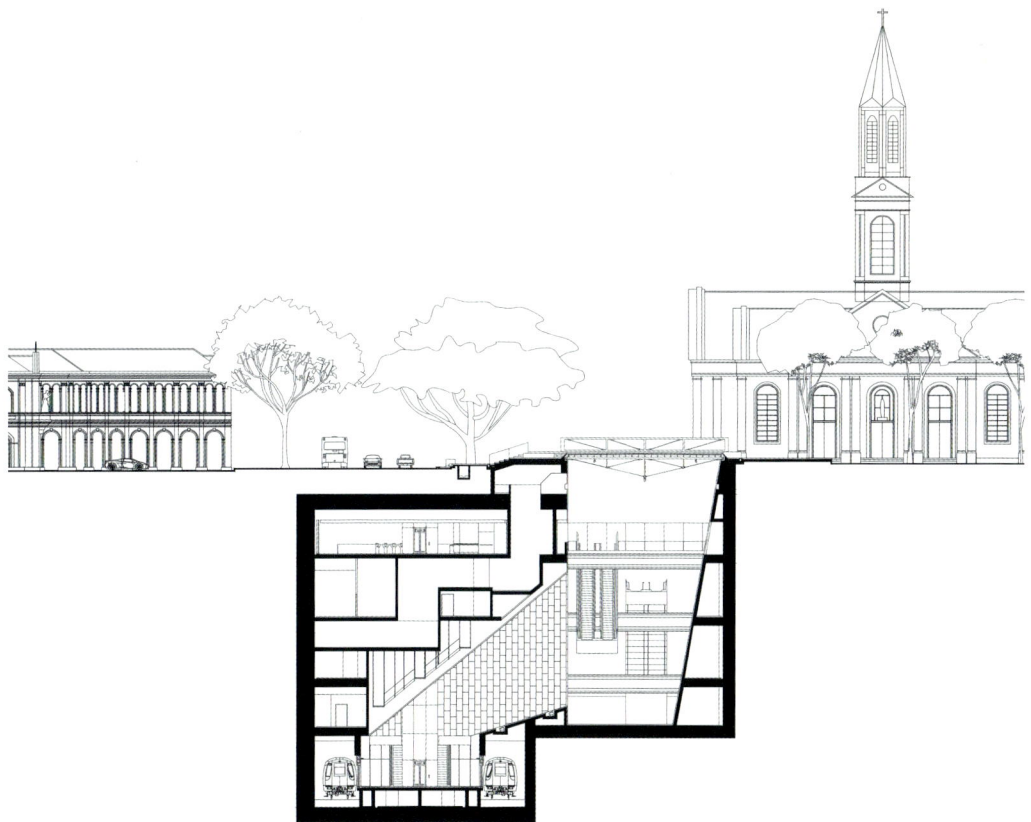

5 10 20 30 m

WOHA: NEW FORMS OF SUSTAINABLE ARCHITECTURE

↑
The under-
ground void of
the station can
be viewed at
night through
the water-
covered glass
roof. The central
axis is perfectly
aligned with
the entry to the
Singapore Art
Museum.

→
The roof
comprises
four layers of
multi-laminated
glass panels,
supported by
lightweight
stainless-steel
tension trusses.

→ Views to the
surrounding
historic buildings
over the roof
of the station
demonstrate
the minimal
visual impact
of the design.

The reflection
pools on the
station's glass
roof and the
surrounding
plaza enhance
the precinct's
sense of civic
decorum without
intruding on
the vistas.

Stadium
MRT Station

KALLANG, SINGAPORE, 2000—08

→
A sky–lit canyon
is contained
between two
sheer aluminium
walls, one of
which leans in
a curve towards
the other.

In a moment of extraordinary serendipity, WOHA won the competition[1] twinned with their successful Bras Basah MRT Station entry, and you could say that the two schemes were the same, but different: '*We did think of them as one project, both during the competition and in design development.*' While the grand interior of Bras Basah station has a relatively sober disposition, clad neatly in limestone, its counterpart at the Stadium station has shimmer and verve, sparked by the gleam of its aluminium skin. As at Bras Basah, the site and the massing had significant civic obligations, although on the reclaimed waterfront of Kallang, the neighbouring structures were of a markedly different vintage and style to those of the inner-city precinct. The station was built adjacent to the circular National Stadium (soon to be demolished and replaced by a domed arena) and the sculpturally assertive Indoor Stadium, designed by Kenzo Tange. The external demeanour took a cue from the glistening silver appearance of Tange's structure, while the plan entered into a subtle reiteration of the stadium's ring, and when viewed after the completion of the new stadium (which also has a lightweight metallic composition), the entire precinct appears neatly homogeneous.

The true joy, however, was to be found inside the station, which essentially comprises one great curvilinear void. The crescent-shaped plan was a bold and simple gesture, a broad brushstroke that set up the intrigues to be seen inside the void, squeezed and splayed between walls clad in ribbed aluminium. The great interior volume – a canyon, no less – is dramatically scaled and slightly intimidating, with one of the two long walls looming large over the passengers as a convex bulk tapering down from the slender, partially glazed roof to the wider breadth of the platform. The invigorating silvery brightness is heightened by the finely delineated treatment of the aluminium cladding (inspired by the incised lines of Dong Son rain drums from Vietnam), which sparkles and flickers in the light shining down from above. WOHA had taken canyons and ravines as their inspiration, and they aspired to a 'lovely light-filled hidden valley' ambience, yet bathed in a shimmering aquatic glow and coloured bottle-green by light reflected from the stone floor tiles, the sunken platform level may be underground, but it also feels like it's underwater.

1 Initiated by the Land Transport Authority in conjunction with the Singapore Institute of Architects, the two competitions were judged separately, and WOHA were up against a large field of local and international architects. At the time, such competitions were unheard of in Singapore, and they were then discontinued for many years.

Sunlight streams directly through the elongated aperture above the canyon, it rakes across the walls and floor, and the subterranean volume is transformed into a natural environment. Both in its context and in its assembly, this station is the only WOHA project ever built without nature, if by nature we mean greenery. But the structure is consummately organic, with a sinuous plan, a diaphanous skin and an overtly topographic 'quarried' metaphor as its parti: '*We specifically talked about using natural forms as a way of creating a journey into the underworld.*' WOHA were thinking of the city as an organism, and one wonders whether, if the station had been designed at a later date, WOHA would have inserted gardens and foliage: a move that may well have diminished the impact of carving out such a monumental and elemental landform from the bowels of the earth.

WOHA: NEW FORMS OF SUSTAINABLE ARCHITECTURE

←
The curving northern external wall of the entry volume is clad with finely ribbed aluminium panels.

→
The above-ground entry volume flares out at both ends to accommodate the large crowds attending events at the adjoining stadia.

↓
Longitudinal section. Concourse-level plan. Cross-section.

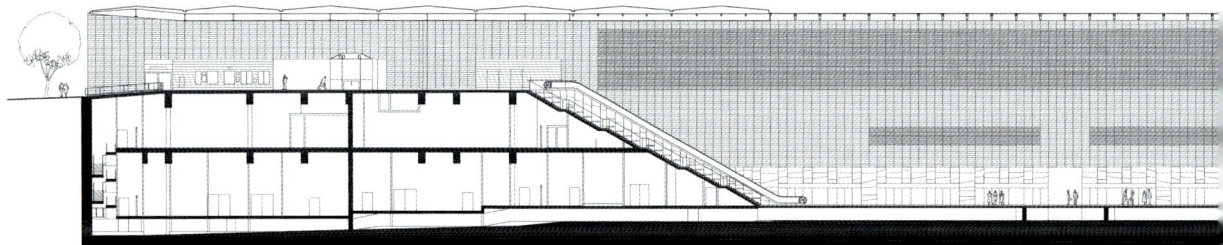

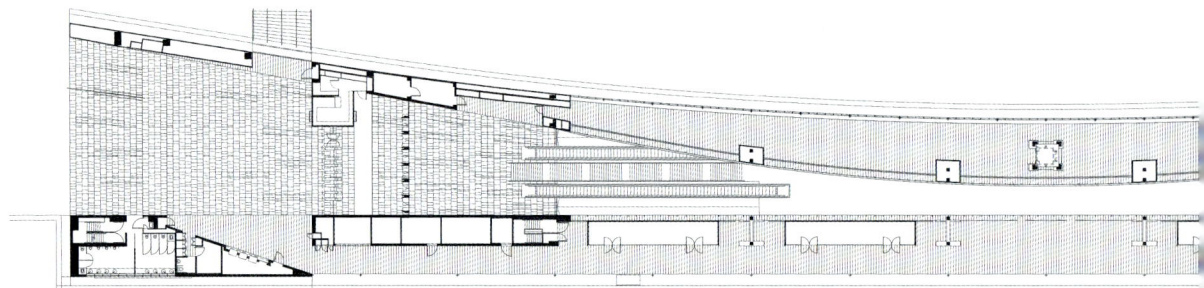

WOHA: NEW FORMS OF SUSTAINABLE ARCHITECTURE

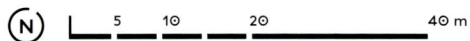

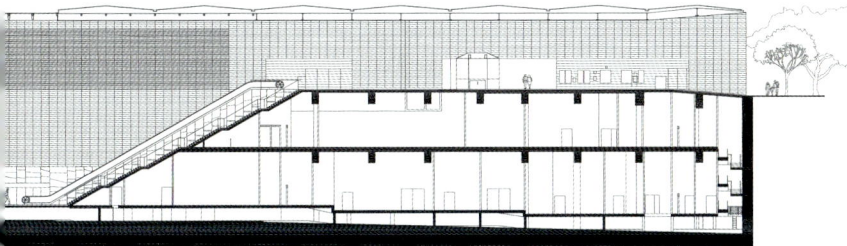

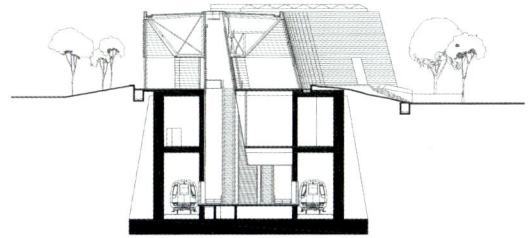

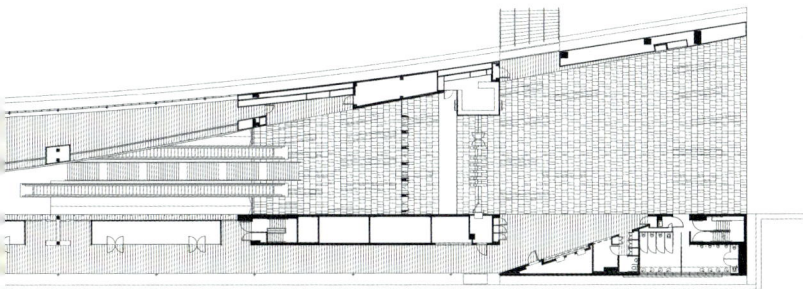

← ←
Calligraphic
concept sketch
of the plan.

←
The descent
into the canyon
presents a vista
of multiple
vanishing points,
with curved,
straight and
diagonal lines
converging at
various heights.

→
Before passen–
gers descend by
escalator to the
broad spaces of
the platform, the
concourse level
is 'squeezed' by
the convex wall
in order to set up
a dynamic spatial
sequence.

← A narrow crescent–shaped skylight stretches high above the platform.

↑ Looking up from the platform to the western end, with the convex northern wall bulging ever closer to its perpendicular counterpart.

← In the middle of the day, direct sunlight casts shadows that shift as ribbed patterns across the perpendicular southern wall.

WOHA: NEW FORMS OF SUSTAINABLE ARCHITECTURE

vertical light

Section.

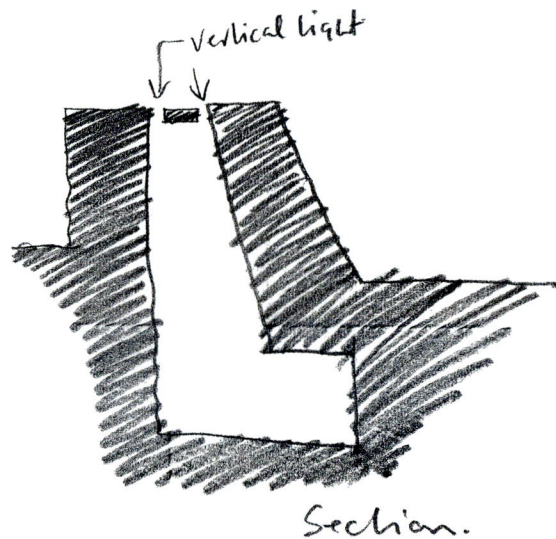

↑
The interplay
between the
two walls is
evident from
the platform,
covered in
quartz agglom-
erate panels with
an underwater
colour cast.

↗
Shadow patterns
created by
direct sunlight
rake across
the ribbed
aluminium
panels above
the platform.

←
Concept sketch.

WOHA: NEW FORMS OF SUSTAINABLE ARCHITECTURE

↑
A detail of an
aluminium
wall, showing
the horizontal
lines etched by
direct sunlight,
interspersed
with shadows
from struts
and reflections
from the glass
skylight.

→
Concept sketches.

striations
pick up light

wall
elevation

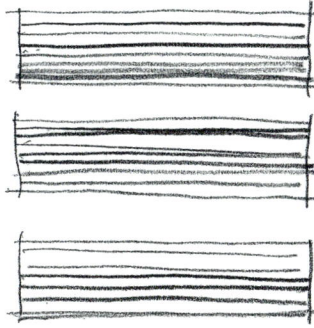

louvres with different
height striations

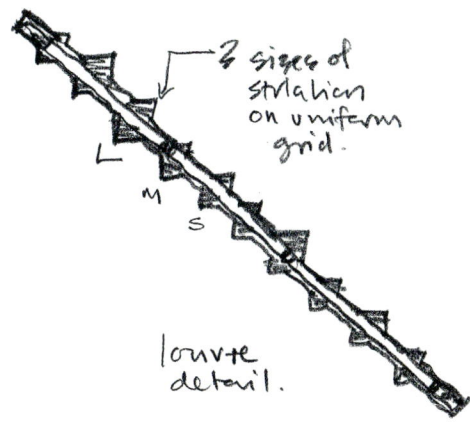

2 sizes of
striation
on uniform
grid.

L
M
S

louvre
detail.

Alila Villas Uluwatu

BALI, 2003—09

'The Uluwatu landscape was so interesting, it was dry and arid ... nothing like traditional Bali. Our client thought it was time to do something different in Bali, and we took advantage ... we suggested a sustainable resort. As we had always thought that resorts should be more socially responsible, we proposed that Alila Villas Uluwatu should have a sustainable brand, which would differentiate it from most of the existing resorts. As Indonesia was not technologically advanced, it would have been too difficult to implement a complex sustainability programme, so we focused on old-fashioned passive green methods. We dramatically reduced the need for air-conditioning with cross-ventilation and broad overhangs, and we harvested water with rain-gardens, soakaways, and retention ponds and tanks. Streams run down the hillside into the retention ponds and the water is then circulated through the site. The landscape only used local plants and all the materials came from Bali or Java. We used local labourers and craftspeople, all the timber was recycled, and huge rubble walls were built from the stone excavated on site during construction. The shallow hipped roofs don't need downpipes; they have a loose top layer of pumice-stone volcanic rocks, which provides natural insulation and soaks up the rainwater ... so then we had flowering roofs.'

A resort commissioned in the scrubby and stony landscape of Uluwatu, on the southern tip of Bali, provided WOHA with their first opportunity to address sustainability on a sweeping scale in a *tabula rasa* setting, and it proved to be something of a game-changer for the hospitality industry, showing that luxury and conscientious environmental awareness were not incompatible. Wong Mun Summ and Richard Hassell had been employed at Singapore-based Kerry Hill Architects for over four years in the early 1990s, where they had worked on more than thirty hotel and resort projects, and they were well versed in the prerequisites of luxury and well prepared to provide the playground desired by the clientele. Here in Uluwatu, the overriding obligations were now to produce a prototype for what might be termed 'sustainable luxury', and to provide an environmentally-driven masterplan for what was effectively a small town. When the resort was completed, the impact of the programme for sustainability was initially overshadowed by its architectural attributes. All the

> **WOHA were unmistakably designing to create something beautiful, but as the resort became well known and well publicized, the programme for sustainability was documented in subsequent architectural discourse and it became apparent that the singular tectonic appearance was very much an expression of that overriding intention.**

structures built across the sprawling site shared an architectural language; a vocabulary of roughly hewn yet crisply detailed forms that WOHA had contrived to combine in an instantly identifiable fashion, as a brand or trademark, if you like. The architects' oft-quoted observation that they imagined Mies van der Rohe and Carlo Scarpa paid a visit to a Majapahit emperor provides a pretty accurate summation of the resort's style, where the exotic and the imperious meet the rational and modernist, overlaid with a hint of the sublime. WOHA were unmistakably designing to create something beautiful, but as the resort became well known and well publicized, the programme for sustainability was documented in subsequent architectural discourse and it became apparent that the singular tectonic appearance was very much an expression of that overriding intention.

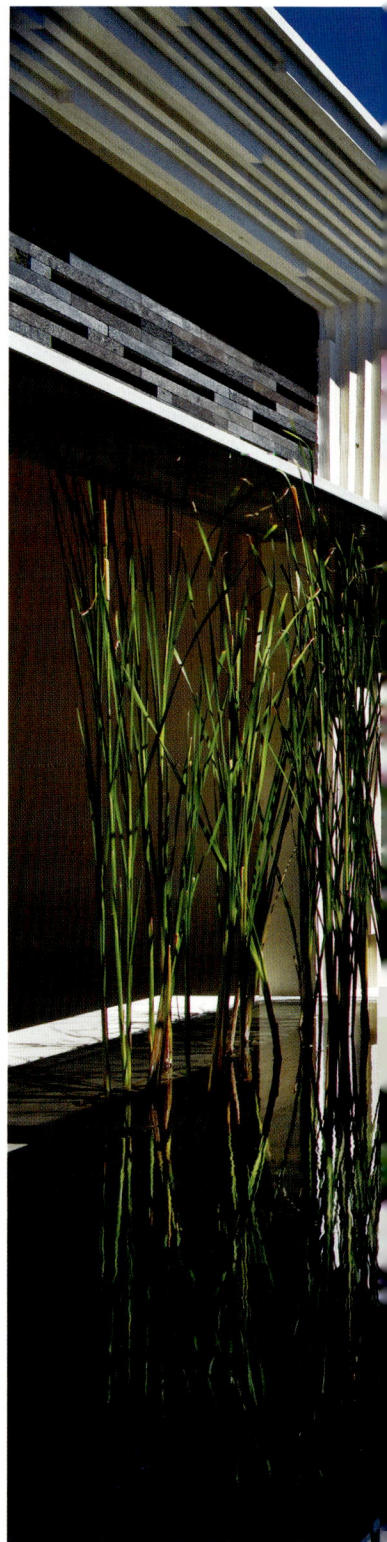

WOHA: NEW FORMS OF SUSTAINABLE ARCHITECTURE

182

Below the layers of guest rooms arrayed on a hillside, the public areas — on a flat expanse at the edge of a cliff — have a grandly sumptuous yet intimately scaled demeanour. The monumental intricacy of the colonnades and their entablatures are set within a balmy series of shallow water features, a tropical tribute to Scarpa, and the heavy rusticated stonework is countered by a Miesian homage of elegant, capacious pavilions ordered by slender metal columns. Yet the architecture transcends homage: WOHA were blending such abstracted appropriations in order to complement their own design elements, most of which had a vernacular flavour derived from the rugged Uluwatu context. Ranged in rows on a steep slope, the guest villas were a triumph for passive ventilation strategies, with strong cooling winds drawn through permeable single-room spaces that opened out wide to the views of the ocean. Each villa had a crafted timber cabana — a diminutive version of those found in the public areas — placed at the end of a swimming pool and perched above the stone rubble walls rising above the access path for the row of guest rooms below. On the gently terraced roofs of all the structures, an untamed volcanic landscape of blackened pumice stones nurtures sporadic, and uncultivated, displays of local plant life.

WOHA had an all-encompassing remit with this commission, built to their own masterplan, and it was clearly evident upon completion that WOHA had designed every last detail across the expanse of the site and in the resort: architecture, landscaping, environmental strategies, hydrology, interior design, furniture and lighting. As they had 'wanted to do much more than just create playgrounds for the rich', the overall design should not be judged in terms of self-indulgence or as luxury for its own sake, as it was instead a consummate tribute to the innate correctness of vernacular structure and form. It comprised a very timely demonstration of more-than-acceptable sustainability and effectively inaugurated a continually evolving approach, one where aesthetics and the provision of a materialist lifestyle can be harmoniously intertwined with a now-necessary ecological programme.

←
Looking towards the sea from the lobby, with a shallow pool edged by colonnades built from creamy white stone.

← Viewed from the public areas at the base of the hillside, the timber cabanas of the guest villas rise above walls built from stone excavated during construction.

→ Seen in a photo taken during final construction, a large hilltop villa looks over the one-bedroom villas below.

→ The living pavilions of the larger pavilions are placed at right angles to the bedroom wing. The architectural style could be described as 'rusticated Miesian'.

→ Each one-bedroom villa, with its own swimming pool, was designed with both view-maximization and cross-ventilation in mind.

As seen on a larger villa at the top of the hillside, the low–pitched terraced roofs of the resort are covered with volcanic pumice rock.

N

10   50   100   200 m

Masterplan.

← The angled and recessed pilasters of the colonnade are built from 50 mm–square lengths of *batu jogia putih* stone. The entablature is inlaid with the darker *batu candi*.

↘ Sunlight passes through the stone screens of the passage-ways within the colonnades of the public areas.

← Angled and fluted pilasters were used in the private colonnades of the larger villas.

→ Thrown into relief by the bright Balinese sunlight, the fluted pilasters of the public colonnades were used as a continuous textural motif.

→→ A lantern suspended by steel rods above the lobby is comprised of spindles made from cast bronze.

↓ In the shape of Hindu spindles, brass spacer beads on poles are used as ornamental screens throughout the resort.

←
The clerestory walls of the restaurant were surfaced with copper stamps used for batik printing, which were sourced from the factories just before they were melted down.

↑
Leading to the sea from the lobby, a series of ornamental pools and gardens were enclosed by the colonnades and pavilions of the public areas.

←
A terraced retention pond and a white stone staircase at the foot of the hillside.

→
Shallow reflec-
tion pools edged
with stepped
stone form
a Balinese-
inflected
homage to
Carlo Scarpa.

↓
Rainwater
cascades beside
the stairways on
the hillside down
to retention
ponds before
being recycled
throughout the
resort.

↑
Looking towards the lobby from the pool areas above the cliff edge.

→
The planning of the public areas was very formal, with a right-angled geometry that continues through both the architecture and the landscaping.

←
A 'sunset cabana' was cantilevered over the edge of the cliff as a lookout and a culmination of the public landscaping sequence.

→
The broad arms
of the public
area's colon-
nades reach
out through
a spindly
savannah-like
landscape typical
of the Uluwatu
region.

The Met

BANGKOK, 2003—09

If WOHA's legacy can be measured out with prototypes, the parti (the determining idea) of this machine for sustainable high-rise living was probably the most clearly delineated and unambiguously expressed of them all. As views of The Met can be had from all over Bangkok, and as the architecture did not conceal its programme of performance, the monumental rationality of the building's massing stands as an elemental demonstration of just how the implementation of passive energy use can be achieved on a massive (mega-city) scale.

WOHA had firmly articulated their vision for sky cities with the Duxton Plain competition entry in 2001, so it was intriguing, to say the least, to see how the ideas and strategies might actually work in practice. After amending an initial proposal for eight towers with varying heights, the as-built scheme for The Met adopted the Duxton Plain model of essentially identical high-rise blocks, which all rose to sixty-six storeys. Linked by sky bridges and sky streets, the towers were staggered on a self-shading plan and segregated by soaring voids that stimulated wind-flow and thermal cooling in all directions. The high-level public spaces and the apartments would thus be naturally ventilated and cooled in an elemental manner, made possible by the immensity of the structural elements and voids.

> **As views of The Met can be had from all over Bangkok, and as the architecture did not conceal its programme of performance, the monumental rationality of the building's massing stands as an elemental demonstration of just how the implementation of passive energy use can be achieved at a massive (mega-city) scale.**

In stark contrast to the almost brutal rawness and uncompromising bulk of its overall form when seen from a distance, the composition of The Met appears delicate and ethereal when viewed at close quarters in the Silom district of central Bangkok. The façades of the north and south elevations are crisply delineated by gleaming metallic strips, the deep-set balconies are dotted with blooming frangipanis, and the two narrow east and west walls are clad with a mosaic of coloured panels and inlaid stainless-steel mirrors: '*We didn't think that "decorative" and "uncompromising" should be mutually exclusive.*' WOHA were here 'domesticating the megastructure', an approach that would be vital to the acceptance of ultra-high-density vertical living. The Duxton Plain proposal for public housing had been underpinned by WOHA's notion of a high-rise compound with layers of sky villages that functioned as though they were at street level, and although this complex was not so communal, the apartments in The Met were envisaged as if they were earthbound houses. The public areas have a laid-back, convivial air, with residents meeting up on sky streets that extend across the breadth of the complex on three evenly spaced levels. Those streets — with timber decking, granite walkways and water gardens — feel far removed from the chaotic city life way down below, as the stultifying heat has been supplanted by remarkably cool and occasionally very strong winds, which also refresh and cross-ventilate the permeable individual apartments.

Of course, the delights of a new way of living remained hypothetical until The Met was actually completed, but as the succession of high-rise apartments built to date in Bangkok had been notoriously under-nurtured, both in terms of liveability and design, WOHA could thus present their visions of a desirable lifestyle to a receptive audience. As it transpired, The Met proved to be a very popular development: its apartments rarely come up for sale, and its residents actively maintain its facilities and appearance. It is revealing to note that nearly ten years after completion, the frangipanis on the balconies are blooming better than ever, as is the great green wall of flowering vines that wraps around the nine-storey car park podium,[1] and it becomes clear that when environmental sustainability has been implemented in a manner that delights the resident, the future of high-density mega-city living can be seen in a newly optimistic light.

1 Above-ground car parks are a mandatory building component in flood-prone Bangkok. In Singapore, WOHA have also (when possible) placed car parks above ground rather than below, as the costs are considerably lower and podiums are naturally ventilated. It is hoped that providing car parks will no longer be a consideration sometime in the near future.

→ The south elevation viewed from the gardens of a traditional teak-house.

WOHA: NEW FORMS OF SUSTAINABLE ARCHITECTURE

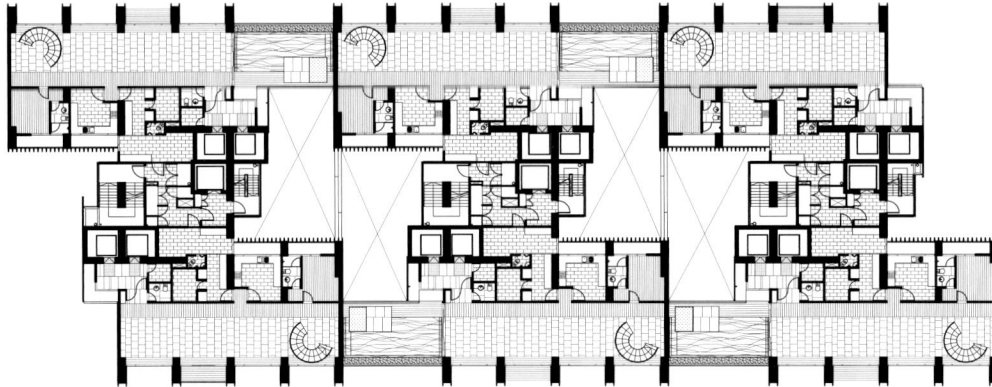

←
55th floor plan.
41st floor plan.
30th floor plan.

→
Sections.

N   5   10   20 m

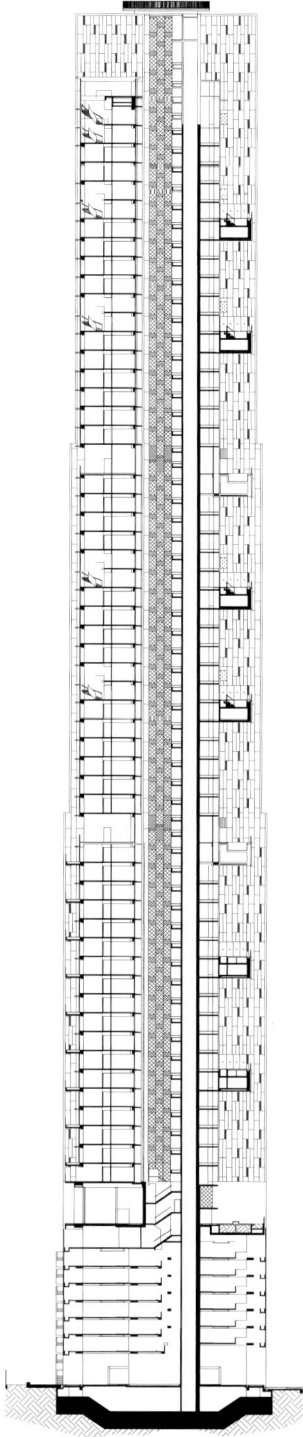

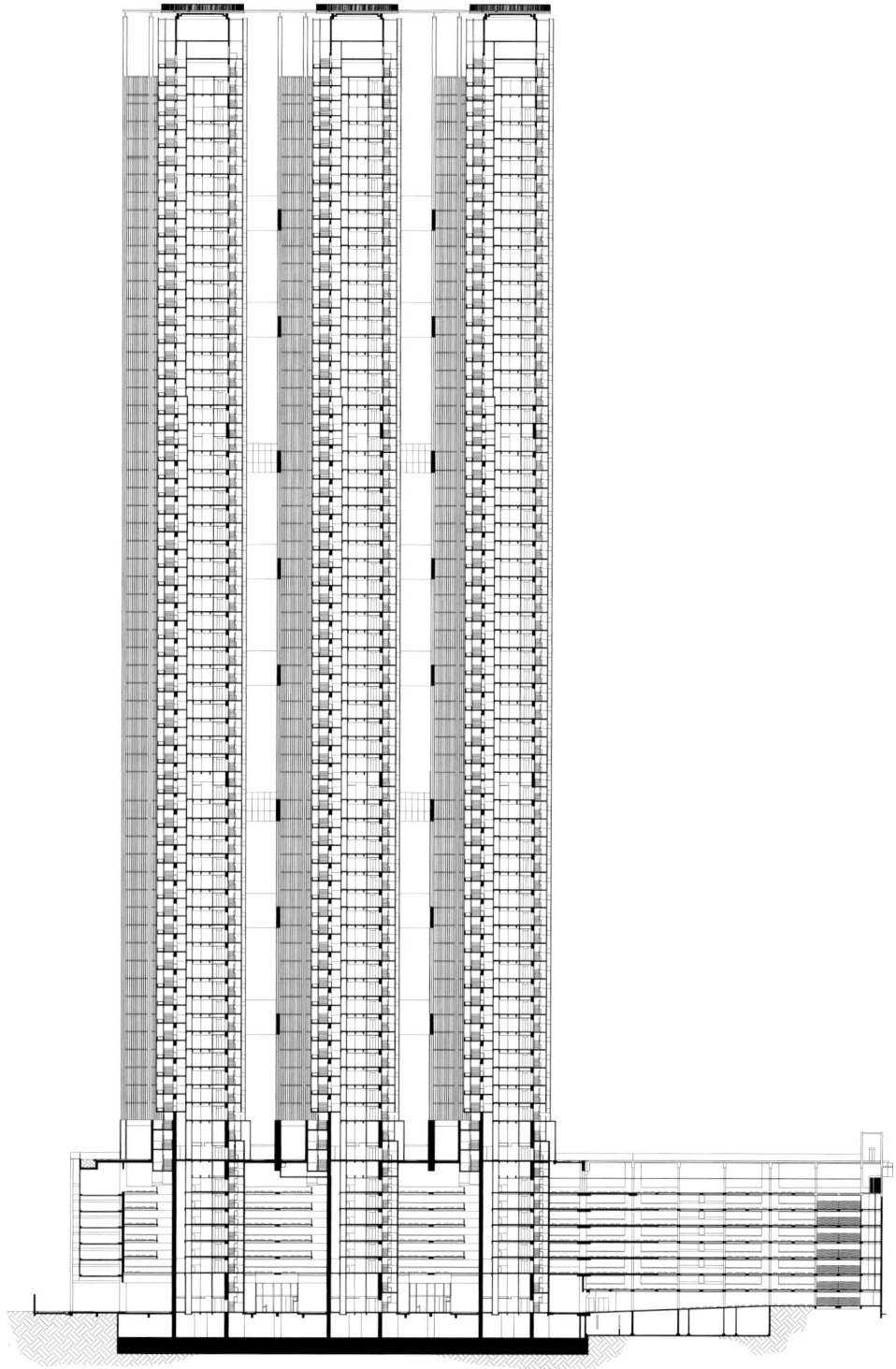

10   20   50 m

← By pulling the six towers apart, public and private areas are cooled by breezes drawn through the voids.

→ Soaring voids between the towers rise the height of the sixty-six-storey development from the ninth-floor podium.

↘ The massive vertical slots admit sunlight as well as cooling breezes throughout the apartment towers.

←
Outdoor rooms
in the lower–
level apartments
are adorned
by frangipanis,
seen between
columns that
extend as
buttresses
towards the
base of the
towers.

→
Common decks
span the width
of the building
on three levels
as breeze–filled
sky streets for
all residents.

↘
The entry to the
car park podium
demonstrates
the consistency
of the building's
structural
grid, whereby
horizontal vistas
have a similar
perspective
to the vertical
views.

WOHA: NEW FORMS OF SUSTAINABLE ARCHITECTURE

↖
←
A 50-metre lap pool is located on the roof of the nine-storey car park podium, providing residents with resort-style relief from Bangkok's congestion.

→
As seen on the northern façade, frangipani trees on the balconies provide the development with an unexpectedly domesticated appearance.

← The structure operates as a 'cooling machine' for the apartments, high above streets where the temperature averages 35°C.

→ North elevation. The vertical voids that separate the towers stimulate wind flow and generate thermal cooling.

School of the Arts

SINGAPORE, 2005—10

L ocated on a prominent site at the city end of Orchard Road, the School of the Arts has an unexpected and possibly confounding presence. Its notionally over-scaled bulk should loom large over the streets and adjoining parkland, but, obfuscated by greenery, the massing is incongruously fragmented and its aesthetic is difficult to define in conventional terms. It is a very different building, deriving its formal appearance both from its uncompromising approach to environmental sustainability and from WOHA's intrinsic desire to build for a city-as-garden. The building was the first large-scale public demonstration of WOHA's strategies for building in the tropics, and a most conspicuous exposition it turned out to be. In broad terms, those strategies were utilized to provide comprehensive shading and cross-ventilation, encourage communal integration, install greenery as a significant architectural component and, in the process, introduce a garden city morphology to a high-density urban environment.

The parti, the essential design motivation from which all else flowed, was the structural and spatial arrangement devised to ventilate the building without using air-conditioning. The School of the Arts was constructed as a wind machine, funnelling Singapore's light breezes into a multiplicity of openings and accelerating their passage through a continuous network of walkways, stairways and public spaces that had no air-traps or dead-ends. The building was segmented into two layers (academic floors above and public spaces below), and each comprised what might be called a labyrinth for tropical liveability: they were large, permeable volumes that required little artificial cooling, and they actively sought to encourage social interaction. In his rejection of modernist absolutism, the word 'labyrinth' was used by Aldo van Eyck in the 1960s for schemes where buildings might comprise a series of 'villages' under one roof, uniting a variety of functions, activities and services. Van Eyck had an overriding social agenda, he had an abiding interest in anthropology, and he repeatedly advocated that architects think of space and time as place and occasion. This was an outlook shared by WOHA, and it has been integral to all their work as a practice.

WOHA here conflated their humanist thinking with the need for sustainable design, conceiving of the school as a 'labyrinthine' matrix that could be calibrated to enhance a building's environmental performance. A three-dimensional sequence of interlocking spaces and connections was not only an effective construct for boosting human interaction, but it

1   In the book *Garden City Mega City*, WOHA explain the process: 'Horizontal Breezeways – extending the length or breadth of a building's mass – perform as no-dead-end corridors that can be shaped as funnels to hasten the speed of the breezes passing through. These breezeways are orientated to channel the prevailing winds through the structure, aided by deflectors and scoops.'

> **The School of the Arts was constructed as a wind machine, funnelling Singapore's light breezes into a multiplicity of openings and accelerating their passage through a continuous network of walkways, stairways and public spaces that had no air-traps or dead-ends.**

could also serve as a mechanism to increase the velocity of the air that flowed from one end of a breezeway to the other. The breezeways would dramatically cool and refresh a building in the sweltering tropics, and the school's spatial configuration was thus attuned to accelerate and maximize cross-ventilation.[1] It is fascinating to view the upper (academic) levels in operation, as the ebb and flow of students follows the patterns of the cooling breezes, as if they were gusts of wind, and the correlation between sociable and sustainable architecture is graphically displayed. As a corollary, one is always aware of the external environment, seen at all times from all directions, and this notion of phenomenological integration with the greater city would be critical to the continuing evolution of WOHA's ideas for urban architecture.

WOHA: NEW FORMS OF SUSTAINABLE ARCHITECTURE

↑
View from
the southeast,
showing the
clearly expressed
layering of six
academic floors
above the public
performance
areas.

The building's form is a clear expression of its elemental structure, which immediately sets this architecture apart from the prevailing 'hide the components behind the cladding' paradigm. The elevations were completely literal and self-explanatory, with a thoroughly organic feature that changed with the seasons: the six floors of the upper stratum were clad on their most visible façades by cloaks of verdant vines that formed flowering environmental screens. The lower stratum can be seen as WOHA's first public step in the direction of topographic architecture, where the organic reference was geological rather than botanical. If the upper levels were notable for the capaciousness of the open-air voids and their exposure to the outside world, the lower public areas have an almost claustrophobic air. A series of cavernous passageways appear to have been 'carved' — with an expressionist thrust — through shards of roughly hewn stone, and as with several other of their nearby projects, WOHA were intent upon reactivating inner-city connectivity while establishing a street-level identity for the school.

The School of the Arts is one of WOHA's seminal projects. It was something of an experiment and it worked, especially for the students, not least because the interior spaces felt like outdoor spaces and they were very comfortable places to be. The natural joys of living had not been replicated or supplanted by artificial means, yet the function and operation of the building as an educational institution was not compromised. '*It turned out exactly as we wanted ... it was our model for designing a public building in a tropical city. We only used air-conditioning in the theatres and IT rooms, and post-occupancy evaluation showed that our natural microclimate was better for students than schools with air-conditioning. So the building performed well on both counts ... sustainability and user satisfaction.*'

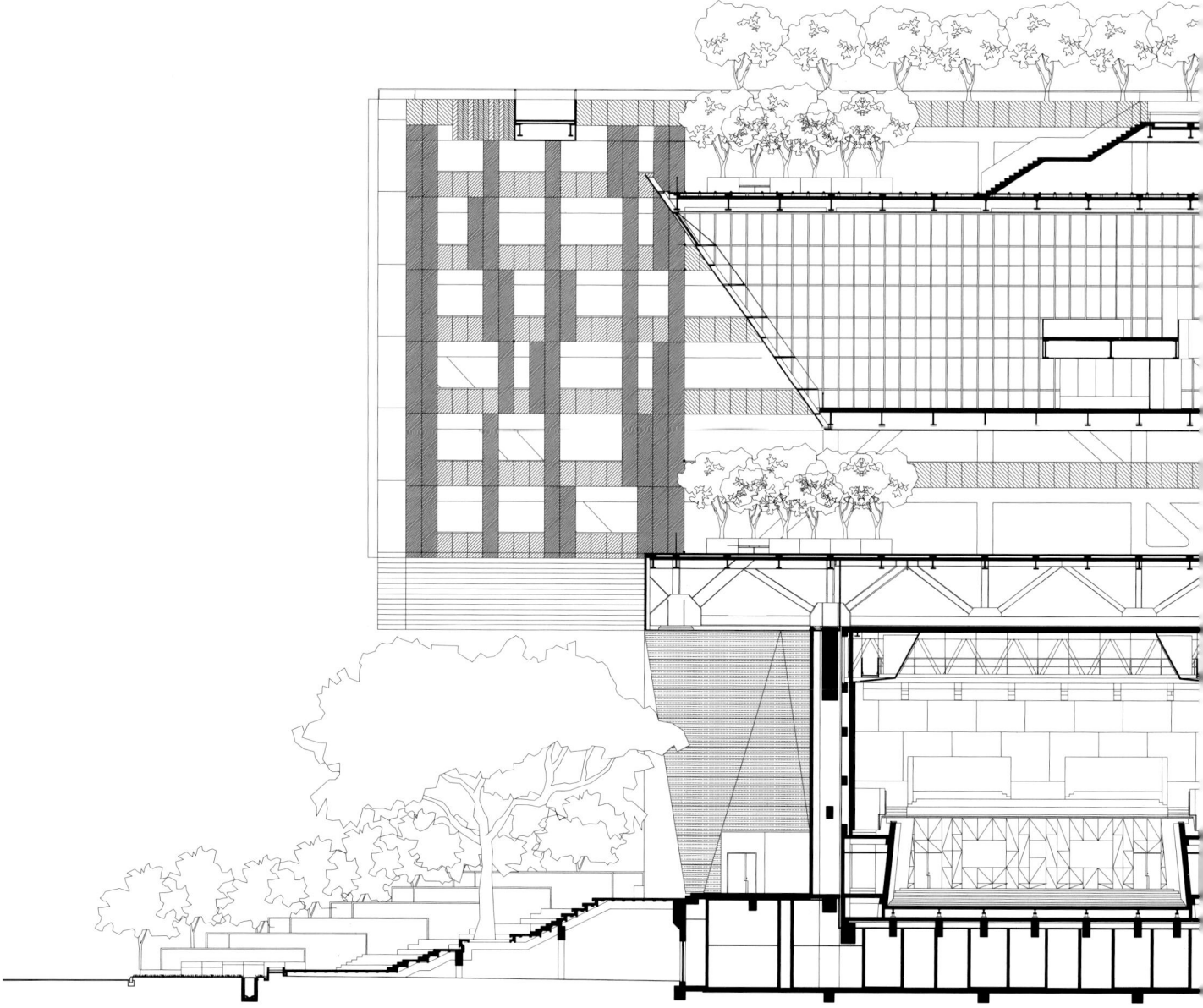

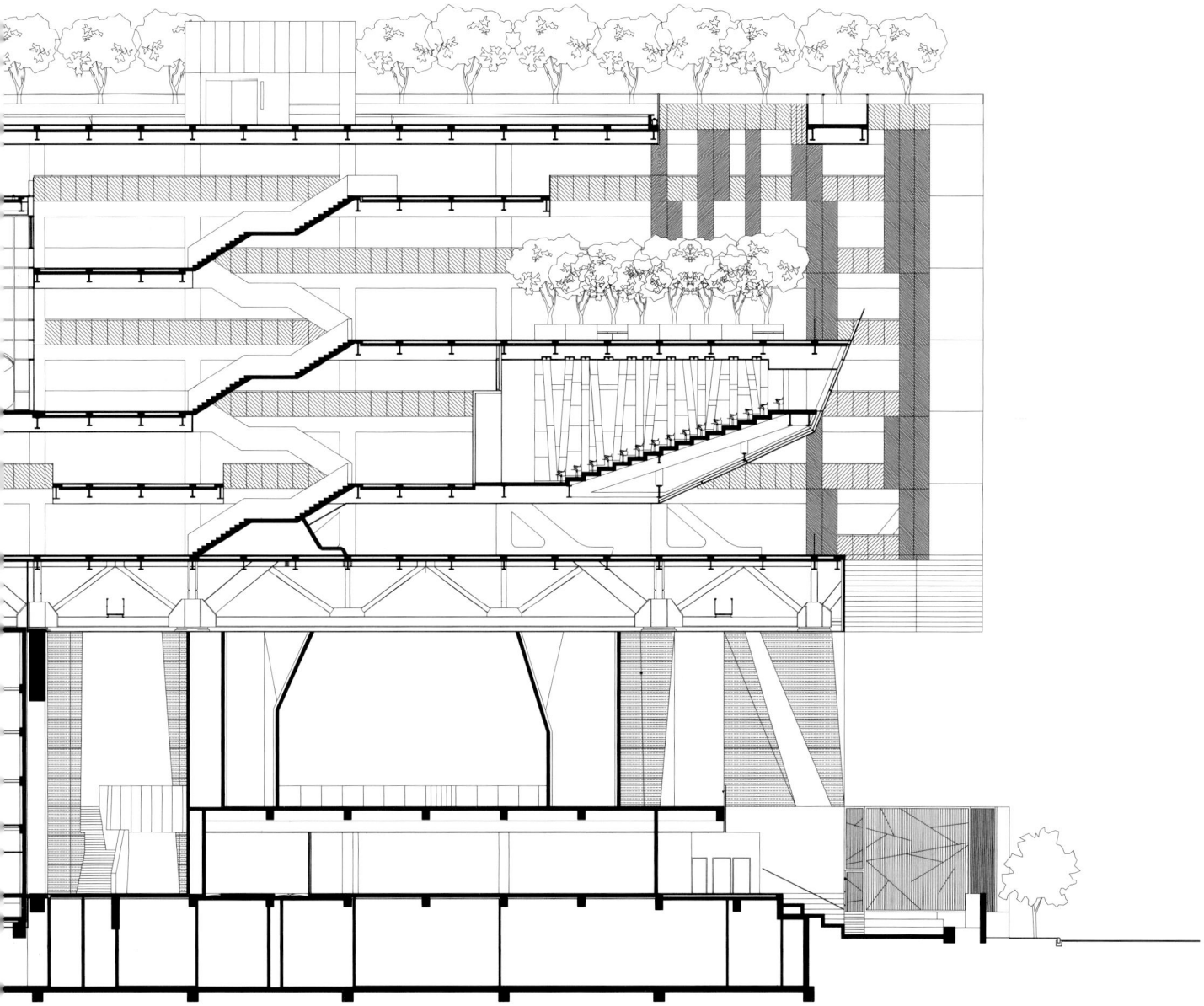

Section.

L__1   5   10   20 m

↑
The art school has no external grounds, so half the building is comprised of in–between spaces, which function as meeting areas and playgrounds.

→
Students enter by escalator on the fifth floor, which serves as an assembly area for the school, looking out to the forested slopes of Fort Canning Park.

→
A steel–plate
spiral staircase
rises above the
fifth floor as the
principal vertical
circulation route.

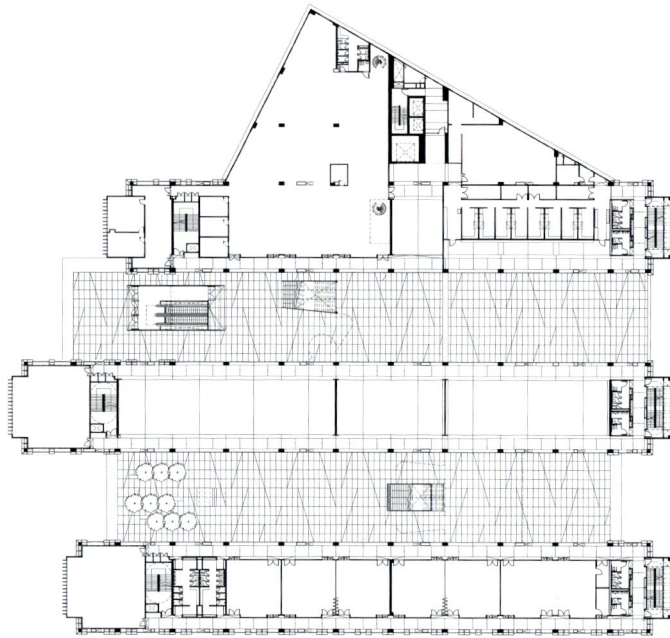

↖
5th floor plan.

↙
2nd floor plan.

→
A landscaped courtyard on the eighth floor overlooks an inner–city precinct to the east.

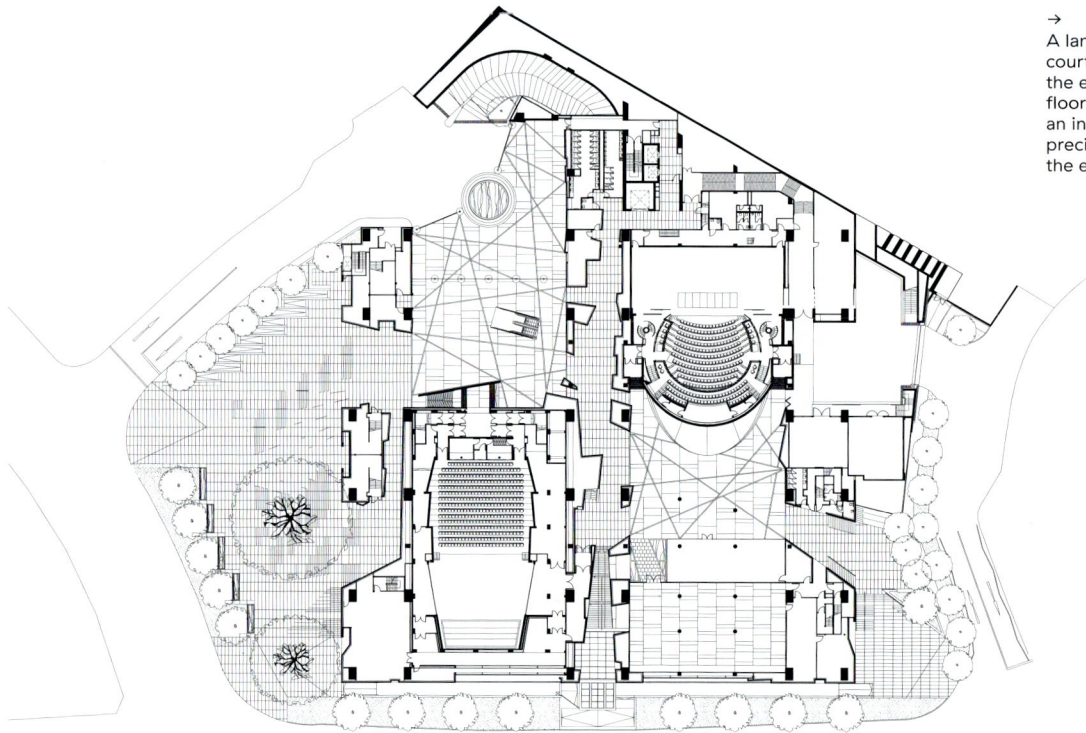

N

10 20   50 m

← Breezes are deflected by the sloping glass wall of the library into the fifth-floor assembly area below.

→ The extensive use of flowering thunbergia vines creates a natural environment and softens the utilitarian appearance of the classroom blocks.

← Looking back into the school on the eighth floor. The spaces and planes on the upper levels were layered to capture the wind flow.

→→ Vines growing from planter boxes are supported by panels of expanded aluminium mesh to form a green wall on the eastern façade.

WOHA: NEW FORMS OF SUSTAINABLE ARCHITECTURE

←
An eastern
street-level
entrance to the
lower levels
passes between
the roughly
hewn walls of
the performance
spaces.

→
The upper
academic levels
are reached by
escalators from
the expressionist
and cavernous
public areas.

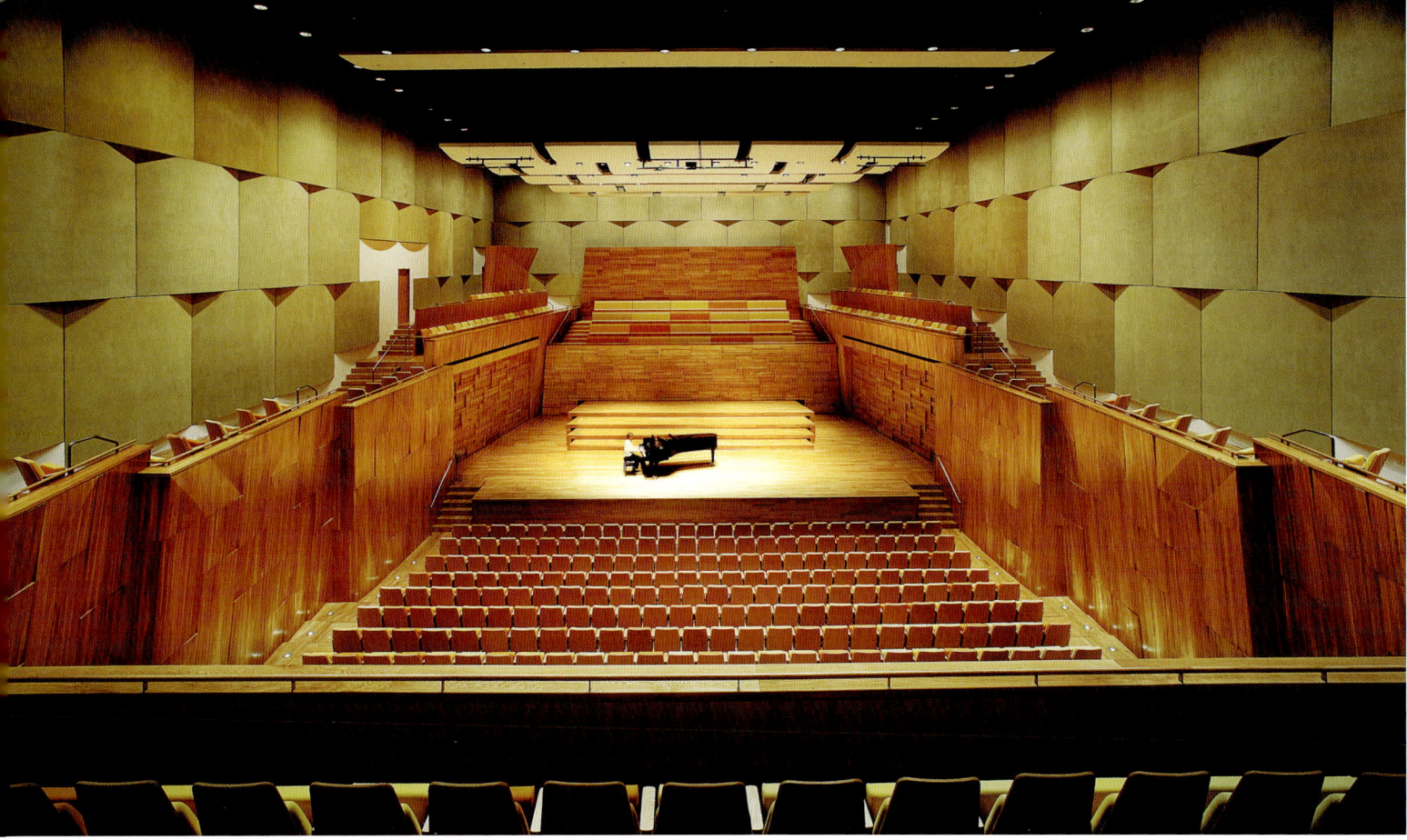

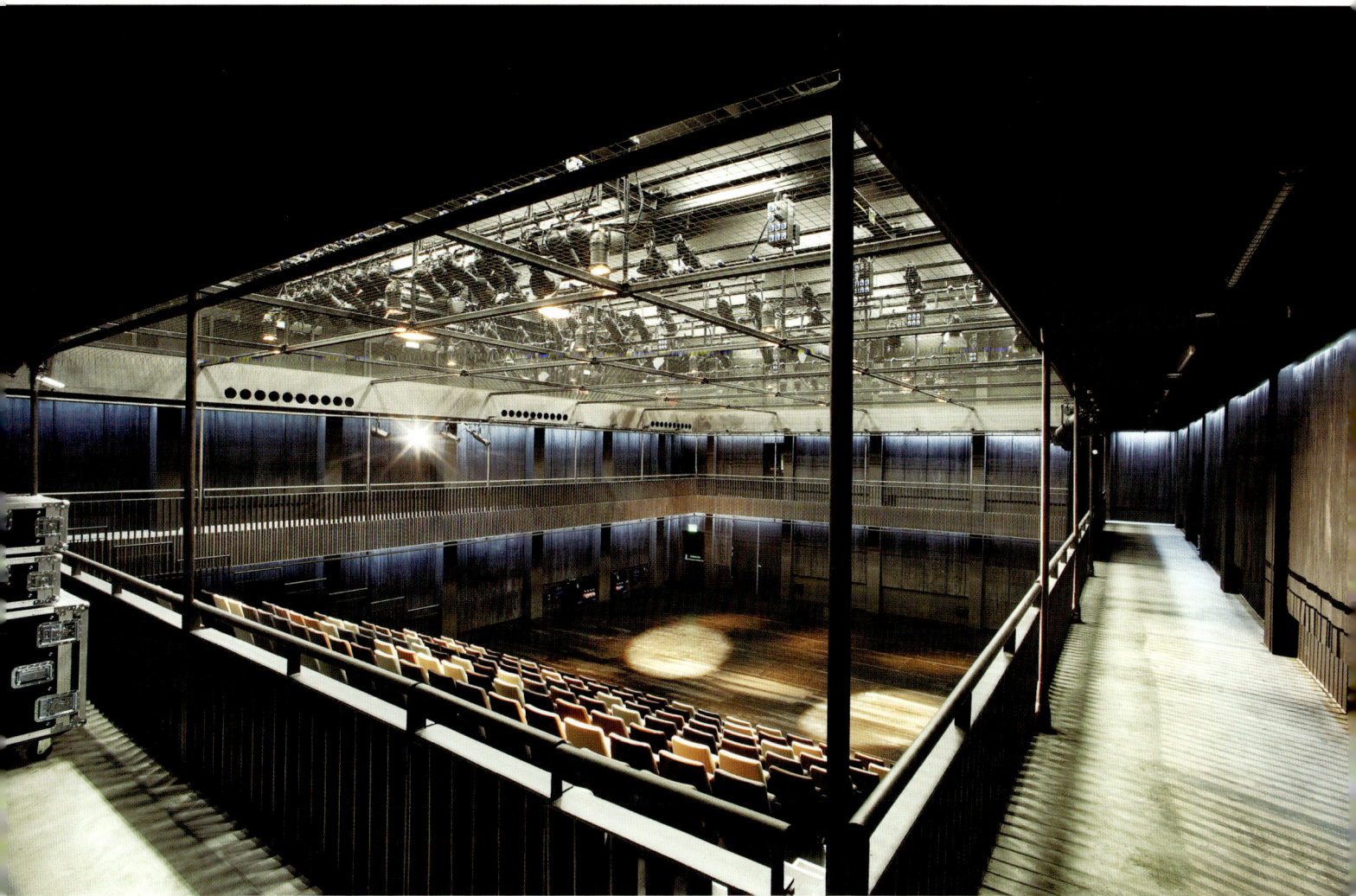

The lower public levels contain three performing arts venues, all designed by WOHA. The black-box theatre has an industrial no-frills appearance, befitting the flexibility of its spatial configurations.

↖ The elegantly formal music auditorium is lined by precast acoustic panels that rise above tapered walls of timber.

→ The intimate drama theatre has a dress-circle plan with brightly coloured fittings.

↑
Strips of recy-
cled plywood
formwork were
used to create
rough ribbed
shards of tawny
rust–coloured
concrete in the
public areas.

↗ →
A claustrophobic
and somewhat
mysterious
sequence of
passageways
on the ground
floor is cooled by
breezes passing
through the
open–ended
volume.

WOHA: NEW FORMS OF SUSTAINABLE ARCHITECTURE

↓
A view from the drop−off area shows the diagonal geom−etries of the school's entry sequence.

↑ →
The southern façade, with three linear one-room-wide classroom blocks — separated by huge horizontal breezeways — rearing up above the public areas.

Parkroyal on Pickering

SINGAPORE, 2007—13

In terms of WOHA's design trajectory, the design of this hotel was notable for many reasons, but in a broad (global) context, the project's completion in 2013 had great impact for one overriding reason: the landscaping. The environmental benefits of designing buildings that performed green were by now widely acknowledged and generally mandated, but the act of incorporating green (trees, shrubs, vines, etc.) as a conspicuous design element had received a few murmurings of criticism. Possibly subconsciously, it may have felt anti-canonical, the casting aside of the revered forms and styles of humankind's hegemony in a sudden reversion to the untamed and natural. Some WOHA projects with trees and gardens – such as Newton Suites (2003–07) and the School of the Arts (2005–10) – had been published widely, but the resonance was muted, and their vertical greenery was regarded as a curiosity rather than a paradigm shift. The images that circulated following the completion of Parkroyal on Pickering changed all that. From many angles, the architecture looked like it was part of the landscape, and the building appeared to be a park in the centre of the city, which in fact it was. It was a compelling sight, and it quite clearly proposed a fresh and timely vision for the future of urban development.

The hotel occupies an entire block on the western edge of the central business district, where banks of high-rise towers meet up with a disparate assortment of housing blocks, shopping malls and heritage precincts, and it sits opposite the lawns and raintrees of Hong Lim Park, also a city block in size. WOHA's elementary intention was to form a visual continuation of that parcel of tropical landscape: *'Hong Lim Park had been donated to the city by a philanthropist, and we felt we should do the same thing ... provide the city with more new greenery.'* The twelve-storey guest room block rises above a five-storey podium, which was 'sculpted' as a rocky landform within which all manner of foliage could thrive. Its crevices and terraces are filled with palm trees, frangipani, hanging vines, grasses and shrubs, all watered by rivulets that course through its folds and layers. In the context of a 21st-century business district, the views of this landscape from the street were singularly unprecedented, but that didn't really feel like anything new: it just felt natural, a seamless extension of the adjoining parkland.

→
Looking down from the top floor to three shelves of aerial gardens placed outside the guest rooms.

WOHA: NEW FORMS OF SUSTAINABLE ARCHITECTURE

The podium was a consummate realization of WOHA's proposals for topographic architecture. The structure acts as a bedrock for the landscaping, which continued to rise between the guest room wings above, where layers of curvilinear concrete shelves were placed at every fourth level to serve as planter beds for further collections of trees, grasses and vines. The guest rooms look directly into these aerial gardens, and to enjoy such an intimate natural panorama in a high-rise cityscape was unexpected, to say the least, not to mention luxuriant. As the noise and pollution would be untenable in a downtown setting, the guest rooms had to be air-conditioned and sealed with glass, so other strategies were required to reduce the energy load. WOHA adopted an E-shaped plan, so that the wings of the tower block would shade one another, and the access corridors were placed out in the fresh air, on the southern façade, as a set of landscaped walkways screened by hanging vines.

Aside from the landscaping, the Parkroyal on Pickering was also notable for its elaborately crafted interior design features and for its civic role in central Singapore. WOHA staged an urban reprise of the Alila Villas Uluwatu resort (2003—09), where they had simply designed everything, and although the process in downtown Singapore could not be quite so all-encompassing (or so rustic), the joinery, light fixtures and built-in furniture are consummately, and self-evidently, crafted by WOHA. Most striking of all were the pert and whimsical 'bird-cage' cabanas on the site-wide recreation deck, and the series of curvaceous mouldings that writhe through and above the public areas, both inside and out. Those sumptuous mouldings (Rococo by any other name) were layered as a grand soffit for the lofty porte-cochère, which serves as a new public gateway between Hong Lim Park and Chinatown, and WOHA were very much aware of such civic possibilities, which they proceeded to treat as obligations. Many of the hotel's attributes were thought of as amenities for the public at large — views of the aerial gardens, newly tree-lined footpaths and increased circulation at street level, never mind the dramatic improvement in ecological performance and environmental remediation — and WOHA were here conscientiously designing for the city as a whole.

As photographs of the hotel — obviously in a city but, somehow, also in a rainforest — were disseminated around the world, along with accompanying data on its sustainability ratings, WOHA's ideas for the future of urban development had now entered the mainstream. Dreaming of cities as natural environments, with trees on buildings, now appeared more viable than ever, and the impact was widespread. WOHA had pushed the boundaries here, and that worked because the building and the architects' vision of a green city looked wonderful.

> **From many angles, the architecture looked like it was part of the landscape, and the building appeared to be a park in the centre of the city, which in fact it was. It was a compelling sight, and it quite clearly proposed a fresh and timely vision for the future of urban development.**

As a piece of
topographic
architecture,
the five–storey
podium was
sculpted
to provide
contoured
ledges for plants
and swathes
of trailing
Phyllanthus.

←
The guest rooms
are accessed
by external
corridors on
the southern
elevation of
the hotel.

↙
The external
corridors have
resort-style
landscaping,
with trop-
ical planting,
bubbling
ponds and
bulging walls
of greenery.

→
The residents
of a large HDB
public housing
complex look
out to hanging
gardens on the
southern façade
of the hotel.

↑
Terraces on the
podium roof
appear as paddy
fields in the city,
interspersed
with waterfalls
and streams.

←
The curvaceous
shelves between
the guest room
blocks support
lush sky gardens
containing a
mixture of
tropical plants
and trees.

← The fifth-floor pool deck viewed from Hong Lim Park, across Pickering Street to the north.

→ Cantilevered at four-floor intervals, the shelves of planting appear as a continuous aerial garden when viewed from above.

↓ Featuring 'bird-cage' cabanas, the pool deck on the podium roof provides a resort-style ambience unexpected in the CBD.

←
The shelves
of plants that
curve between
the upper levels
form a contin-
uation of the
topographical
architecture of
the podium.

→ ↘
Section from
west.
6th floor plan.
5th floor plan.
1st floor plan.

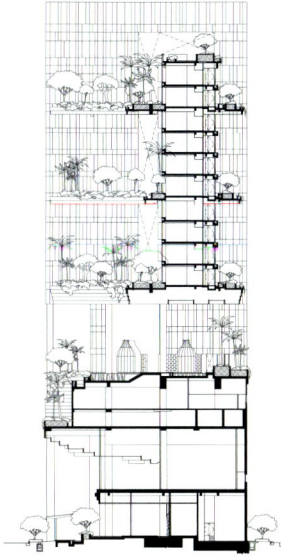

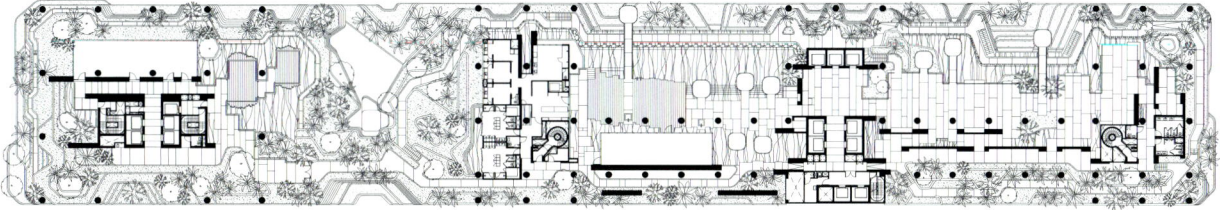

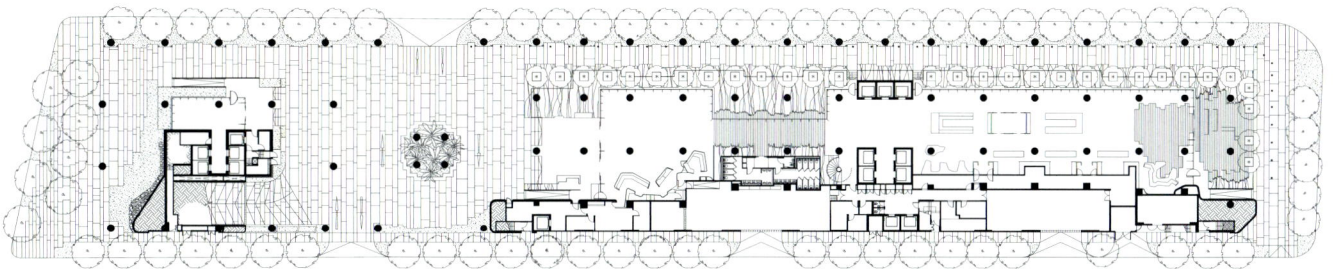

←
Sculpted in
reinforced
concrete, the
contoured
'geological'
striations of the
podium provide
crevices for
abundant plant
growth.

←
Viewed from the
intersection of
Pickering Street
and South Bridge
Road, the guest
rooms rise above
the podium,
supported by a
grid of circular
columns.

←↑
Looking up from the deck on the roof of the podium to the layered shelves of planting outside the guest rooms.

→
Roofed by snaking bands of fluted concrete, the lofty porte-cochère forms a gateway between two discrete inner-city precincts.

← The footpath on Pickering Street is contained within the hotel's landscape, integrating public and private spaces in the downtown location.

→ Viewed from the hotel entry, the porte–cochère is enveloped by layered bands of fluted concrete as a form of treeless topographic architecture.

↘ The contoured exterior forms are continued through the lobby areas as timber mouldings.

←
The top floor
guest lounge
features timber
joinery with
a Japanese
inflection. Light
fittings are
enclosed within
the cabinets.

→
WOHA
designed the
furnishings
and joinery
throughout
the hotel. The
interior spaces
and fittings are
integral to the
overall architec–
tural concept.

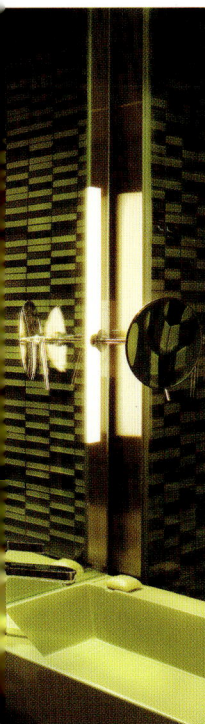

← →
The guest rooms
look directly into
external gardens
placed on large
cantilevered
ledges.

→
Looking from
a cantilevered
cabana to the
swimming pool
and tropical
gardens on the
open-sided
podium roof
deck.

SkyVille @ Dawson

QUEENSTOWN, SINGAPORE, 2007—15

In 2001, WOHA submitted an entry to the Duxton Plain public housing competition with a proposal that was appreciably radical, not to say ground-breaking, in terms of its vertical layering and social programme, but the scheme did not conform to many of the existing regulations and was awarded a merit prize. Six years later – after various regulations had been changed to permit such a typology – SkyVille @ Dawson was commissioned by Singapore's Housing and Development Board (holders of the 2001 competition) and, in light of the bigger picture of Asian mega-city development, it was gratifying to see that WOHA's undeniably humanist agenda had finally gained currency. Located six kilometres to the west of the city centre, the public housing complex is essentially a variation on that Duxton Plain scheme, now composed of three slender forty-seven-storey towers, hollowed out and arrayed on a triple-diamond plan that partially encloses gigantic full-height voids. These voids comprise the invisible core, a huge outdoor space within the structure where residents can live, work and mingle in shaded aerial neighbourhoods, cooled by breezes flowing through in all directions. On every eleventh floor, terraces and gardens spread throughout the complex as new ground levels, which serve as the base for a collection of twelve sky villages, each overlooked and shared by eighty homes (rather than insular apartments). A site-wide sky park on the roof consists of public gardens and terraces, and the idea of treating elevated spaces as though they were common areas at street level had been central to the Duxton Plain proposal, which, critically, posited that a high-rise apartment should feel like a house, a bungalow or a villa, close to gardens, walkways, streets and parks.

→ Communal gardens and walkways are layered at every eleventh level within the huge internal voids.

'SkyVille is the size of a small town, and we wanted people to get to know their neighbours. High-rise developments have never been places to make friends ... we wanted to change all that.'

—WOHA

The purpose of the architecture is not readily apparent until you spend time negotiating the great internal volumes, where the programmatic intention unfolds as a geometric sequence of private gardens and small communal parks, which have elevated vistas of the city skyline in the distance. The spaces and the panoramas are unusual for an apartment complex, and as such, they feel rather intimidating on first impression. It's not until the realization dawns: of how different the environment is and how much it has to offer, that the scale of the programme — both for sociability and sustainability — becomes clear. The architecture of SkyVille @ Dawson is not just different, it is completely distinctive, essentially for the simple reason that it hasn't been done before. As with The Met (2003—09) and the School of the Arts (2005—10), the structure was incontrovertibly a prototype, one that utilized nearly all of WOHA's procedures for sustainable construction in the tropics (as catalogued in the Garden City Mega City project).

WOHA's post-completion assessment of SkyVille @ Dawson is not just architectural; they prefer to rate the project, especially in regard to its user-friendliness. The point to be made is that a complex of this scale, with 960 apartments, is not really to be judged as an architectural artefact, but as a quite sizeable part of the city and as a home and an amenity for thousands of people. WOHA are more intent on publicizing the results of surveys on energy saving and increased social interaction than they are on inserting the building's tectonic attributes into architectural discourse, and in doing so they have taken the next step: they are now focused on the performance of the city, and they are thus thinking as planners and as advocates for a better quality of urban existence. Megastructures are extraordinarily useful for shaping mega-city density — in fact, they are key to making the improvements required for sustainable development. Therefore, WOHA's imperative — as set out with SkyVille @ Dawson — is to prioritize the appeal of the immediate living environments, to humanize the neighbourhoods and, above all, to ensure that they are widely regarded as preferred places to live.

WOHA: NEW FORMS OF SUSTAINABLE ARCHITECTURE

A view from the south shows the apartment blocks rising as a carapace that shelters the hollowed-out spaces within. The gardens on the roof of the car park can be seen below.

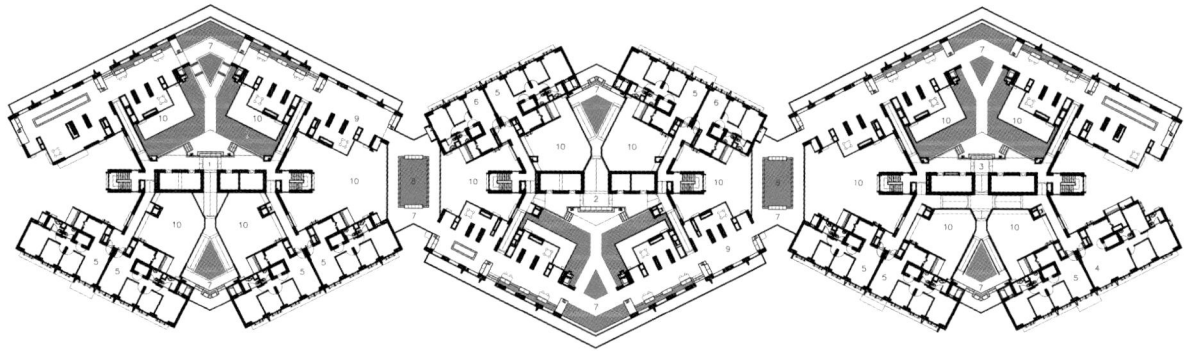

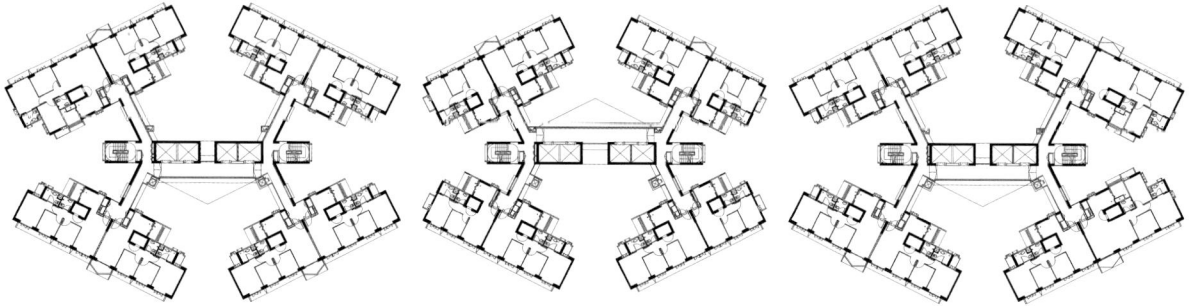

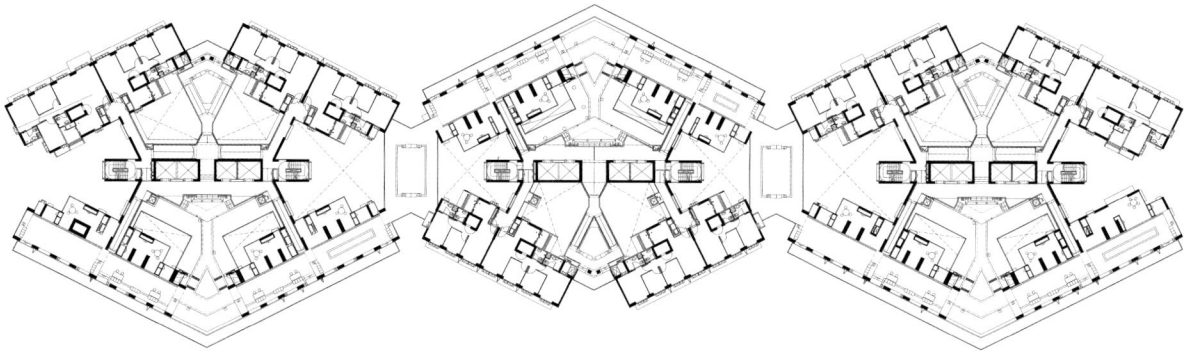

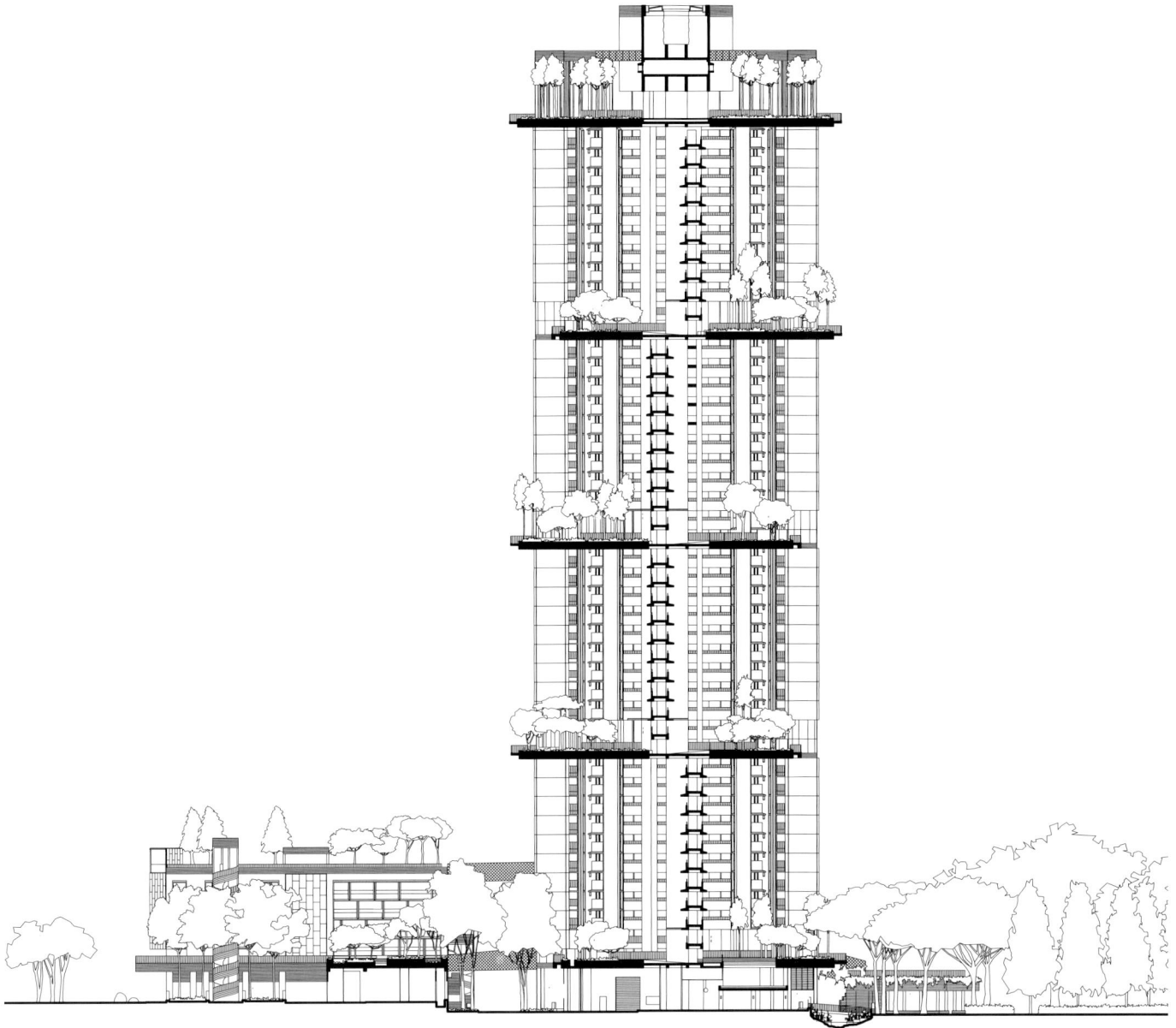

↗
Section.

↖
36th floor plan.
16th—24th
floor plan.
14th floor plan.

←
The porous open-ended structure of the monumental complex seen from the northeast. The photo was taken before construction started on the adjacent sites.

→
Looking from the southeast to the folding façades of the towers, which shield the shaded and breeze-filled community spaces placed inside the full-height voids.

WOHA: NEW FORMS OF SUSTAINABLE ARCHITECTURE

↑
Layers of
rectangular
sky gardens
form part of
the internal
circulation routes
between the
towers.

→
The communal
sky gardens
within the voids
can be viewed
from every
apartment.

→
Terraces with gardens and meeting places extend as sky villages from the lift core to the perimeter lookouts.

↑
Looking up at kite–shaped platforms that serve as sky gardens within the vertical voids.

← →
The layers of
terraces and
gardens offer
the amenity of
street level, with
cooling breezes,
elevated views,
and no conges–
tion.

↘
The aerial
gardens provide
a uniquely safe
and pleasurable
environment
for residents of
all ages.

←
The roof of the
car park was
designed as
a public park
with children's
playgrounds.

↗
With panoramic
views over
Singapore, a park
that spreads
across the entire
breadth of the
roof can be
enjoyed by the
public at large.

→
Looking through raintrees to the northern elevation, showing the open nature of the ground–floor access and circulation routes.

↑
As gardens and meeting places were placed within the open aerial spaces of the complex, lawns to the north are freed up to be used as sporting fields and playgrounds.

→
Shops, a food court and facilities for the local community are located to the south of the towers.

The triple-
diamond plan
and the scale of
the internal voids
can be clearly
seen in this view
of the northern
elevation.

Oasia
Downtown

TANJONG PAGAR, SINGAPORE, 2011—16

As part of Singapore's zealous drive for post-independence modernity, a large portion of the once-disreputable Tanjong Pagar district was designated as a conservation area, which meant that its 19th-century shophouses and unsanitary streets were transformed from rundown and grimy into picturesque and chic. The residents were relocated to HDB public housing blocks, and the boutiques and wine bars moved in. Now the very epitome of Singapore hip, this autonomous low-rise tiled-roof precinct serves as the foreground to a fresh iteration of Tanjong Pagar: a phalanx of high-rise slabs that forms an elongation of the existing central business district. The demarcation is abrupt, and the contrast between the charms and conviviality of the 19th-century streetscapes and the neutral gridded expression of the 21st century is laid bare. The recently built towers were all made with floor plates cantilevered from a central core, they were hermetically sealed by a curtain wall, and it is fair to say that the designs did not set out to extend much in the way of what might be termed civic generosity.

One of the towers, however, is different. Clad in crimson-coloured aluminium mesh and cloaked by flowering vines, the twenty-seven storey Oasia Downtown hotel has no central core, it does not have a solid mass, and it is not shrouded from top to toe by a curtain wall. The plan is square, with the floor plates suspended between piers placed on the four chamfered corners, which contain the elevators and services. The building envelope was sliced apart to form three voluminous atria, stacked atop one another and opened to the elements on two sides, with the plan of the central atrium rotated 180 degrees. Overlooked by two banks of guest rooms and screened by the profusion of greenery on the external mesh, the atria were treated as aerial parklands and they also serve as huge cubic breezeways,[1] channelling the winds that swirl high above ground level. The tower looks remarkable, opened out to delight in (not hide from) the tropical conditions, and swathed by a vertical garden whose blooms flourish and fade according to the seasons.

→ The chamfered corner elevations rise the height of the twenty–seven–storey tower as uninterrupted vertical gardens.

1 WOHA were to call these spaces 'Breezeway Atria', as no name existed for what was a new form of sustainable design. As categorized in their book *Garden City Mega City*: 'Breezeway Atria rise above Multiple Ground Levels as grand vertical volumes, which form three-dimensional shared precincts within the perforated structure of a tropical tower. The atria facilitate constant cross-ventilation and natural lighting, while rejuvenating the lifestyle and social interaction of city residents.'

Like the nearby Parkroyal on Pickering hotel (2007–13), the Oasia Downtown now stands as a photogenic symbol of Singapore's green city credentials and as a conspicuously expressed statement of WOHA's idealistic intentions. Although supremely functional in terms of their typology of hospitality, both buildings can be viewed as 'installations in the city'; as playful yet provocative artistic flourishes designed to subvert the passive abstraction of the surrounding skyline by blatantly injecting greenery — masses of vegetation — as an alternative mode of architecture.

In many ways, the design of Oasia Downtown was more audacious than that of its predecessor. Although the impact of the Parkroyal's extensive landscaping in its urban context was emphatic in its consummation, the orthogonal form of the building could be clearly seen, and the vertical gardens were not all-enveloping by any means. On the other hand, Oasia Downtown seemed to quite wilfully disobey any aspiration to accord with conventional architectural politesse. The tower's outlines were fuzzy, the landscaping–as–cladding was prone to spontaneous (organic) outbursts, and the structure appeared almost clumsy and dishevelled. In fact, you might say that, in spirit, the tower resembled a very large tree; an allusion that — not coincidentally — could be reinforced by its environmental performance.

'Oasia Downtown has a green plot ratio of 1100%, which means that we have eleven times as much greenery as the site in its natural state. The tower has been evaluated by ecologists in comparison with nearby parks, and although the site is only 50 metres square, it has the same amount of biodiversity as those much larger parks ... and it actually performs 30% of the ecosystem services of a lowland rainforest. Now we want to triple that degree of landscaping ... then our building would be as environmentally beneficial as a rainforest. Oasia Downtown has been measured by thermal cameras, and the façade surface temperature was less than half that of the adjoining glass–clad Tanjong Pagar Centre ... 25°C compared with 55°C. Imagine how much cooler the city would be if all the buildings were Oasia Downtowns.'

> **The tower has been evaluated by ecologists in comparison with nearby parks, and although the site is only 50 metres square, it has the same amount of biodiversity as those much larger parks ... and it actually performs 30% of the ecosystem services of a lowland rainforest.**

←
With a markedly
different profile
and colour
palette to its
neighbours,
the tower is
framed by office
buildings to the
southeast.

→
The uncon−
ventional
proportions and
colouration of
the tower form a
very compatible
backdrop to
the rows of
19th−century
shophouses in
Tanjong Pagar.

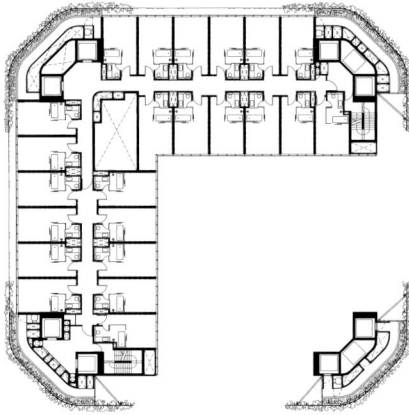

22nd, 23rd, 25th floor plan.

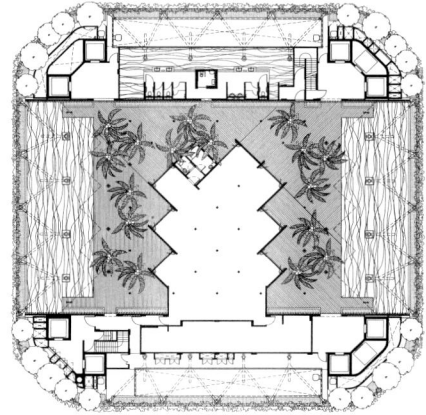

27th floor plan.

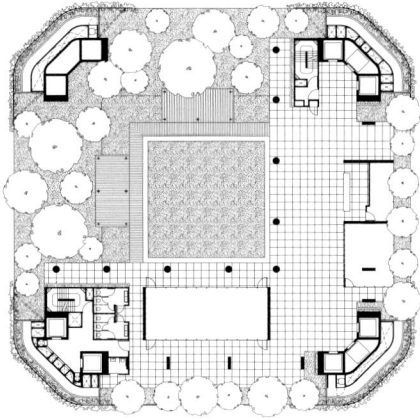

12th floor plan — sky terrace.

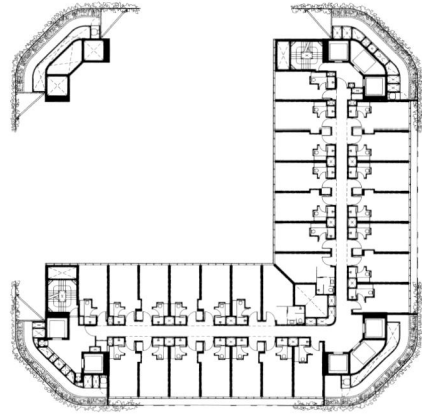

13th—20th floor plan.

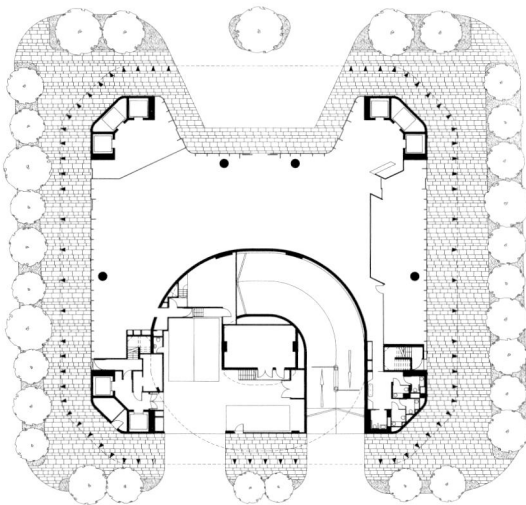

1st floor plan.

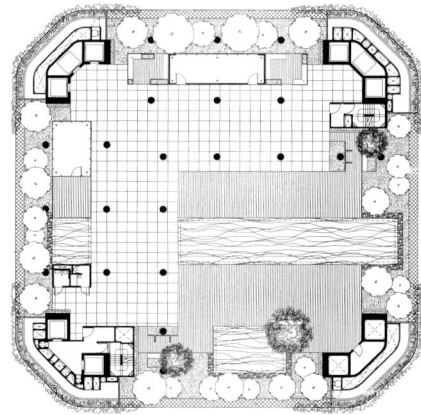

6th floor plan — sky terrace.

Ⓝ   10   20   50 m

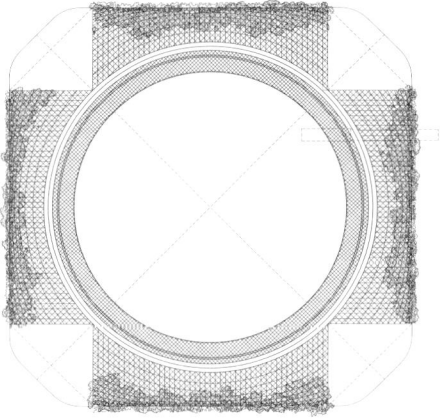

Roof plan.

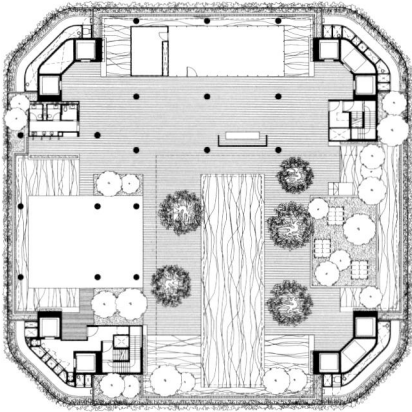

21st floor plan — sky terrace.

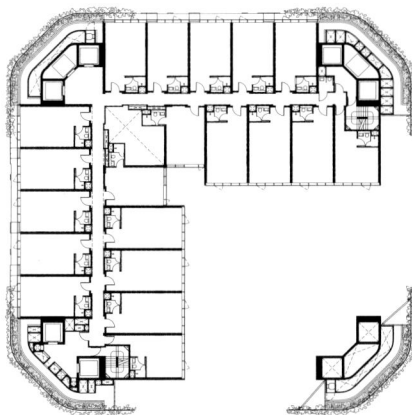

7th—11th floor plan.

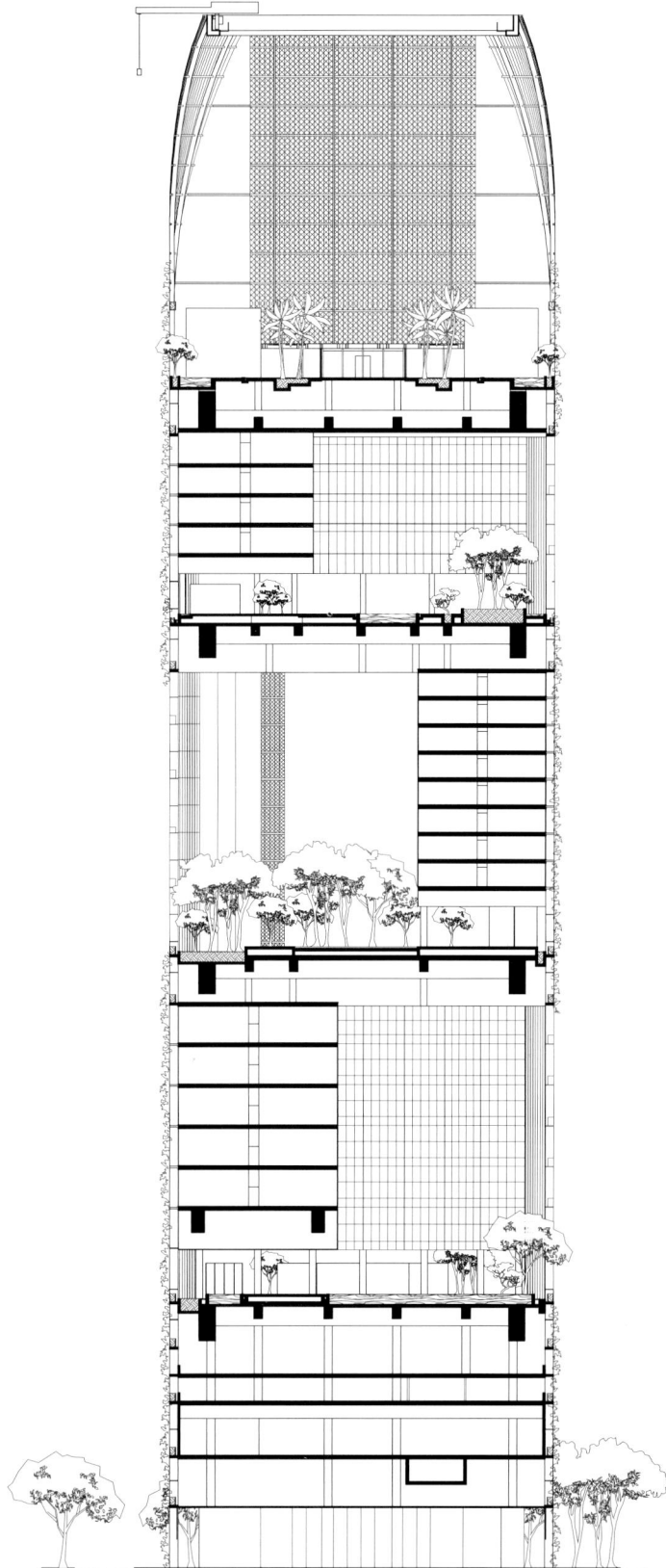

Section.

←
View from
the south–
west during a
period when
plant growth
was relatively
dormant.
The panels of
aluminium mesh
have a variety
of reddish–
toned hues.

→
Looking from
the northeast
at a time when
the plant growth
was flourishing.
Only the guest
room window
elevations are
not cloaked by
greenery.

←
The open-air
courtyard
adjoining the
twelfth-floor
hotel lobby is
ringed by trop-
ical gardens.

→
Looking down
from a guest
room to the
courtyard and
gardens on the
twelfth floor,
contained within
a ten-storey
atrium that was
left open on the
north and east
elevations.

↓
Vines and
creepers
pass through
aluminium mesh
from irrigated
planter boxes
to merge on
the exterior as
great screens
of greenery.

← At its most lush during the summer months, the cloak of greenery presents a street-level vista that could not be described as architectural in the traditional sense.

→ When seen from various angles, the tower does appear to be part of a rainforest. The amount of greenery is eleven times more than that of the site in its natural state.

↓ Shaded public footpaths, framed by vine-clad columns, wrap around the tower as an act of civic beneficence.

↑
Public footpaths
are enclosed
by a botanic
colonnade of
creepers rising
from the ground
to meet those
descending from
planter boxes
above.

↖
The building has
a dichotomous
appearance,
with a rigidly
formal structural
grid overlaid by
wilfully dishev‑
elled swathes of
flowering vines.

→ The tower has
a conspicuous
presence in
the congested
downtown
precinct,
providing office
workers and
apartment
residents with a
very unlikely and
quite remarkable
view.

Looking out from the gardens on the twenty–first floor through a set of expanded mesh screens.

→
View from a guest room to the swimming pool atrium on the twenty–first floor. The building's structural loads were borne by the columns on each of its corners.

↓
The common areas for guests here are completely cross–ventilated, shaded and protected from rain.

Kampung Admiralty

ADMIRALTY, SINGAPORE, 2013—17

For several years, WOHA had been formulating and re-formulating a specific building type for Singapore, a multi-storey structure that could house – in the most sustainable manner possible – a myriad of activities, amenities and services on a single site for the community at large: '*We were aiming to create social and community space from the in-between fabric. It was the opposite of a clear-cut figure-and-ground separation … there is much more room to innovate in the relationships between functions and cellular components.*' The seed for this three-dimensional interstitial thinking had been sown with their winning design in 2005 for the School of the Arts, where all the institution's academic and public functions were linked and layered over ten floors, continuously ventilated by breezes passing through open-ended voids, passageways and staircases. A competition entry in 2008 for the School of Science and Technology placed all the communal and academic facilities – spread over four interconnected and passively ventilated levels – in a standalone orthogonal volume, even though the brief had indicated that the new campus would be housed in a set of buildings. Two further competition entries extended the scope and scale of this idea to the wider community, and indeed to the city at large: the Tampines Community Town Hub (2011) and the Punggol Community Park Station (2013) were formally adventurous and programmatically ambitious, and they were particularly well resolved in a volumetric sense. Both took the form of a large and highly permeable orthogonal block, which contained a variety of amenities and services for the surrounding district, with the Tampines Hub roofed by sporting facilities and the Punggol Station by forested layers of terracing.

With their Kampung[1] Admiralty competition (held by the Housing and Development Board) entry, WOHA presented another iteration, a recalibration of those earlier schemes – and once again, they proposed a single building to house all the facilities as one cellular grouping. The brief comprised four components – a medical centre, a community centre, a retail centre and housing for the elderly – and it had been assumed that the conflicting nature of their requirements would necessitate separate buildings.

→ The rooftop gardens descend as terraces to a central void, which contains gardens for the medical centre and a skylight for the public plaza on the ground floor.

1 *Kampung* is the Malay word for 'village' and has always been used in Singapore to describe small community settlements.

WOHA, however, perceived that the flat, squarish site was perfectly suited to a single block, and if structured accordingly, such a building would be a much more effective means of providing sustainable and sociable high-density development. Their winning proposal was thus not remarkable for its formal architecture so much as its programme of integration through stratification, and when completed, the project met with unqualified praise from the local community, which in this case also meant the Singapore government, who had been very much part of the development process.

WOHA: NEW FORMS OF SUSTAINABLE ARCHITECTURE

The site for Kampung Admiralty lay next to an MRT station, a bus interchange and a rather mundane shopping mall, and it was surrounded by the serried ranks of HDB public housing blocks that spread for miles across the flatlands of northern Singapore. The location was not auspicious, nor particularly enticing, but the networks were functional and efficient, and the area was almost crying out for a focal point and some aesthetic remediation. Forming an extension of the neighbouring mall, the shops and cafés on the ground floor of Kampung Admiralty are entered from a two-storey atrium, roofed by a skylight and open on its sides. Cooled by free-flowing breezes, this lofty, light-filled space now serves as an expansive meeting place (spontaneous and/or formal) for the local community, overlooked by a large food court on a mezzanine level. WOHA had always (and this goes back to their earliest houses) insisted that open sociable spaces were integral to living in the tropics — such areas had, after all, been fundamental components of villages and vernacular compounds — and Kampung Admiralty had presented the opportunity to provide this most desirable civic amenity in a demonstrably egalitarian context. The cool and capacious site-wide atrium was nothing less than a reinstatement of traditional (pre-modernist) Asian architectural planning, as was the abundantly vegetated rooftop park: both were welcoming, accessible and totally tropical.

Arrayed around a central light well, the building's components were layered as horizontal strata: a supermarket and car park lay beneath the ground-floor atrium and the food court, which were roofed by two floors of medical, aged-care and childminding facilities, and capped by eight floors of housing for the elderly. The apartments are contained in two towers, which look out on to bountiful tropical gardens, cascading down a 'hillside' as a terraced mini-rainforest with trails that weave between secluded retreats, communal allotments and recreation areas. An oasis in the drably monotonous high-rise suburbs, this rooftop parkland was one of WOHA's most emphatic and symbolic gestures. It was a more-than-timely 'installation' in the only-too-visible context of the Asian mega-city, and it was beautifully sculpted and landscaped: like Parkroyal on Pickering and Oasia Downtown, it appeared that the building's parti was botanical rather than architectural.

There was, however, much more to the project than the provision of a pleasure garden, and in the broadest sense, the completed complex was possibly WOHA's most unequivocally successful building. Kampung Admiralty was no isolated prototype, as WOHA had here delivered sustainable architecture for an all-inclusive public development whose community benefits and civic function extended well beyond the confines of an individual structure.

> **An oasis in the drably monotonous high-rise suburbs, this rooftop parkland was one of WOHA's most emphatic and symbolic gestures. It was a more-than-timely 'installation' in the only-too-visible context of the Asian mega-city, and it appeared that the building's parti was botanical rather than architectural.**

A view from the west shows the compact nature of a city–within–a–city, which contains layers and levels of community facilities roofed by a public park.

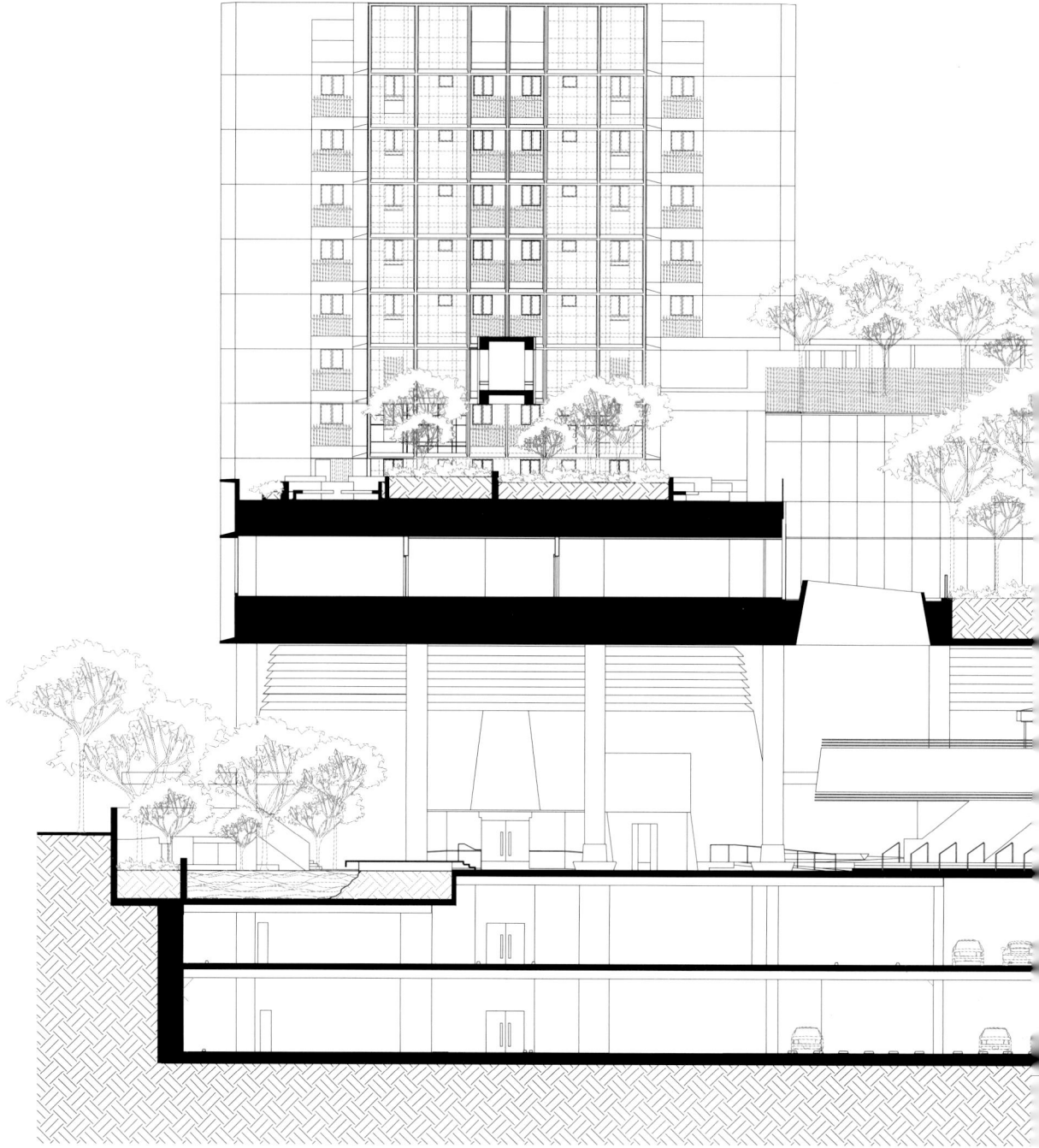

Section.

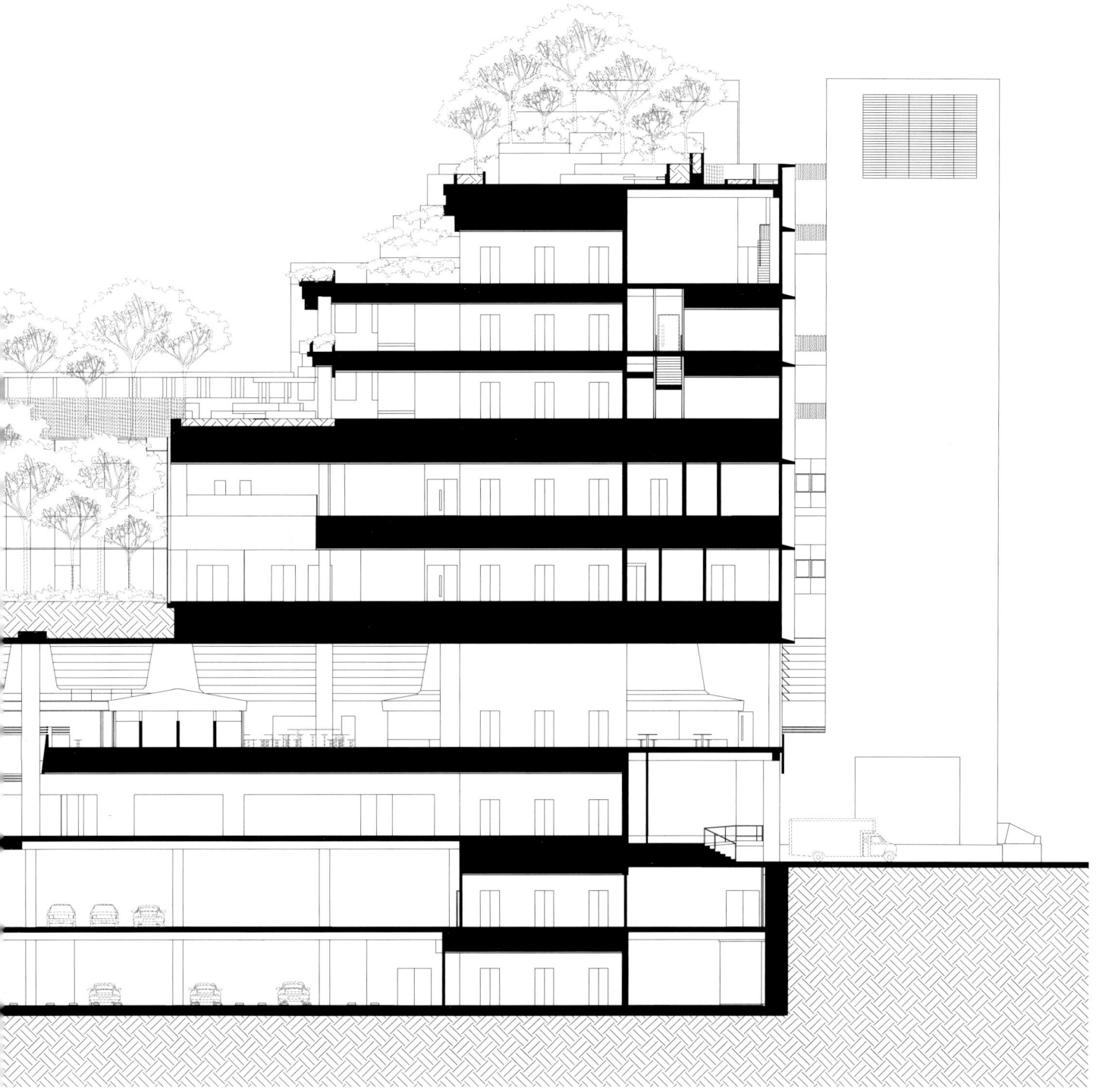

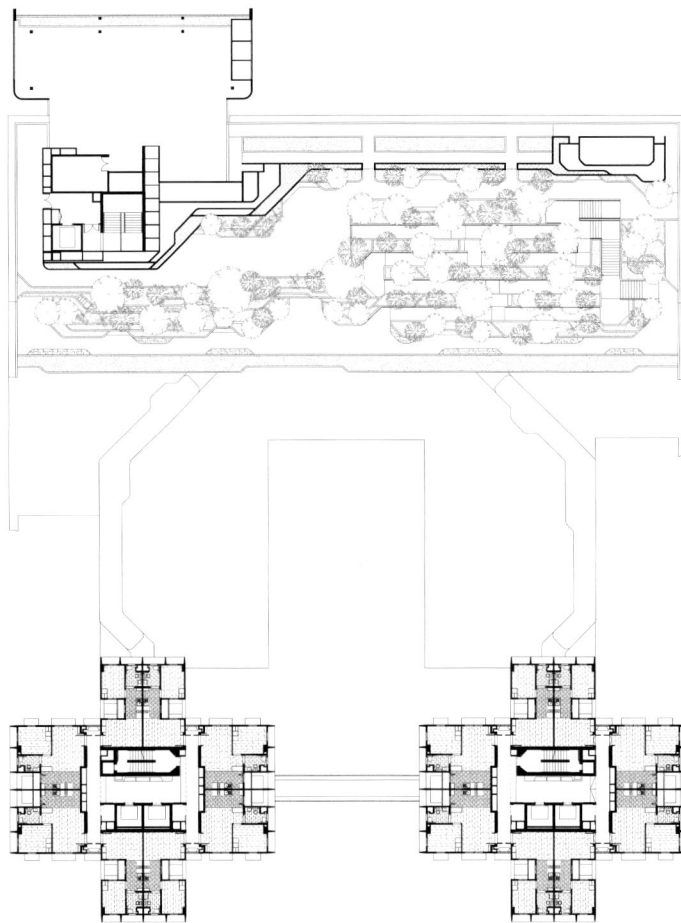

```
|___|___|_____|
5   10          25 m
```

9th floor plan.

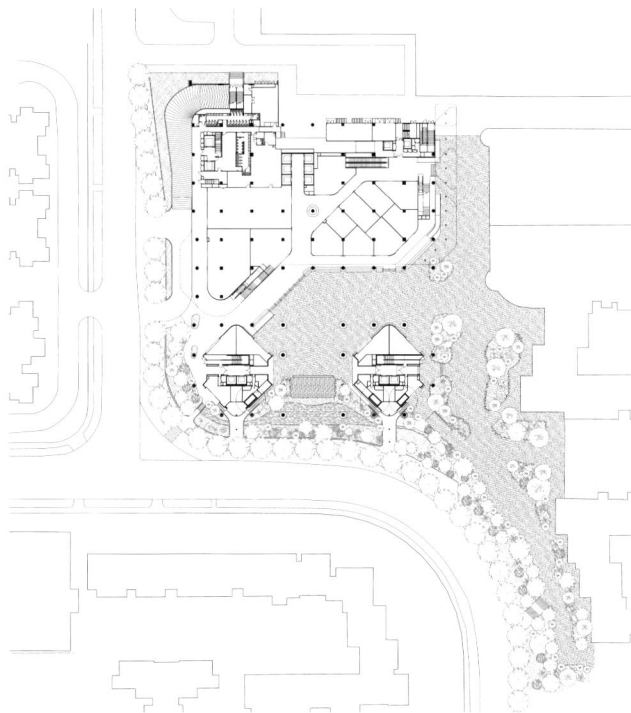

```
 N   |___|___|_____|
    10  20          50 m
```

Site plan.

→
View of the southern elevation showing the public plaza beneath two floors of community facilities and the eight-storey apartment blocks.

← The double-height indoor plaza forms an extension of the existing public spaces of the neighbourhood.

→ Looking down from the mezzanine–level food court to the public plaza, which serves as a gathering place for the local community.

↓ The atrium at street level forms an extension of the shops and circulation routes of the suburb's commercial centre.

The coloured
panels of the
orthogonal
façades are
recessed and
framed to
impose a sense
of architec–
tonic rigour in
an amorphous
suburban
context.

↑
Pathways zigzag through the terraced gardens on the roof, overlooking the apartments for the elderly.

→
The landscape on the roof is so lush that secluded and contemplative retreats can be found in a high−density environment.

←
A playground on the bottom level of the rooftop park. The entire complex was an all−inclusive project with benefits for every member of the local community.

← The medical centre on the third floor looks directly into gardens layered around the central light well.

→ View from the fifth-level parkland showing the central light well at left.

↘ The two apartment towers are surrounded by gardens and communal areas on the fourth floor.

↑ →
The contoured layers of the concrete structure on the rooftop terraces form an aerial version of the topographic architecture used by WOHA for podium designs.

↑
Looking across
the activity
areas in the
fifth-level park
to the terraced
gardens.

Accessible to everybody, the rooftop gardens form an extra-ordinary landscape in the midst of northern Singapore's densely settled high-rise suburbs.

Eleven Selected Projects: Consultants

St Mary of the Angels
Singapore

CLIENT
The Franciscan Friars (The Order of Friars Minor)

CIVIL & STRUCTURAL ENGINEERING
Worley Pte Ltd

MECHANICAL & ELECTRICAL ENGINEERING
AE&T Consultants

QUANTITY SURVEYOR
A. Peter Tan Associates Pte Ltd

MAIN CONTRACTOR
Soil Build Pte Ltd

INTERIOR CONTRACTOR
Shanghai Chong Kee Furniture & Construction Pte Ltd

1 Moulmein Rise
Singapore

CLIENT
UOL Group Limited

MECHANICAL & ELECTRICAL, CIVIL & STRUCTURAL ENGINEER
Meinhardt (Singapore) Pte Ltd

QUANTITY SURVEYOR
KPK Quantity Surveyors (1995) Singapore Pte Ltd

MAIN CONTRACTOR
Shining Construction Pte Ltd

Bras Basah MRT Station
Singapore

CLIENT / PROJECT MANAGER / QUANTITY SURVEYOR
Land Transport Authority

STRUCTURAL ENGINEER
Maunsell Consultants (Singapore) Pte Ltd / WorleyParsons

MECHANICAL & ELECTRICAL ENGINEER / MAIN CONTRACTOR
Woh Hup–Shanghai Tunnel Engineering—NCC JV

LANDSCAPE ARCHITECT
Cicada Pte Ltd

Stadium MRT Station
Singapore

CLIENT / PROJECT MANAGER / QUANTITY SURVEYOR
Land Transport Authority

STRUCTURAL ENGINEER
Maunsell Consultants (Singapore) Pte Ltd

MECHANICAL & ELECTRICAL ENGINEER
Meinhardt (Singapore) Pte Ltd

LANDSCAPE ARCHITECT
Cicada Pte Ltd

MAIN CONTRACTOR
Nishimatsu Construction / Lum Chang JV

Alila Villas Uluwatu
Bali

CLIENT
PT. Bukit Uluwatu Villa

MECHANICAL & ELECTRICAL ENGINEER
PT. Makesthi Enggal Engineering

CIVIL & STRUCTURAL ENGINEER
Worley Parsons Pte Ltd / PT. Atelier Enam Struktur

ECOLOGICALLY SUSTAINABLE DESIGN CONSULTANT
Sustainable Built Environments

LIGHTING CONSULTANT
Lighting Planners Associates

QUANTITY SURVEYOR
PT Kosprima Sarana Kuantitama

LANDSCAPE CONSULTANT
Cicada Pte Ltd

MAIN CONTRACTOR
PT. Hutama Karya

The Met
Bangkok

ARCHITECTS IN ASSOCIATION
Tandem Architects LLC

CLIENT
Pebble Bay Thailand Co. Ltd

MECHANICAL & ELECTRICAL ENGINEER
Lincolne Scott Ng Pte Ltd

CIVIL & STRUCTURAL ENGINEER
Worley Pte. Ltd

QUANTITY SURVEYOR
KPK Quantity Surveyors (1995) Singapore Pte Ltd

LANDSCAPE ARCHITECT
Cicada Pte Ltd

MAIN CONTRACTOR
Bouygues Thai Ltd

School of the Arts
Singapore

CLIENT
Ministry of Communications and Information

MECHANICAL & ELECTRICAL ENGINEER
Lincolne Scott Ng Pte Ltd

CIVIL & STRUCTURAL ENGINEER
Worley Parsons Pte Ltd

QUANTITY SURVEYOR
Rider Levett Bucknall

LANDSCAPE ARCHITECT
Cicada Pte Ltd

THEATRE ACOUSTICS
Arup Acoustics / Theatreplan LLP

LIGHTING CONSULTANT
Lighting Planners Associates

MAIN CONTRACTOR
Tiong Aik Construction Pte Ltd

Parkroyal on Pickering
Singapore

CLIENT
UOL Group Limited

HOTEL DEVELOPER
Pan Pacific Hotels Group

CIVIL & STRUCTURAL ENGINEER
TEP Consultants Pte Ltd

MECHANICAL & ELECTRICAL ENGINEER
BECA Carter Hollings & Ferner (S.E. Asia) Pte Ltd

QUANTITY SURVEYOR
Rider Levett Bucknall LLP

LIGHTING CONSULTANT
Lighting Planners Associates (S) Pte Ltd

LANDSCAPE CONSULTANT
Tierra Design (S) Pte Ltd

MAIN CONTRACTOR
Tiong Seng Contractors (Pte) Ltd

SkyVille @ Dawson
Singapore

CLIENT
Housing & Development Board

CIVIL & STRUCTURAL ENGINEER
LBW Consultants LLP

MECHANICAL & ELECTRICAL ENGINEER
BECA Carter Hollings & Ferner (S.E. Asia) Pte Ltd

QUANTITY SURVEYOR
Davis Langdon KPK (Singapore) Pte Ltd

LANDSCAPE CONSULTANT
ICN Design International

MAIN CONTRACTOR
Hor Kew Private Limited

Oasia Downtown
Singapore

CLIENT
Far East SOHO Pte Ltd

CIVIL & STRUCTURAL ENGINEER
KTP Consultants Pte Ltd

MECHANICAL & ELECTRICAL ENGINEER
Rankine & Hill (S) Pte Ltd

QUANTITY SURVEYOR
Rider Levett Bucknall

LANDSCAPE CONSULTANT
Sitetectonix Pte Ltd

LIGHTING CONSULTANT
Lighting Planners Associates (S) Pte Ltd / The Lightbox Pte Ltd

MAIN CONTRACTOR
Woh Hup (Private) Ltd

Kampung Admiralty
Singapore

CLIENT
Housing & Development Board

CIVIL & STRUCTURAL ENGINEER
Ronnie & Koh Consultants Pte Ltd

MECHANICAL & ELECTRICAL ENGINEER
AECOM Pte Ltd

QUANTITY SURVEYOR
Davis Langdon KPK (Singapore) Pte Ltd

LANDSCAPE CONSULTANT
Ramboll Studio Dreiseitl Singapore Pte Ltd

MAIN CONTRACTOR
Lum Chang Building Contractors Pte Ltd

Project Chronology
(Year of Initial Design)

2021
Ismaili Centre, Singapore (in progress)
MSUN One City Residential Development, Bao'an, Shenzhen (in progress)
Shanghai Vanke Future City 2 Masterplan, Shanghai (in progress)
TCL Headquarters, Shenzhen (competition entry)
Tianjin University GTSI Campus, Shenzhen (competition entry)

2020
NS Square Floating Platform, Singapore (in progress)
Chengdu Er Jiang Si Mixed-Use Development, Tianfu, Chengdu (in progress)
Bukit Timah — Rochor Green Corridor Phase 1, Singapore (in progress)
Enabling Village Extension, Singapore (in progress)
Elderly Community, Xi'an (in progress)
Aquatique Pattaya Hotel and Entertainment Development (in progress)
Cairns Street Residential Development, Brisbane (in progress)
Shanghai Vanke Future City Masterplan, Shanghai
Petaling Jaya Master Plan, Malaysia (unbuilt)
Longhua Urban Revamp, Shenzhen (competition entry)
Springleaf Precinct Masterplan, Singapore (competition entry)
Kallang-Kolam Ayer Industrial Estate, Singapore (competition entry)
Harry Butler Institute Environmental Education Centre Design, Australia (competition entry)
Shenzhen Xiaomeisha Mixed-Use Development, China (competition entry)
Sanya Regent Mixed-Use Development, China (competition entry)
Fifty-Fifty City, masterplan proposal, Singapore (unbuilt)
HDB Redhill Development, Singapore (unbuilt)

2019
Nassim Residential Development, Singapore (in progress)
Racecourse Masterplanning Competition, Singapore (competition entry)
Karawaci Masterplan, Tangerang, Indonesia
Shanghai Qingpu Masterplan, Shanghai
Prapanca Masterplan, South Jakarta
Founders' Memorial, Singapore (competition entry)
OCT 2nd Headquarters, Kunming (unbuilt)
OCT Headquarters, Shenzhen (competition entry)
Bukit Timah Integrated Development, Singapore (unbuilt)
ZTE Headquarters, Shenzhen (competition entry)
Hangzhou Future Green City (competition entry)
Vanke Headquarters, Shenzhen (competition entry)

Singapore Science Park Cluster 1, Singapore (competition entry)

2018
Meyer House, Singapore (in progress)
Forbes Residences, Perth (in progress)
Ascott Reit LYF, Co-Live Residences, One North, Singapore (in progress)
New Bridge Road Conserved Building — Additions and Alterations, Singapore (in progress)
Alila Villas Okinawa Masterplan, Okinawa, Japan (unbuilt)
Huacheng Taipei Residential, New Taipei City (unbuilt)
Prince Bay Shenzhen Competition (unbuilt)
OCT International Art and Cultural Centre Competition, Shenzhen (unbuilt)
World Expo Pavilion, Singapore Pavilion for World Expo 2020, Dubai
Vanke Group Headquarters Competition, Shenzhen (unbuilt)

2017
Singapore Institute of Technology (SIT) Campus — Plot 1, Punggol North (in progress)
Punggol Digital District, Singapore (in progress)
The Tre Ver Condominium, Singapore (in progress)
Rifle Range Road Park, Singapore (competition entry)
Mandai Eco-Accommodation, Singapore (competition entry)

2016
Design Orchard, Orchard Road, Singapore
E2C Campus, Redhill Road, Singapore
Punggol Creative Cluster & Learning Corridor Masterplan, Singapore

2015
Holland Village, Singapore (competition entry)
Market Street — Sky Forest City Tower, Singapore (competition entry)
The Rail Corridor, Singapore (competition entry)
Mandai Eco-Lodge, Singapore (competition entry)
Pan Pacific Orchard, Singapore (in progress)
Integrated Transport Hub, Jurong, Singapore (competition entry)

2014
Singapore Institute of Technology Masterplan, Singapore
Enabling Village, Singapore
Vanke Yun City, Shenzhen
Self-Sufficient City — Integrated New Town Masterplan, Jakarta (unbuilt)
443 Queen Street, Brisbane (in progress)
Liveability Blueprint for Tampines by Centre for Liveable Cities, MND, Singapore
Barangaroo South, Sydney (competition entry)
EDIS Masterplan — Tropical Urban Business Park, Penang (competition entry)

2013
The Hedberg, Hobart, Sky Green, Taichung

Extension to Crowne Plaza Hotel Changi Airport, Singapore
Alila Villas Uluwatu Additions, Bali (in progress)
Mixed-Use Development at Senopati, Indonesia (unbuilt)
Tea Bone Zen Mind, Singapore (unbuilt)
Geothermal Power Station, Biliran, Philippines (unbuilt)
Mixed-Use Development at Kemang Raya, Indonesia (unbuilt)
Community Park Station, Punggol, Singapore (competition entry)
Tengah New Town Masterplan, Singapore (competition entry)
Artillery Avenue Sentosa, Singapore (competition entry)
Kampung Admiralty, Singapore
NUS School of Design and Environment, Singapore (competition entry)
Orchard Road Presbyterian Church, Singapore (competition entry)
Gospel Light Christian Church, Singapore (competition entry)

2012
Alila Villas Uluwatu Suites, Bali (in progress)
The Park, Mumbai (in progress)
Rosewood Phuket Resort, Phuket
Neihu Office Tower, Taipei (unbuilt)
Henninger Turm, Frankfurt, Germany (competition entry)
Peruri Green, Jakarta (competition entry)
Silver Kris Lounges, Singapore (competition entry)

2011
Oasia Hotel Downtown, Singapore
Church of St Mary of the Angels: Phase Two, Singapore (in progress)
Mixed-Use Development at Raidung, Hyderabad (unbuilt)
Mixed-Use Development at Ophir Road, Singapore (unbuilt)
BRAC University, Dhaka (in progress)
Permeable Lattice City, Singapore (unbuilt)
Community Town Hub, Tampines, Singapore (competition entry)

2010
Ogilvy & Mather Office Fit-Out, Singapore
Capitol Theatre, Singapore (competition entry)
Student Housing for Singapore University of Technology & Design (competition entry)
32 Carpenter Street, Singapore
The Grove, Guangzhou
Industrial Development at Sungei Kadut Street 3, Singapore (unbuilt)
New Cuffe Parade, Mumbai (in progress)
Huaku Sky Garden, Taipei
Residential Development at Ardmore Park, Singapore (unbuilt)

2009
Space Asia Hub, Singapore
Cluny Park Extension, Singapore
46/47 North Canal Road, Singapore
Alila Villas Bintan, Indonesia (in progress)
Design 2050, Singapore (unbuilt)
Mixed-Use Development, Jaipur (unbuilt)

2008
House at Sukhumvit, Bangkok

Capitamall Tianfu, Chengdu
Resort at Salt Cay, Turks and Caicos Island (unbuilt)
School of Science and Technology, Singapore (competition entry)

2007
SkyVille @ Dawson, Singapore
Parkroyal on Pickering, Singapore
Sarang House, Singapore
National Art Gallery, Singapore (competition entry)
Offices at New Bridge Road, Singapore (unbuilt)
Resort at Cape Paradise, Phuket (unbuilt)
Silver Cliff, Sentosa, Singapore (unbuilt)

2006
The Pano, Bangkok
29 HongKong Street, Addition and Alteration, Singapore
Conserved Shophouse at Cairnhill Road, Singapore
Cicada Office, Singapore (completed)
Goodwood Residence, Singapore
InterContinental Hotel & Resort, Sanya, Hainan
Crowne Plaza Hotel Changi Airport, Singapore
Resort at Chiang Mai, Thailand (unbuilt)
Ginowan Hotel, Japan (unbuilt)
Addition and Alteration to Hyatt Regency, Johor Bahru (unbuilt)
Residential Development at 29 Leonie Hill, Singapore (unbuilt)
Gardens by the Bay, Singapore (competition entry)

2005
Hansar, Bangkok
School of the Arts, Singapore
Iluma, Singapore
Genexis Theatre, Fusionopolis, Singapore
Resort at Pattaya, Thailand (unbuilt)
Grand Formosa Regent, Taipei (unbuilt)
A12 Hotel, Taipei (unbuilt)
Apartments at Scotts Road, Singapore (unbuilt)
UNSW Asia, Singapore (competition entry)
Masterplan and Concept for Marina Bay Integrated Resort, Singapore (competition entry)

2004
The Hyde, Sydney
Wilkie Edge, Singapore
Masterplan for Resort and Villa at Emerald Bay, Phuket
Development Project at Hampshire Road, Singapore (unbuilt)
Singapore Association of the Visually Handicapped (unbuilt)
Tong Watt Road Development, Singapore (unbuilt)

2003
House at Cluny Park Singapore
NOMU, Singapore
The Met, Bangkok
Alila Villas Uluwatu, Bali
Newton Suites, Singapore
Masterplan for Resort at Pulau Rebak, Langkawi (unbuilt)
Commercial Development at Jalan Bangka Raya, Kemang Jakarta (unbuilt)
Freedom Park in Pretoria, South Africa (competition entry)

SMU Hostel, Singapore
(competition entry)

2002
Odeon Towers Extension, Singapore
Tan Quee Lan Suites
House at Leedon Park, Singapore
(unbuilt)
Alila Ubud Villas, Bali (unbuilt)
High–Rise Apartment at Grange
Garden, Singapore
Lasalle SIA College of the Arts,
Winstedt Road, Singapore
(competition entry)

2001
Conservation Shophouse at 175 Telok
Ayer Street, Singapore
House in Bukit Bayu, Kuala Lumpur
(unbuilt)
Bishopsgate Interiors (unbuilt)
Four Good Class Bungalows at
Belmont Road, Singapore (unbuilt)
Detached Houses at Cluny Road,
Singapore (unbuilt)
Queensland Gallery of Modern
Art, Brisbane (competition entry)
Duxton Plain Public Housing,
Singapore (competition entry)
Condominium at Claymore Road,
Singapore (competition entry)

2000
House at Rochalie Drive, Singapore
Three Houses at Berrima Road,
Singapore
Gilstead Brooks, Singapore
Bras Basah MRT Station, Singapore
Stadium MRT Station, Singapore
Terrace Villa, Kuala Lumpur (unbuilt)
Detached House at Sime Park Hill,
Singapore
Singapore Management University,
Victoria Street, Singapore
(competition entry)

1999
Chinese High School Boarding House,
Singapore
Church of St Mary of the Angels,
Singapore
House at Maple Avenue, Singapore
House at Hua Guan Avenue,
Singapore
1 Moulmein Rise, Singapore
Teneriffe Cluster Housing
Development (as 2BY4 Architects
in Association)
Pulai Springs Resort, Malaysia (unbuilt)
Residence at Poolai, Malaysia
(unbuilt)

1998
Black and White Bungalows at Mount
Pleasant, Singapore
Three Houses at Victoria Park Road,
Singapore
Interiors for Office at Keong Siak
Street, Singapore (completed)
Interior Fit–Out for Industrial and
Commercial Bank in Tianjin, China
Masterplan for Resort Hotel in
Republic of Maldives (unbuilt)
Eighteen Housing Units at Sanur, Bali,
Indonesia (unbuilt)
Residence at Jalan Arnap, Singapore
(unbuilt)

1997
Detached House at Jalan Seruling,
Singapore
Three Houses at Camborne Road,
Singapore

Condominium Development at Palm
Grove Avenue Singapore
House in Jakarta, Indonesia (unbuilt)

1996
Good Class Bungalow at Bishopsgate,
Singapore
Four Semi–Detached Houses at
Linden Drive, Singapore
Queen Astrid Park, Singapore
(unbuilt)
Goh Residence, Malaysia (unbuilt)
Hotel and Villa Development on Pulau
Bersah, Malaysia (unbuilt)
Town Houses in Jakarta (unbuilt)

1995
Conserved Shophouse at Emerald
Hill Road, Singapore
House at Merryn Road, Singapore
Masterplan for Resort and Spa at
Pulau Tengah, Malaysia (unbuilt)

1994
12 Houses at Watten Estate Road,
Singapore

Exhibitions

2019
'Future and the Arts' exhibition,
MORI Art Museum, Tokyo

2018
'In Search of Southeast Asia through
the M+ Collections' exhibition,
M+ Museum, West Kowloon,
Hong Kong
'Best High–Rises' exhibition,
Deutsches Architekturmuseum,
Frankfurt, Germany
'Best Tall Buildings' exhibition,
organized by Council on Tall
Buildings and Urban Habitat
(CTBUH), Chicago Architecture
Center, Chicago
'Garden City Mega City' exhibition,
Austin Central Library, Texas

2017
'Garden City Mega City' exhibition,
Museo de la Ciudad, Mexico City
'20 Under 45: The Third Edition'
exhibition, Urban Redevelopment
Authority, Singapore

2016
'Garden City Mega City' exhibition,
The Skyscraper Museum, New
York City
'Fragments of an Urban Future'
installation, 15th International
Venice Architecture Biennale,
Palazzo Bembo, Venice

2013
'Breathing Architecture' exhibition,
Mobile Museum–Seed Project,
Taipei

2012
'Breathing Architecture' exhibition,
Taichung INFO–BOX, Taichung

2011
'Breathing Architecture' exhibition,
Deutsches Architekturmuseum,
Frankfurt, Germany
'Water: Curse or Blessings!?'
exhibition, Aedes Gallery, Berlin

2009
'20 Under 45: The Next Generation'
exhibition, Urban Redevelopment
Authority, Singapore

2008
'Liebe Deine Stadt — Sayang
Singapore' exhibition, WOHA
Office, Singapore

2007
'WOHA Reflects' exhibition,
WOHAGA, Singapore

2006
'Exotic — More or Less' exhibition,
Aedes Gallery, Berlin
'Exotic — More or Less' exhibition,
Urban Redevelopment Authority,
Singapore

2005
'DesignMonth at Singapore Pavilion'
exhibition, World Expo Japan
'SingaporEdge' exhibition, organized
by DesignSingapore Council, London
'Second Nature' exhibition, Changi
Airport Terminal 2, Singapore
'WOHA' exhibition, WOHA Office,
Singapore

2004
9th International Venice Architecture
Biennale, Singapore Pavilion, Venice

1999
McDonald's exhibition, Singapore

Awards

2021
→ Kampung Admiralty, Singapore
President's Design Award —
Design of the Year. Awarded by
DesignSingapore Council and Urban
Redevelopment Authority
ULI Awards for Excellence: Asia
Pacific — Winner. Awarded by
Urban Land Institute

→ Sky Green, Taichung
CTBUH Best Tall Building Award —
Award of Excellence. In the 100–m
to 199–m height category, awarded
by Council on Tall Building & Urban
Habitat
CTBUH Best Tall Building Award —
Award of Excellence. In the
Residential/Hotel category,
awarded by Council on Tall
Buildings and Urban Habitat
Green Good Design Award —
Winner. Awarded by The Chicago
Athenaeum and The European
Centre for Architecture Art Design
and Urban Studies

2020
→ Kampung Admiralty, Singapore
Asia Pacific Leadership in Green
Building Awards — Shortlist.
Under the Leadership in Sustainable
Design and Performance
(Institutional) category, awarded by
World Green Building Council
International Urban Project Award
— shortlist. Organised by *Bauwelt
Berlin* and *WA World Architecture*
magazine, Beijing

→ Sky Green, Taichung
19th SIA Architectural Design Award
— Building of the Year. Awarded by
Singapore Institute of Architects
19th SIA Architectural Design Award
— Design Award. Awarded by
Singapore Institute of Architects
Good Design Award — Winner.
Awarded by The Chicago
Athenaeum and The European
Centre for Architecture Art Design
and Urban Studies
World Architecture Festival (China)
Awards — Excellent Design
Award winner. Awarded by World
Architecture Festival

2019
→ Design Orchard, Singapore
Good Design Award — Winner.
Awarded by The Chicago
Athenaeum and The European
Centre for Architecture Art Design
and Urban Studies

→ Enabling Village, Singapore
ARCASIA Awards for Architecture
— Mention. Under Category D
(Conservation Projects) category,
awarded by Architects Regional
Council Asia (ARCASIA)

→ Huaku Sky Garden, Taipei
Green Good Design Award —
Winner. Awarded by The Chicago
Athenaeum and The European
Centre for Architecture Art Design
and Urban Studies

→ Kampung Admiralty, Singapore
18th SIA Architectural Design
Awards — Design Award. Under the
Commercial (Mixed Development)
category, awarded by SIA
ARCASIA Awards for Architecture
— Mention. Under Category B-4
(Specialized Buildings) category,
awarded by Architects Regional
Council Asia (ARCASIA)
Best Tall Mixed-Use Building —
Winner. Awarded by Council on
Tall Buildings and Urban Habitat,
Chicago, Illinois
Green Good Design Award —
Winner. Awarded by The Chicago
Athenaeum and The European
Centre for Architecture Art Design
and Urban Studies
SGBC–BCA Sustainability Leadership
Awards — Design Award. Under
the Leadership in Sustainable
Design and Performance
(Institutional), awarded by
Singapore Green Building Council
and the Building and Construction
Authority, Singapore
Urban Habitat Award (Single–Site
Scale) — Winner. Awarded by
Council on Tall Buildings and Urban
Habitat, Chicago, Illinois

→ Parkroyal on Pickering, Singapore
SGBC–BCA Sustainability Leadership
Awards — Design Award. Under
the Leadership in Sustainable
Design and Performance
(Commercial), awarded by
Singapore Green Building Council
and the Building and Construction
Authority, Singapore

→ SkyVille @ Dawson, Singapore
ARCASIA Awards for Architecture

WOHA: NEW FORMS OF SUSTAINABLE ARCHITECTURE

— Mention. Under Category A–2 (Multiple Family Residential Complexes) category, awarded by Architects Regional Council Asia (ARCASIA)

2018

→ **Huaku Sky Garden, Taipei**

Good Design Award — Winner. Awarded by The Chicago Athenaeum and The European Centre for Architecture Art Design and Urban Studies

World Architecture Festival — Shortlisted. Under the Housing, Large Scale — Completed category, awarded by World Architecture Festival

→ **Kampung Admiralty, Singapore**

HDB Design Award — Winner. Under the Completed Project — Mixed Development category, awarded by Housing & Development Board

International Chapter Architecture Awards — Commendation for Commercial Architecture. Awarded by The Australian Institute of Architects

World Architecture Festival — Winner. Under the Mixed Use — Completed category, awarded by World Architecture Festival

World Architecture Festival — World Building of the Year. Awarded by World Architecture Festival

→ **Oasia Hotel Downtown, Singapore**

Best Tall Building Asia & Australasia — Winner. Awarded by Council on Tall Buildings and Urban Habitat, Chicago, Illinois

Best Tall Building Worldwide — Winner. Awarded by Council on Tall Buildings and Urban Habitat, Chicago, Illinois

President's Design Award — Design of the Year. Awarded by DesignSingapore Council and Urban Redevelopment Authority

Urban Habitat Award — Finalist. Awarded by Council on Tall Buildings and Urban Habitat, Chicago, Illinois

2017

→ **Enabling Village, Singapore**

Design for Asia Award — Grand Award with Special Mention. Awarded by Hong Kong Design Centre

→ **Floating University: BRAC University Campus, Dhaka**

LafargeHolcim Awards Asia Pacific — Bronze Winner. Awarded by LafargeHolcim Foundation for Sustainable Construction

→ **Kampung Admiralty, Singapore**

NParks Skyrise Greenery Award — Winner, Outstanding and Excellence Award. Awarded by National Parks Board, Singapore

→ **Oasia Hotel Downtown, Singapore**

17th SIA Architectural Design Awards — Design Award. Under the Commercial (Mixed Development) category, awarded by SIA

17th SIA Architectural Design Awards — Building of the Year.

Under the Commercial (Mixed Development) category, awarded by SIA

2017–18 ULI Global Awards for Excellence — Winner. Awarded by Urban Land Institute

Emporis Skyscraper Awards — 3rd Place. Awarded by Emporis

Good Design Award — Winner. Awarded by The Chicago Athenaeum and The European Centre for Architecture Art Design and Urban Studies

Green Good Design Award — Winner. Awarded by The Chicago Athenaeum and The European Centre for Architecture Art Design and Urban Studies

International Chapter Architecture Awards — Commended. Under the Commercial Architecture category, awarded by Australian Institute of Architects

NParks Skyrise Greenery Award — Winner, Excellence Award. Awarded by National Parks Board, Singapore

→ **SkyVille @ Dawson, Singapore**

Green Good Design Award — Winner. Awarded by The Chicago Athenaeum and The European Centre for Architecture Art Design and Urban Studies

International Chapter Architecture Awards — Winner. Under the Residential Architecture — Multiple Housing category, awarded by Australian Institute of Architects

→ **Wong Mun Summ and Richard Hassell — WOHA**

Designer of the Year Asia. Awarded by Maison&Objet

2016

→ **Church of St Mary of the Angels, Singapore**

World Architecture Festival — Finalist. Under the Mixed-Use (Completed) category, awarded by World Architecture Festival

→ **Enabling Village, Singapore**

16th SIA Architectural Design Awards — Design Award. Under Special Categories, awarded by SIA

BCA Universal Design Award — Winner (Platinum). Awarded by Building and Construction Authority, Singapore

President's Design Award — Design of the Year. Awarded by DesignSingapore Council and Urban Redevelopment Authority

→ **Floating University: BRAC University Campus, Dhaka**

World Architecture Festival — Finalist. Under the Education (Future Projects) category, awarded by World Architecture Festival

→ **Goodwood Residence, Singapore**

16th SIA Architectural Design Awards — Honourable Mention. Under the Residential Projects category, awarded by SIA

Green Good Design Award — Winner. Awarded by The Chicago Athenaeum and The European Centre for Architecture Art Design and Urban Studies

→ **Kampung Admiralty, Singapore**

World Architecture Festival — Winner. Under the Commercial Mixed-Use (Future Projects) category, awarded by World Architecture Festival

→ **Parkroyal on Pickering, Singapore**

16th SIA Architectural Design Awards — Design Award. Under the Commercial Projects category, awarded by SIA

→ **SkyVille @ Dawson, Singapore**

16th SIA Architectural Design Awards — Design Award. Under the Residential Projects category, awarded by SIA

BCA Universal Design Award — Winner (Platinum). Awarded by Building and Construction Authority, Singapore

Good Design Award — Winner. Awarded by The Chicago Athenaeum and The European Centre for Architecture Art Design and Urban Studies

HDB Design Award — Winner. Under the Completed Project — Housing category, awarded by Housing & Development Board

President's Design Award — Design of the Year. Awarded by DesignSingapore Council and Urban Redevelopment Authority

The International Highrise Award — Finalist. Awarded by City of Frankfurt, Deutsches Architekturmuseum and DekaBank

World Architecture Festival — Finalist. Under the Housing (Completed) category, awarded by World Architecture Festival

→ **Space Asia Hub, Singapore**

16th SIA Architectural Design Awards — Honourable Mention. Under Special Categories, awarded by SIA

→ **Vertical Stacked City, Shenzhen**

World Architecture Festival — Finalist. Under the Office (Future Projects) category, awarded by World Architecture Festival

2015

→ **48 North Canal Road, Singapore**

Building of the Year Award — Winner. Under the Offices category, awarded by ArchDaily

Green Good Design Award — Winner. Awarded by The Chicago Athenaeum and The European Centre for Architecture Art Design and Urban Studies

→ **Goodwood Residence, Singapore**

WAN Asia Award (Residential) — Winner. Awarded by World Architecture News.com

→ **Kampung Admiralty, Singapore**

HDB Innovative Design Award — Winner. Under To-Be-Built Mixed Development category, awarded by Housing & Development Board, Singapore

Landscape Excellence Assessment Framework (LEAF) — Outstanding Project. Awarded by National Parks Board

→ **Parkroyal on Pickering, Singapore**

Landscape Excellence Assessment Framework (LEAF) — Outstanding Project. Awarded by National Parks Board

MIPIM Asia Awards — Gold Winner. Under the Best Hotel and Tourism Development category, awarded by Reed MIDEM

Urban Habitat Award — Winner. Awarded by Council on Tall Buildings and Urban Habitat, Chicago, Illinois

→ **SkyVille @ Dawson, Singapore**

Landscape Excellence Assessment Framework (LEAF) — Certificate of Recognition. Awarded by National Parks Board

Universal Design Mark Award — Gold Plus (Design). Under Residential (New) category, awarded by Building and Construction Authority

2014

→ **Goodwood Residence, Singapore**

Best of Year Awards — Honoree. Under the Residential (Other) category, awarded by *Interior Design* magazine

Good Design Award — Winner. Awarded by The Chicago Athenaeum and The European Centre for Architecture Art Design and Urban Studies

World Architecture Festival — Shortlisted. Under the Housing (Completed) category, awarded by World Architecture Festival

→ **Parkroyal on Pickering, Singapore**

Design for Asia Awards — Grand Award. Awarded by Hong Kong Design Centre

Green Good Design Award — Winner. Awarded by The Chicago Athenaeum and The European Centre for Architecture Art Design and Urban Studies

Iconic Awards — Best of Best Winner. Under the Architecture (Public) category, awarded by German Design Council

International Architecture Awards — Winner. Under the Commercial category, awarded by Australian Institute of Architects

2013

→ **48 North Canal Road, Singapore**

URA Architectural Heritage Award — Winner. Under Category B — Integrated 'Old and New' Developments, awarded by URA

→ **Newton Suites, Singapore**

Asia Pacific Property Awards — Highly Commended. Under the Best Apartment category, awarded by the International Property Awards

Asia Pacific Property Awards — Highly Commended. Under the Best Residential High Rise Development category, awarded by the International Property Awards

→ **Parkroyal on Pickering, Singapore**

9th Annual Hospitality Design Awards — Finalist. Under the

Hotel (Luxury/Upscale) category, awarded by *Hospitality Design* magazine

Best of Year Awards — Winner. Under the Hotel (Public Space) category, awarded by *Interior Design* magazine

CTBUH Best Tall Building Awards (Asia and Australasia) — Finalist. Awarded by Council on Tall Buildings and Urban Habitat

Gold Key Award for Excellence in Hospitality Design — Honourable Mention. Under Best Hotel — Luxury / Upscale category, awarded by International Hotel / Motel & Restaurant Show

Good Design Award — Winner. Awarded by The Chicago Athenaeum and The European Centre for Architecture Art Design and Urban Studies

INSIDE Festival — Winner. Under Hotels (Interior) category, awarded by INSIDE Festival

NParks Skyrise Greenery Award — Winner, Outstanding Skyrise Greenery Project Award. Awarded by National Parks Board, Singapore

President's Design Award — Design of the Year. Awarded by DesignSingapore Council and Urban Redevelopment Authority

WAN Hotel of the Year Award — Winner. Awarded by World Architecture News.com

World Architecture Festival — Finalist. Under the Hotels (Large) category, awarded by World Architecture Festival

World Architecture Festival — Finalist. Under the Office category, awarded by World Architecture Festival

→ Ogilvy & Mather Office Fit-Out, Singapore

Green Good Design Award — Winner. Awarded by The Chicago Athenaeum and The European Centre for Architecture Art Design and Urban Studies

→ Sarang House, Singapore

Green Good Design Award — Winner. Awarded by The Chicago Athenaeum and The European Centre for Architecture Art Design and Urban Studies

→ Space Asia Hub, Singapore

Green Good Design Award — Winner. Awarded by The Chicago Athenaeum and The European Centre for Architecture Art Design and Urban Studies

→ The Met, Bangkok, Thailand

Aga Khan Award for Architecture — Shortlisted. Awarded by Aga Khan Trust for Culture

2012

→ Hansar, Bangkok

Green Good Design Award — Winner. Awarded by The Chicago Athenaeum and The European Centre for Architecture Art Design and Urban Studies

→ InterContinental Sanya Resort, Hainan

Good Design is Good Business China

Awards — Merit Award Winner. Awarded by *Architectural Record* magazine, USA

Green Good Design Award — Winner. Awarded by The Chicago Athenaeum and The European Centre for Architecture Art Design and Urban Studies

→ Space Asia Hub, Singapore

Best of Year Awards — Honoree. Awarded by *Interior Design* magazine

URA Architectural Heritage Award — Winner. Under Category B — Integrated 'Old and New' Developments, awarded by URA

World Architecture Festival — Finalist. Under the New and Old category, awarded by World Architecture Festival

→ Wilkie Edge, Singapore

Green Good Design Award — Winner. Awarded by The Chicago Athenaeum and The European Centre for Architecture Art Design and Urban Studies

2011

→ Alila Villas Uluwatu, Bali

International Architecture Award — Winner. Awarded by The Chicago Athenaeum and The European Centre for Architecture Art Design and Urban Studies

RIBA International Awards — Winner. Awarded by Royal Institute of British Architects

ULI Awards for Excellence: Asia Pacific — Finalist. Awarded by Urban Land Institute

→ Bras Basah MRT Station, Singapore

International Architecture Award — Winner. Awarded by The Chicago Athenaeum and The European Centre for Architecture Art Design and Urban Studies

→ Hansar, Bangkok

CTBUH Best Tall Building Award — Finalist. Awarded by Council on Tall Buildings and Urban Habitat

→ InterContinental Sanya Resort, Hainan

'Best New Resort in China'. Awarded by TTG China Travel Awards

'Best Resort Hotel'. Awarded by 'Gold List Award of China Tourism'

Best of Year Awards — Winner. Under the Hospitality: Hotel: Large category, awarded by *Interior Design* magazine

'China's Top 10 Most Popular New Opening Hotels of 2011'. Awarded by '8th Golden-Pillow Award of China Hotels'

Gold Key Award for Excellence in Hospitality Design — Winner. Under Best Hotel Design–Resort category, awarded by International Hotel / Motel & Restaurant Show

Gold Key Award for Excellence in Hospitality Design — Winner. Under the Spa category, awarded by International Hotel / Motel & Restaurant Show

'The Best Resort in China'. Awarded by *World Traveler* magazine

---

World Architecture Festival — Finalist. Under the Holiday category, awarded by World Architecture Festival

→ Ogilvy & Mather Office Fit-Out, Singapore

Best of Year Awards — Honoree. Under the Office: Large category, awarded by *Interior Design* magazine

→ School of the Arts, Singapore

Best of Year Awards — Winner. Under the Educational — International category, awarded by *Interior Design* magazine

Green Good Design Award — Winner. Awarded by The Chicago Athenaeum and The European Centre for Architecture Art Design and Urban Studies

International Architecture Award — Winner. Awarded by The Chicago Athenaeum and The European Centre for Architecture Art Design and Urban Studies

President's Design Award — Design of the Year. Awarded by DesignSingapore Council and Urban Redevelopment Authority

RIBA International Awards — Winner. Awarded by Royal Institute of British Architects

The Jørn Utzon Award for International Architecture — Winner. Awarded by Australian Institute of Architects

→ The Met, Bangkok

Green Good Design Award — Winner. Awarded by The Chicago Athenaeum and The European Centre for Architecture Art Design and Urban Studies

International Architecture Award — Winner. Awarded by The Chicago Athenaeum and The European Centre for Architecture Art Design and Urban Studies

RIBA Lubetkin Prize — Winner. Awarded by Royal Institute of British Architects

2010

→ Alila Villas Uluwatu, Bali

10th SIA Architectural Design Awards — Honourable Mention. Under the Commercial Projects category, awarded by SIA

10th SIA Architectural Design Awards — Honourable Mention. Under the Interior Architecture category, awarded by SIA

6th Annual Hospitality Design Awards — Finalist. Under the Resort category, awarded by *Hospitality Design* magazine

Asia Pacific Interior Design Awards — Bronze Winner. Under the Hotel Space category, awarded by Hong Kong Interior Design Association

Asia–Pacific Interior Design Biennial Awards — Winner. Under Best Aesthetics Conception Award, awarded by Asia Pacific Federation of Architects/Interior Designers

Asia–Pacific Interior Design Biennial Awards — Winner. Under Best Design Client Award, awarded by Asia Pacific Federation of Architects/Interior Designers

---

Asia–Pacific Interior Design Biennial Awards — Winner. Under Outstanding Design Award, awarded by Asia Pacific Federation of Architects/Interior Designers

BCI Green Design Award — Green Leadership Award Winner. Under the Commercial category, awarded by BCI Asia Construction Information Pte. Ltd.

Design for Asia Award — Bronze Award. Awarded by Hong Kong Design Centre

Earth-Minded Awards — First Place Winner. Under Hospitality Projects, awarded by *Hospitality Design* magazine and the American Society of Interior Designers

Gold Key Award for Excellence in Hospitality Design — Winner. Under the Best Hotel Design category, awarded by International Hotel / Motel & Restaurant

Good Design Award — Winner. Awarded by The Chicago Athenaeum and The European Centre for Architecture Art Design and Urban Studies

National Commendation for International Architecture — Commended. Awarded by Australian Institute of Architects

ULI Awards for Excellence: Asia Pacific — Finalist. Awarded by Urban Land Institute

World Architecture Festival — World Holiday Building of the Year. Under the Holiday category, awarded by World Architecture Festival

→ Bras Basah MRT Station, Singapore

10th SIA Architectural Design Awards — Design Award. Under the Industrial, Transport & Infrastructure Projects category, awarded by SIA

Design for Asia Award — Bronze Award. Awarded by Hong Kong Design Centre

Land Transport Excellence Awards — Winner. Under the Best Design Infrastructure, Project Partner Category, awarded by Land Transport Authority, Singapore

National Award for International Architecture — Winner. Awarded by Australian Institute of Architects

RIBA International Awards — Winner. Awarded by Royal Institute of British Architects

→ Genexis Theatre, Singapore

Asia–Pacific Interior Design Biennial Awards — Winner. Under Best Commercial Space Award, awarded by Asia Pacific Federation of Architects / Interior Designers

→ Iluma, Singapore

World Architecture Festival — Finalist. Under the Shopping (Including Mixed Use) category, awarded by World Architecture Festival

→ InterContinental Sanya Resort, Hainan

'Best New Opening Resort'. Awarded by Golden Chair Award of China MICE Industry

'Best Newly-Opened Hotel in Greater China Region'. Awarded by *Travel & Leisure* magazine

→ LTA Circle Line Competition, Singapore

BCA Construction Excellence Awards. Building and Construction Authority

→ Newton Suites, Singapore

MIPIM Awards — Finalist. Under the Residential Developments category, awarded by Reed MIDEM

ULI Awards for Excellence: Asia Pacific — Winner. Awarded by Urban Land Institute

→ NOMU, Singapore

10th SIA Architectural Design Awards — Honourable Mention. Under the Special categories — Retrofitting, awarded by SIA

→ Parkroyal on Pickering, Singapore

World Architecture Festival — Finalist. Under the Future Projects (Commercial) category, awarded by World Architecture Festival

→ School of the Arts, Singapore

World Architecture Festival — World Learning Building of the Year. Under the Learning category, awarded by World Architecture Festival

→ SkyVille @ Dawson, Singapore

HDB Innovative Design Award — Winner. Under To-Be-Built category, awarded by Housing & Development Board, Singapore

→ Stadium MRT Station, Singapore

International Architecture Award — Winner. Awarded by The Chicago Athenaeum and The European Centre for Architecture Art Design and Urban Studies

President's Design Award — Design of the Year. Awarded by DesignSingapore Council and Urban Redevelopment Authority

→ The Hyde, Sydney

UDIA NSW Awards for Excellence — High Density Development Award Winner. Awarded by Urban Development Institute of Australia (UDIA) New South Wales

→ The Met, Bangkok

BCI Green Design Award — Green Leadership Award Winner. Under the Residential Architecture — Multiple Houses category, awarded by BCI Asia Construction Information Pte. Ltd.

RIBA International Awards — Winner. Awarded by Royal Institute of British Architects

The International Highrise Award — Winner. Awarded by City of Frankfurt, Deutsches Architekturmuseum and DekaBank

The Jørn Utzon Award for International Architecture — Winner. Awarded by Australian Institute of Architects

→ The Pano, Bangkok

Emporis Skyscraper Awards — 4th Place Finalist. Awarded by Emporis

→ WOHA, Singapore

SIA-Getz Architecture Prize for Emergent Architecture — Winner. Awarded by Singapore Institute of Architects and Getz Brothers

2009

→ Alila Villas Uluwatu, Bali

Best of Year Awards — Winner. Under the Hospitality: Hotel-Resort category, awarded by Interior Design magazine

Green Good Design Award — Winner. Awarded by The Chicago Athenaeum and The European Centre for Architecture Art Design and Urban Studies

→ Bras Basah MRT Station, Singapore

World Architecture Festival — World Transport Building of the Year. Under the Transport category, awarded by World Architecture Festival

→ Conserved Shophouse at Cairnhill Road, Singapore

URA Architectural Heritage Award — Winner. Under category B — Integrated Old and New Development, awarded by URA

→ Crowne Plaza Changi Airport, Singapore

3rd LIAS Awards for Excellence — Silver Winner. Awarded by Landscape Industry Association (Singapore)

Design & Engineering Safety Excellence Awards, Merit Award, Commercial Category. Awarded by Building and Construction Authority

ULI Awards for Excellence: Asia Pacific — Winner. Awarded by Urban Land Institute

→ Genexis Theatre, Singapore

Best of Year Awards — Winner. Under the Institutional category, awarded by Interior Design magazine

President's Design Award — Design of the Year. Awarded by DesignSingapore Council and Urban Redevelopment Authority

World Architecture Festival — Finalist. Under the Interiors and Fit-Out category, awarded by World Architecture Festival

→ LTA Circle Line Competition, Singapore

Design and Engineering Safety Excellence Awards. Awarded by Building and Construction Authority

→ Newton Suites, Singapore

3rd LIAS Awards for Excellence — Gold Winner. Awarded by Landscape Industry Association (Singapore)

FIABCI Prix d'Excellence Awards — First Runner Up. Under the Residential Category, awarded by The International Real Estate Federation

Green Good Design Award — Winner. Awarded by The Chicago Athenaeum and The European Centre for Architecture Art Design and Urban Studies

International Architecture Award — Winner. Awarded by The Chicago Athenaeum: Museum of Architecture and Design and The European Centre for Architecture Art Design and Urban Studies

MIPIM Asia Awards — Winner. Under the Residential Developments category, awarded by Reed MIDEM

ULI Awards for Excellence: Asia Pacific — Finalist. Awarded by Urban Land Institute

→ The Met, Bangkok

CTBUH Best Tall Building Award — Finalist. Awarded by Council on Tall Buildings and Urban Habitat

Emporis Skyscraper Awards — Bronze Award Winner. Awarded by Emporis

President's Design Award — Design of the Year. Awarded by DesignSingapore Council and Urban Redevelopment Authority

World Architecture Festival — World Housing Development of the Year. Under the Housing category, awarded by World Architecture Festival

2008

→ Crowne Plaza Changi Airport, Singapore

9th SIA Architectural Design Awards — Honourable Mention. Under the Residential Projects category, awarded by SIA

Cityscape Asia Real Estate Awards — Best Developer. Under the Residential Built category, awarded by Cityscape Asia

Development of the Year — Winner. Awarded by Hotel Investment Conference Asia Pacific (HICAP)

World's Best Airport Hotels — Finalist. Awarded by ForbesTraveler.com

→ Newton Suites, Singapore

Award for International Architecture — Winner. Awarded by Australian Institute of Architects

CTBUH Best Tall Building Award — Nominated. Awarded by Council on Tall Buildings and Urban Habitat

Design for Asia Award — Gold Award. Awarded by Hong Kong Design Centre

Emirates Glass LEAF Awards — Finalist. Under the Residential Building of the Year — Multiple Building Level category, awarded by the Leading European Architects Forum

President's Design Award — Honourable Mention. Awarded by DesignSingapore Council and Urban Redevelopment Authority

SIA-NParks Skyrise Greenery Awards — Design Award. Awarded by SIA and National Parks Board, Singapore

The International Highrise Award — Finalist. Awarded by City of Frankfurt, Deutsches Architekturmuseum and DekaBank

World Architecture Festival — Finalist. Under the Home, Housing Category, awarded by World Architecture Festival

→ Stadium MRT Station, Singapore

9th SIA Architectural Design Awards — Design Award. Under the Industrial, Transport & Infrastructure Projects category, awarded by SIA

Award for International Architecture — Winner. Awarded by Australian Institute of Architects

World Architecture Festival — Finalist. Under the Transport category, awarded by World Architecture Festival

→ Wong Mun Summ and Richard Hassell — WOHA

President's Design Award — Designer of the Year. Awarded by DesignSingapore Council and Urban Redevelopment Authority

2007

→ 1 Moulmein Rise, Singapore

Aga Khan Award for Architecture — Award Winner. Awarded by Aga Khan Trust for Culture

President's Design Award — Design of the Year. Awarded by DesignSingapore Council and Urban Redevelopment Authority

→ Alila Villas Uluwatu, Bali

MIPIM Architectural Review Future Project Awards — Commended. Under the Retail & Leisure category, awarded by The Architectural Review

→ Church of St Mary of the Angels, Singapore

The Kenneth F. Brown Asia Pacific Culture and Architecture Design Award — Honourable Mention. Awarded by School of Architecture

→ Gilstead Brooks, Singapore

President's Design Award — Honourable Mention. Awarded by DesignSingapore Council and Urban Redevelopment Authority

→ Newton Suites, Singapore

Emporis Skyscraper Awards — Silver Award Winner. Awarded by Emporis

2006

→ 1 Moulmein Rise, Singapore

ARCASIA Awards for Architecture 2005-2006 — Special Recognition. Under Category A-2: Multiple-Family Residential, awarded by ARCASIA

→ Church of St Mary of the Angels, Singapore

President's Design Award — Design of the Year. Awarded by DesignSingapore Council and Urban Redevelopment Authority

→ Gilstead Brooks, Singapore

8th SIA Architectural Design Awards — Design Award. Under the Cluster Housing category, awarded by SIA

Asian Habitat Award for Planning and Designing — Winner. Awarded by Asian Habitat Society

→ House at Rochalie Drive, Singapore

ARCASIA Awards for Architecture 2005—2006 — Gold Medal. Under Category A-1: Single-Family Residential, awarded by ARCASIA

RAIA National Awards — Joint Award Winner. Under The RAIA International Award, awarded by RAIA

→ Odeon Towers Extension, Singapore

8th SIA Architectural Design Awards — Honourable Mention. Under the Shopping Centres category, awarded by SIA

→ **Tan Quee Lan Suites, Singapore**
8th SIA Architectural Design Awards — Honourable Mention. Under the Mixed Developments category, awarded by SIA

AR Awards for Emerging Architecture — Honourable Mention. Awarded by *The Architecture Review*

URA Architectural Heritage Award — Winner. Under Category B — Integrated Old and New Developments, awarded by URA

→ **The Met, Bangkok**
Asian Habitat Award for Planning and Designing — Winner. Awarded by Asian Habitat Society

MIPIM Architectural Review Future Project Awards — Winner. Under the Tall Buildings category, awarded by *The Architectural Review*

→ **Three Houses at Victoria Park Road, Singapore**
International Architecture Award. Awarded by The Chicago Athenaeum: Museum of Architecture and Design

→ **WOHA, Singapore**
ARCASIA Awards for Architecture 2005—2006 — Overall Commendation Award. Awarded by ARCASIA

2005

→ **1 Moulmein Rise, Singapore**
FIABCI Prix d'Excellence — Award Winner. Under the Residential category, awarded by International Real Estate Federation

→ **Duxton Plain Public Housing Development, Singapore**
MIPIM Architectural Review Future Project Awards — Highly Commended. Under the Residential category, awarded by *The Architectural Review*

→ **Gilstead Brooks, Singapore**
Cityscape Architectural Review Awards, Dubai — Award Winner. Under the Residential category, awarded by Cityscape and *The Architectural Review*

→ **School of the Arts, Singapore**
Singapore Arts School Competition — Winner. Awarded by Ministry of Information, Communications & the Arts

→ **UNSW Asia, Singapore**
UNSW Asia (Singapore), Round 1, Limited Architectural Competition — Merit Award. Awarded by University of New South Wales, Australia

2004

→ **1 Moulmein Rise, Singapore**
7th SIA Architectural Design Awards — Award Winner. Under the Residential Projects/Apartments & Condominiums category, awarded by SIA

ar+d Awards — Commended.

Awarded by *The Architectural Review*

Cityscape Architectural Review Awards, Dubai — Commended. Under the Residential Building category, awarded by Cityscape and *The Architectural Review*

→ **Church of St Mary of the Angels, Singapore**
7th SIA Architectural Design Awards — Award Winner. Under the Institutional Projects/Religious Buildings category, awarded by SIA

7th SIA Architectural Design Awards — Award Winner. Under the Interior Design/Commercial category, awarded by SIA

9th SIA–ICI Colour Awards — Gold Award. Under the Architecture category, awarded by SIA

9th SIA–ICI Colour Awards — Gold Award. Under the Interior category, awarded by SIA

International Prize Dedalo Minosse for Commissioning a Building, Italy — Highly Commended. Organized by ALA — Assoarchitetti, Vicenza, Italy

→ **Conserved Shophouse at 175 Telok Ayer Street, Singapore**
9th SIA–ICI Colour Awards — Silver Award. Under the Conservation category, awarded by SIA

Young Entrepreneur of the Year Award. Awarded by Australian Chamber of Commerce, Singapore

→ **Conserved Shophouse at Emerald Hill Road, Singapore**
ARCASIA Awards for Architecture — Gold Award. Under the Conservation Projects category, awarded by ARCASIA

→ **House at Hua Guan Avenue, Singapore**
7th SIA Architectural Design Awards — Honourable Mention. Under the Residential Projects/Semi–Detached Houses category, awarded by SIA

→ **House at Merryn Road, Singapore**
ARCASIA Awards for Architecture — Honourable Mention. Under the Residential Projects category, awarded by ARCASIA

→ **House at Rochalie Drive, Singapore**
7th SIA Architectural Design Awards — Honourable Mention. Under the Residential Projects/Individual Houses category, awarded by SIA

9th SIA–ICI Colour Awards — Gold Award. Under the Architecture category, awarded by SIA

→ **Odeon Towers Extension, Singapore**
9th SIA–ICI Colour Awards — Bronze Award. Under the Architecture category, awarded by SIA

→ **Teneriffe Cluster Housing Development (as 2BY4 Architects in Association), Singapore**
7th SIA Architectural Design Awards — Honourable Mention. Under the A5 Cluster Housing category, awarded by SIA

→ **Three Houses at Berrima Road, Singapore**

7th SIA Architectural Design Awards — Honourable Mention. Under the Residential Projects/Individual Houses category, awarded by SIA

2003

→ **Conserved Shophouse at 175 Telok Ayer Street, Singapore**
URA Architectural Heritage Awards. Awarded by Urban Redevelopment Authority

→ **House at Maple Avenue, Singapore**
4th SIA Micro Design Awards — Bronze Award. Under the Internal Building Components category, awarded by SIA

4th SIA Micro Design Awards — Silver Award. Under the Roof Structure category, awarded by SIA

→ **House at Rochalie Drive, Singapore**
Architecture + Cityscape Awards, Dubai — Highly Commended. Under the Housing and Residential category, awarded by Cityscape

→ **Three Houses at Berrima Road, Singapore**
4th SIA Micro Design Awards — Bronze Award. Under the Roof Structure category, awarded by SIA

2002

→ **Duxton Plain Public Housing Development, Singapore**
Duxton Plain Public Housing International Architectural Design Competition — Merit Prize. Awarded by URA

→ **Three Houses at Victoria Park Road, Singapore**
World Architectural Awards — Finalist. Awarded by World Architecture

2001

→ **'Beyond the Golden Arches' — Exhibition at the National Museum, Singapore**
6th SIA Architectural Design Award — Honourable Mention. Under the Interior Design — Commercial category, awarded by SIA

→ **Conserved Shophouse at Emerald Hill Road, Singapore**
6th SIA Architectural Design Award — Honourable Mention. Under the Conservation category, awarded by SIA

→ **Four Semi–Detached Houses at Linden Drive, Singapore**
6th SIA Architectural Design Award — Honourable Mention. Under the Terrace/Semi–Detached Houses category, awarded by SIA

→ **House at Merryn Road, Singapore**
6th SIA Architectural Design Award — Honourable Mention. Under the Interior Design — Residential category, awarded by SIA

→ **Three Houses at Victoria Park Road, Singapore**
6th SIA Architectural Design Award — Winner. Under the Individual Houses category, awarded by SIA

The SIA–ICI Colour Awards — Silver

Award. Under the Architecture category, awarded by SIA

2000

→ **LTA Circle Line Competition, Singapore**
LTA Marina Line Boulevard Station Design Competition, Singapore — First Prize. Awarded by Land Transport Authority

LTA Marina Line Museum Station Design Competition, Singapore — First Prize. Awarded by Land Transport Authority

→ **Singapore Management University Competition, Singapore**
SMU Urban Design Competition — Honourable Mention. Awarded by Singapore Management University

1999

→ **Conserved Shophouse at Emerald Hill Road, Singapore**
Royal Australian Institute of Architects International Award. Awarded by RAIA

1995

→ **House at Meyer Road, Singapore**
Asia Pacific Interior Design Award, Hong Kong

Staff

Founding Directors
Wong Mun Summ
Richard Hassell

Directors
Esther Soh Hui Sim
Pearl Chee Siew Choo
Chan Ee Mun
Sim Choon Heok
Alina Yeo Hwee Hua
Schirin Taraz-Breinholt
Phua Hong Wei
Darren Chen Jingzhi

Senior Associates
Mappaudang Ridwan Saleh
Goh Soon Kim
Herbert Salim
Adithya Rangharajan
Eng Wang Kwoon
Goh Hui Hoon

Associates
Sofwan
Chang Chee Choon
Dominic John Broadhurst
Oscar Goldron Korintus
Heffrence Teow Hai Png

Specialist Associates
Jose Nixon Sicat Guiao
Justina Tan Kheng Jun
Christina Ong Eng
Kwong Lay Lay
Serena Khor Li Ling
Evelyn Ng Chwee Hwa

Collaborators
Abdullah Bin Hashim, Adell Lesly Vass, Aimee Melissa Lucy Eves, Alan Lai Niap Kiun, Alan Lau Kor Loong, Alen Low Chan Foong, Alen Nikolovski, Alex Tan Cheng Huat, Alvin Oh Szu Chuang, Amanda Chng Kai Lin, Amber Dar Wagh, Amelia Diane Dass, Amod Subhash Tikhe, Anapat Chanadisai, Andre Kumar Alexander, Andrew MacLennan, Andrew Thornton Jones, Ang Chow Hwee, Anthony Wang Weixian, Anna Reidy Miss, Antonius Richard Rusli, Arbenz Christina, Arlinda Hapsawardhani Tresnadharana, Arthur Gunawan, Ayutt Mahasom, Babud Csaba, Bala Ecknaathh, Balaiyan Sivakumar, Barcoma Jbrien Cezar, Bashirul Mughni, Ben Redmond, Benita Tan Shixin, Benjamin Chi, Benjamin Chong Mun Choen, Bernard Lee Kwee Jie, Bianca Isabel Sarthou Mateo, Bibi See Geok Luan, Billy Novia Prima, Burapa Prommul, Caroline Victoria, Caroline Wongsosaputro, Cecilia Cristina C Castro, Chan Hui Wom, Cheah Poon Kwan, Cheerful Lin, Chen Pengfeng, Chen Qisen, Chen Shunann, Chen Zebin, Cheng Xin Wei Julian, Cherry Lim Chua, Cheryl Rabiah Yunus, Chew Yi Tian (Chloe), Chiang Zhi Han Kenneth, Chitdanai Chatchawanwong, Chok Jia Jun, Chou Mei, Chris Lohavaritanon, Christina Chng Yi Li, Christopher Browne, Christopher Wijatno, Chua Gong Yao, Chung Gyeong Oh, Chung Weixian, Craig Harvey Sheppard, Crystal Heng Suet Teng, Cynthia Liau Siao Lin, Cynthia Lim Mei Lin, Daniel Fung Khai Meng, Daisy Ong Kim Yun, Daniel James Laster, Daniel Tan Guan Zhong, Daryl Venpin, Dechatiwat Tanakrit, Declan Liam Reilly, Dela Cruz Al Perry Warren, Dennis Edward Radtke Jr, Dennis Kwek Zhanhao, Dennis Piasan Formalejo, Derek Tan Soong Yi, Desmond Ong, Dharmaraj Subramaniam, Donovan Soon Choon Siong, Edlyn Chong Siew Ling, Edric Choo Poo Liang, Edrick Bryan Perez Paguio, Eduardo Banaag Franco Jr., Elavarasi Rajapackiyam, Eleonora Estrella, Elizabeth Danielle Hardie, Elizabeth Michael Regina, Ellaine Victorio Ponce, Elvin T Alcata, Eow Wan Lin, Eric Dimitri Barthole, Erwin Sukamto, Etienne Vétillart, Evelyn, Evi Syariffudin, Faith Lim Rui En, Fandel Yannis, Fang Jing, Fann Zhi Jian, Federico Diego Valdivieso, Francis Goh Muk Hsiung, Fu Yingzi, Gabriella Patai, Gan Chien Huey, George Fung Kok Joo, Gerald Norman Richardson, Germain Goh Hui Mei, Gigih Nalendra, Girish Waman Kuwalekar, Gladys Wong Lok Yan, Go Marlon Agluba, Goh Chee Hou, Goh Kai Shien, Goh Shu En, Sarah, Graham Robert Hogg, Guo Bisheng, Gwee Tong Mui, Hannes Juergen Hofmann, Han Jeongwon, Hatch Gillian Mary, Helen Cheng, Helen Liu Yan, He HanChao, Hendriko Teguh, Heng Cheng Sin, Henri Tung Kwok Wah, Hermijanto Johan, Ho Chan Ping Chris, Ho Soo Ying, Hong Feng Lin, Huang Yue, Ian Malcolm Donlan, Ikje Cheon, Indra Pramana, Ingyin Kay Thi, Iyan Darmaja Mulyadi, Jacelyn Fooh, Jacquelyn Lee, Jadesupa Pipatsuporn, Jain Renee Cecilia, James Dale Bautista Miranda, Janita Han Pei Ling, Jane Kung, Janet Tan Mui Wah, Jascha Oakes, Jason Men Cheng Feng, Jason Tan Hong Yang, Jeremy Paul Richey, Jessica Xie Xi, Jocelyn Kee Beng Keng, Joey Kang Yew Ping, John Paul Rodulfa Gonzales, Jonathan David Choe, Jonathan Lynn Krizan, Jonathan William Guy Hooper, Jean-Marc Couffin, Joanne Lim Jiawei, John Kevin Chandra, Jonathan Ng Ming-En, Jonathan Tan Wei Jian, Joseph Buan Go, Josephine Isip Samaniego, Joshua Chong Chern Chek, Joshua Seow Tzi Yue, Joseph Ho You Fat, Joshua Ang Le Qiang, Joshua Woon Zhi Xian, Joyce Sng Hwee Puay, Kam Xue Jun, Kanokwan Innara, Kenneth Wong Wen Bin, Khajorn Jaroonwanit, Kiki Raditya, Kim Sehyeon, Kim Seon Hee, Kim Young Beom, Koh Eng Keong Jerry, Koh Wei Ling, Kok Yu Wen, Evanne, Krista Yeong Shilin, Lai Soong Hai, Lai Wei Song, Lasbrey Andrew Thomas, Larissa Tan Jia Yi, Lau Wan Nie, Lee Cheow Yeh, Lee Hao Ning Priscilla, Lee Jian Ming, Lee Jin Ting, Lee Kwang Min, Lee Li Leng, Lee Shing Yi, Lee Si Hui, Esther, Lee Tae Jin, Lefort India Perrine Valentine, Leng Leem Wuai (Adeline), Li Chen, Liak Yuan Zhi, Liam Shu-Ling Rachel, Liam Yuexin Jolene, Liaw Xiao Bin, Liew Yuqi, Lim Chun Keat, Lim Hui Zhen (Zanne), Lim Min Syn, Lim Sheau Huay, Lim Shu Ling, Lim Wei Rong (Kate), Lim Yee Sze, Lim Yin Chao, Lim Yong Kheng, Lim Yu-Tang John, Lin Bolt, Lin Desheng Dillon, Lin Liping, Lin Mu Hon (Zamen), Ling Shi Yin, Lisa Yun Li-Tsan, Lo Jia Yi, Lo Ying-Hsien (Rita), Loh Ghim Chong, Loh Tze Yang, Glenn, Loo Quan Le, Looi Chee Kin, Low Jo Ann, Low Yun Jie Adelaine, Luke Tan Shixin, Luu Dieu Khanh, Ma Xiao, Machado Martins Da Silva Pedro Miguel, Mahmudova Günay, Mangklapruk Kanop, Maria Antonia Loneza Nieva, Maria Arlene Valdez Dy, Maria Sara Tan Yu Wen, Marut Kaewroong, Matheson Andrew, Mathew Robert Devendorf, Matthew James Shang, Matthias Benz, Maxine Ong, Mehnaz Ahmed, Melissa Lim Sze Yu, Merlinda Song Li Ming, Michelle Hoe Shu Min, Michelle Valencia Santoso, Miikka Temmo Antero Leppanen, Mohamad Zamri Bin Arip, Mohd Noor Zarina, Mok Yin Tou Agnes, Monthathip Rattanawisitkul, Muhamad Nicco Bin Homaili, Muhammad Halim Bin AB Wahab, Muhammad Nazirul Bin Salleh, Muhammad Sagitha, Nabila Larasati Pranoto, Narpal Singh S/O Jigeet Singh, Natalie Cheung Ai Wen, Neo Jun Hao, Kevin Josiah, Ng Hiok Hoe, Ernest, Ng Jing Lin (Flora), Ng Qiao Chu Abigail, Ng Si Hoa (Kelvin), Ng Sook Fen, Ng Wei-Huong, Joshua, Ng Wen Qi, Ng Xin Yi, Laura, Ng Yi Xu (Eric), Ngai Yuen Chak (Savio), Nicholas Shane Oen Gomes, Nick Puah Guanlong, Ning Xianlin, Novita Johana, Nuntida Owatranphorn, Nutchanun Boontassaro, Ong Baolin, Jonathan, Ong Ker Shing, Ong Shu Sheng, Ong Ying Lun Belle, Parinot Kunakornwong, Park Sun Min Melany, Pamela Choo Li Fang, Pasana Mark Anthony Cruz, Peechaya Mekasuvanroj, Peh Suet Ying, Madalyn, Pham Sing Yeong, Philip Andrew Holub, Philip Chiang, Phoebe Tan Nga Suat, Pholkrit Sangthong, Phua Yun Nong, Phyllis Chua Whee Ming, Piboon Amornjirawong, Priscilla Foo Huili, Puiphai Khunawat, Punpong Wiwatkul, Qiu Yuting, Quek Wan Juan, Gabrielle, Quentin Morgan Clement Lefort, Quentin Sim Xiu Jun, Rainbow Lee Hong Xuan, Ranjit Wagh, Rapeepun Thongprywong, Rashidah Bte Daud, Rayanna Chan, Raymond Ang, Raymond Fong Kok Hoong, Richard Kuppusamy Chien-Ming, Rita Qian Sheng, River Law Kang Jie, Rizaldy Malabanan, Robie Michaell Sanchez Agustin, Rohana Bte Bardi, Ruedee Pavasiriporn, Russell Lee Ken Tian, Rutchai Suksakorn, Sabrina Foong, Samantha Seet Xiang Ling, Sacha Leong Huai-Ern, Sakina Binte Mohamed Halim, Sanghvi Jhanvi Yogesh, Sara Wang Yijun, Sean Alistair Edwards, Sean Chia, See Jian Fa, Seetoh Khan Pang, Serena Tan Yang Leng, Severine Nathalie Eliane Fagnoni, Setha Saipipatpanit, Shaad Hassan Zaidi, Shandy Loh Lee Choo, Shariffa Faridah Binte Mohamed Taha Alsagoff, Shaun Yeo Kee Aik, Shirley Yeo Wei Lee, Shirlyn Tan Soo Hiang, Sharne Jerhn Dta Sulaiman, She Qianyan, Shefali Lal, Shen Hanmo (Max), Shirley Goh Hooi Hiang, Stephanus Cordliepe Nel Johannes, Sim Chiew Khoon, Sim Wei Yih, Shalom Choong Foong Ling, Simeon Chua Cher Yang, Simopoulou Olympia Konstantinou, Sirisan Nivatvongs, Sompon Chanmantana, Stella Mary George Aloysius, Stella Tu Sidian, Stephen Deane Sargent, Stephen Lee Wee Bing, Su Zheng Mei, Suchon Pongsopitsin, Sulaini Bte Jonied, Supachai Khiewngam, Suraiya Dechkumpol, Susan Tan, Suzanne Chayavichitsilp, Swensline Yang Cheng Cheng, Tam Wing Nga (Rosy), Tan Anlong, Cliff, Tan Chee Sing, Tan Cher Ming, Tan Chiew Hong, Tan Huey Jiun, Tan Jia Xian, Tan Jing Min, Tan Seok Xian, Tan Szue Hann, Tan Wei Ru Cherin, Tan Yi Qing, Tan Yoke Eng, Tan Yuan Ling, Rebecca, Tang Chia Ling, Tanya Talwar, Tay I-Lin, Tay Lee Kuan, Roy, Techit Romraruk, Teo Zi Tong, Terence Chew Wei Liang, Terence Chan Wing Huat, Tham Cheng E, Tham Wai Hon, Thirawit Sinutok, Tiang Yu Ping, Timothy Tan Yit Ching, Tiaw Zuo Eng (Joanne), Tina Leong Kai Ling, Toh Hua Jack, Tommy Hui Shui Cheung, Tommy Tang Peng Hong, Tomoyuki Yokoi, Tong Li Shi, Tran Ngoc Ban, Tran Thi Thuy Tien, Tran Thien Huong, Tzeng Heng Foong, Vanessa Ong Weixian, Veronica Lee Shin Kiat, Victoria Scoullar Meadows, Vernace Tay Guo Zhi, Vince Ong Choon Hoe, Vivien Kwang Yuin Fang, Vicky Lee Wei Kee, Wan Pow Chween, Wang Chenhao, Wang Chong, Wang Qi, Wasinee Prasongsumrit, William Chuo, William Zorca, Winnie, Wong Chun Fei, Wong Weilun, Davis, Wu Kansheng, Xie Yuhan, Yang Han, Yap Shan Ming, Ye Hanyu, Yee Hui Xian, Yeung Yim Yu, Yong Pei Yee, Yu HanSik, Yudhi Aristan, Zeng Zhibin, Zhang Jing, Zhang Linwang, Zhang Wenjie, Zhao Meng, Zhao Zhen Jia, Zhou Yubai, Zhuang Chao, Zhuang Mingtong

About the Author
Patrick Bingham-Hall has written many books on architecture and urban planning, with a particular focus on contemporary Asia. He is also an acclaimed architectural photographer.

On the front cover: SkyVille @ Dawson, photo by Patrick Bingham-Hall
On the back cover: Above: Kampung Admiralty, Singapore /
Centre: Oasia Downtown, Singapore / Below: Parkroyal on Pickering,
Singapore, all photos by Patrick Bingham-Hall

First published in the United Kingdom in 2022 by
Thames & Hudson Ltd, 181A High Holborn, London WC1V 7QX

Photographic Credits
All photographs taken by Patrick Bingham-Hall, except as listed below
Marek Swoboda: p. 17 below
Tim Griffith: pp. 18—19; 21 left; 22—23; 30 left; 120; 139; 141; 142; 146—147; 155 below; 156; 177
Albert Lim: pp. 29; 30 above right, centre right
Kuomin Lee: p. 90
Darren Soh: p. 94 centre right
K. Kopter: p. 134

Edited by Patrick Bingham-Hall
Designed by Spread. Tomoko Sakamoto – David Lorente / spread.eu.com

British Library Cataloguing-in-Publication Data
A catalogue record for this book is available from the British Library

ISBN   978-0-500-02530-7

Printed in Singapore by 1010 Printing

FSC® C016973
MIX
Paper from
responsible sources
www.fsc.org

Be the first to know about our new releases,
exclusive content and author events by visiting
thamesandhudson.com
thamesandhudsonusa.com
thamesandhudson.com.au